Are You Experienced?

ARE YOU EXPERIENCED?

The inside story
of the
Jimi Hendrix Experience

by

Noel Redding and **Carol Appleby**

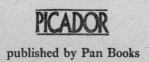

PICADOR

published by Pan Books

First published 1990 by Fourth Estate Ltd
This Picador edition published by Pan Books Ltd,
Cavaye Place, London SW10 9PG

3 5 7 9 8 6 4 2

ISBN 0 330 31923 X

Printed in England by Clays Ltd, St Ives plc

Contents

Dedication   *vii*

 1   Dreams and Schemes   *1*

 2   Managers, Money and Music   *20*

 3   Evreux to Monterey to The Monkees   *30*

 4   Round Two   *62*

 5   Round Three   *96*

 6   Last Straw   *119*

 7   Win Some, Lose Some   *133*

 8   Redding vs the World   *165*

 9   Yameta or Bust   *185*

10   Are You Experienced?   *204*

Afterword   Carol Lines by B.P. Fallon   220

Photo Credits   223

Index   225

This book is dedicated to my most wonderful love – whom I'll never forget or see again: Carol Eva Appleby, 6 November 1946 to 26 June 1990. No words can express my pain. I'll try my hardest, darling Carol.
I love you,
N.

For saving my life, thanks to: Carol Robinson, Jenny, Jim O'Neil, Niall and Claire Quin, Peter and Gail Cantwell, Olive Finn, Martin and Catherine Kingston, the Shanley family of Clonakilty, Kieth Beattie, Mike McCarthy, Mick Avery, Don, Frank Winston, the O'Donovan family, De Barra's, Michael and Catherine Ryan, the Ambulance Service and Regional Hospital, Cork, all my family, Margaret, Vick and Ants, and many, many more; and for help with the book, Grāinne O'Brien, Michael Smith, Dina Anastasio and Sid and Carol.
Thank you all – God bless,
N.

Chapter One

Dreams and Schemes

You gotta have a dream,
If you don't have a dream,
How you gonna have a dream come true?
ROGERS AND HAMMERSTEIN

TWANG twang! Ouch! Twang! Twang! Twang! Twoing . . . As a solo instrument the Jew's harp leaves a lot to be desired.

But because my French teacher at St Leonard's Primary School, Hythe, Kent, England, had doubted my ability to play a tune on one, I found myself in 1954 at nine years of age nervously proving my claim (and winning some time off from lessons) with a successful if tooth-chipping rendition of *Tom Dooley*. From then on I dreamed, first cautiously then flamboyantly, of being a Musician.

'Don't worry, Mum', I'd say, 'I'm going to be a musician and earn LOTS of money.'

She'd give me one of those indulgent mother-type smiles and ask what I thought LOTS was. Did I mean ten pounds in an evening?

'I mean hundreds!'

From that point music was allowed to be considered along with technical drawing as a possible career, though architecture was definitely Mum-favoured for the steady £30 weekly it would earn me.

Luckily my older brother Anthony and younger sister Vicki could supply their share of distractions and Mum was never able to keep the pressure to be practical on me for long. Mum (who is rarely called Margaret by those who know and love her) had her hands full raising us on her own with help from her Swedish mother Nellie Berggren, Gran, who lived with us. Like all good Grans she could be counted on to take our part in arguments and attempts to stretch the rules a bit.

My second musical venture was the violin. The school offered lessons and I followed my best friend Dave Tearell into the class. I was surprised to discover I liked violin and Mum did her bit by making a little pillow for my chin rest.

I succeeded in getting an A pass for Harvey Grammar School with three other boys named David (my middle name), getting the news on St David's Day. This was a *serious* school with a mile-long list of punishable rules that even followed you home. I once got the cane for taking my cap off on a sweltering bus ride home, you had to be in the Fifth Form before you could do that, or loosen your tie. Getting into Grammar School made Mum happy but not me. No music there. Not even violin classes. Only something called 'Music Class', which was really history in disguise and very off-putting.

Outside, it was mandolin-by-book, until one fateful day at the Seabrook school bus stop when a neighbour, a teacher, joined us with a strangely shaped instrument case. Overwhelmed by curiosity, I conquered my shyness long enough to ask what it was. She opened the case right there and showed me her Spanish guitar. I was completely fascinated. With Mum's permission, I made an embarrassed visit that evening to see how it worked. I held it (afraid I'd break it) while she showed me a couple of chords.

That was the end of the mandolin. I started pleading for a guitar for my birthday, but Mum thought it would be another flash-in-the-pan. As we were eternally hard up, the thought of £6.65 going for nothing was not appealing. And since my birthday was on Christmas Day, my dreams looked like going unfulfilled. But somehow Mum managed it by swopping in the mandolin at the Helping Hand shop in Folkestone, and within a week I was driving her distracted with my latest two-chord accomplishment.

At thirteen, I discovered pop music and groups. The excitement was too much. The very first entry in my 1958 Lett's Schoolboy's diary is 'Rock and Roll is jolly good!'

At school I met Pete Kircher. We weren't friends until the day he said, 'I hear you have a guitar. I have one, too.' The next Saturday he cycled three miles to my house (because my Mum loved to hear us) with his guitar strapped on his back (later he would also balance his amp on the handlebars) so we could play together. Pete hadn't discovered tuning yet and his guitar was set to a loose open chord which enabled him to play away with one finger. I tuned him up proper and we started saving for a record player – my half coming from a double paper round (and to this day I'll never know how I got up at 6.15 a.m. for so long).

I became aware of Radio Luxembourg and BBC's Saturday Club

and heard *Swagger* by Joe Brown, *Jada* by Johnny and the Hurricanes, *FBI* by The Shadows, and lots of Eddie Cochran, Buddy Holly, Elvis, Gene Vincent, Chuck Berry, Tommy Steele, Cliff Richard, and Lonnie Donegan. This music changed my world. I totally loved American music! A fews years on, 'the Big Three' – Ray Charles and Johnny Kidd and The Pirates – would add to my fascination. As TV became more available (though not affordable for us, so I'd go to the local shop and watch the display one in the window), the Everly Brothers on the Perry Como Show impressed me no end. And when I heard *Green Onions* by Booker T, my whole life changed.

Now there were concerts and record parties. I'll never forget the day in May '59 when I managed to see Billy Fury and Cliff Richard at the Folkestone Odeon, and got both of their autographs by climbing (though horrified of heights) up the outside of the building to their second-floor dressing room window. I was made to wait, hanging on to the window ledge for dear life, while the book was signed and somehow I got back down. In June I actually spoke to Cliff Richard! And I still have the autographs.

In October '59 I got my first amplifier – a Grampion eight watt costing twenty guineas – thanks to Mum, who was now running a guest house in the village of Seabrook, Kent, and keeping chickens in the yard. The following week I bought a pickup for my acoustic and played 'electric' for the very first time.

Pete and I continued to rehearse and I gathered enough courage to take my guitar to the Hythe Youth Club to play my skiffle repertoire *in front of people* – *The Bol Weevil Song,* Laurie London's *Got The Whole World in His Hands,* and Ricky Nelson songs.

Finally, the day came when I actually got paid for playing. It was an East Kent Bus Company do in Cheriton – two shillings and tea. Me on guitar, John Andrews on bass (both through my eight-watt amp with one ten-inch speaker plugged into an unearthed ceiling light socket), and Mick Goody on snare drum (no snare), hihat, and another snare drum as tomtom. No stopping me now. . .

A summer selling ice cream from a bicycle cart along the seafront followed by a winter working behind the coffee bar at Morelli's, saving every penny, earned me a REAL electric guitar – a Futurama. In February 1960 I joined my first band, The Strangers. It was all my dreams come true. So when I got thrown out – 'Too many guitarists' (three) – I was devastated and cried. Mum told me she'd heard it was because I was the youngest but played the best. That helped.

Going the way of many musicians-to-be, I transferred to art school – and soon stopped studying to form my own band. I called it The

Lonely Ones, and within a few months we had taken all the gigs off The Strangers. It featured Bob Hiscox on rhythm, and John 'Andy' Andrews on bass. Drummers were rare and we did without until we discovered Mick Wibley. Pete joined as vocalist and it was great because he looked like Eddie Cochran in his tight, white jeans with hair long enough (all of two inches) to earn him the nickname of 'Hair'.

In the off season, the guest house sitting room became our rehearsal room and was always crowded with instruments. Luckily our neighbours were an elderly, nearly deaf couple and a family of music-lovers. The room was always full of local music-oriented people: musicians, friends and (best of all) *girls*.

Two of Mum's lodgers, Tom and Peter – Irish men working for Murphy's laying electric cables – were wonderful to us. They were the best of friends but that never stopped them from knocking the shit out of each other after a long night out on the town and spending the morning apologising and carrying each other to work. They chauffeured us to gigs in their flashy Ford Zodiac, helped if we needed it, waited in the nearest pub until we had finished, then delivered us home.

We were soon playing at the Two I's Coffee Bar in Soho (where Tommy Steele had been discovered) for £2.10s a night, the Leas Cliff Hall, the Deal Astor and the Empress Ballroom. By the summer of '62, Colin 'Buster' Osmonds from Pat Barlow (soon to be Neil Landon) and the Cheetahs had replaced Mick on drums.

The *Folkestone Herald* gave us great press which boosted our egos no end. We decided to make a record. With the help of Dennis Stokes of Hayton Manor, Stanford, who had recently turned his hobby into a business by setting up five mikes in his living room, we recorded four songs. We thought it would take an hour – it took three and a half. We were amazed at how difficult it was to record a song so you wouldn't cringe when you listened back. Having got used to PA mikes we rediscovered mike fright and just couldn't get *What a Crazy World We Are Living In* right. The first take wasn't too bad – until half way. The second was hopeless. After an equally dismal third attempt, we abandoned it. And so on. And these were songs we breezily played every night for hundreds of people!

Finally we tried *Dark Town Strutters Ball*. Perfect first time. We ran through an instrumental – faultless! But the tension was building and by the time the lead came round for *Last Stage West* I had to say, 'Don't look at me or I won't be able to do it.' We finally finished doing *Yes Sir, That's My Baby* in one go and collapsed in relief.

The Lonely Ones were now recording artists. We had twelve whole copies pressed for local jukebox use – as in Mr Mousourou's Caprice Espresso Bar where we'd hang out listening to all the new records. Because I was an art student, Mr Mousourou asked me to paint a mural. Full of it, I created a larger-than-life, splashy-coloured jive session in, according to the local papers, a 'suave sort of Cubist' style which stayed there for years.

We sweated through auditions. My first was for a local talent show and I was so nervous that my hand locked on the guitar neck in a frozen E chord on *Move It*, and nothing I could do would move it. At fifteen my constant companion the *NME* encouraged me to try again. I convinced Mum that the only way to relax was to keep at it. Was she surprised (me, too!) when I was offered a two-year world tour doing cabaret at £15 per week all expenses paid – starting in Hong Kong. But I was underage and after a phone call and some serious discussions between the manager and Mum it was decided that I really should refuse the offer. In truth, I felt too young to leave home and happy enough just to be asked.

It was the Spring of 1962 when at sixteen, fed up with lessons and the attitude of the teachers, I quit art school. Once in the early days, Pete, Serge Viatkin (a raver before his time and the first person I knew who shaved his head) and I knocked 'em out at a school concert. The headmaster congratulated us publicly and then invited us to his office for a really stern lecture and a warning to stop all this music nonsense and study more. Exams were important; music wasn't. We had already been in trouble for hanging out in amusement halls listening to the jukeboxes. I discussed the whole thing with my Uncle John Berggren, who during his visits became my substitute father since my parents had divorced before I had got to know my own father. He simply said, 'If you want to go pro, go ahead and just *do it*.'

How could I go to school when we were gigging nearly every night? But Colin had a regular day job and finally left us drummer-less. One desperate night, Pete said he'd have a go. He simply sat down and played. A complete natural! He even sang at the same time! That was that. And because he related to the guitar we both got into exploring the rhythms possible between guitar and drums – especially with me currently listening to my idol, Mick Green.

The Lonely Ones only did the latest chart songs. The crowds ate it up and one review stated, 'When the Lonely Ones played *Let's Twist* everyone deserted their plates of sausages and mash to perform the exotic movements.' We played it eight times that night!

We carried gear up three long flights of stairs to the Co-Op Hall Thursday Club. Then there was the 'Big Beat Ball' at the Leas Cliff

Hall, Folkestone, where the dancers could turn the sprung floor into a trampoline. We auditioned for ITV's *Home Grown* and made the short-list. Then for Ron Golding, Vince Hill's manager.

Once I waited all day to see Marty Wilde (then touring with drummer Brian Bennett, guitarist Jim Sullivan and bassist Licorice Locking) so I could ask for an opinion of my playing. When I finally saw him I was too shy to ask and ended up with his autograph – again.

But the best thing about being in the band was the girls – until everyone wanted to take their girlfriends along to the gigs. 'Drive slower, my girlfriend doesn't feel well,' someone would say when we were late already (probably due to a girlfriend who wasn't ready) and rushing to get there on time. As we got more sophisticated, we'd only give lifts to girls who at least kissed goodnight. A 'No' would get her banned and her name on the 'Prick Teasers List'. Finally, several million complications later, we made a rule: No girlfriends to gigs. It was the best way of finding out whether a guy was dedicated or just horny. I was both.

A newspaper called me the best guitarist in Kent! A friendly rivalry developed between us and Dover's Big Beats – they had a great bassist in Jim Leverton – which kept both bands pushing ahead. We even staged a mock battle in Folkestone for press purposes. But eventually local rivalry wasn't enough and I knew that to expand I'd have to leave the Kent area.

About this time, Pat Barlow/Neil Landon, formerly of The Cheetahs, was singing with The Thunderbolts in London. This band boasted bassist Teddy Wadmore, co-writer with another of my idols, Johnny Kidd, on songs like *Please Don't Touch*. (I once managed to meet Johnny and Mick Green at the same time. I always tried to stay and talk. This time I gained access to the dressing room where I was allowed to have a go on Mick's guitar. It was wonderful until – horror of horrors – I broke a string.) So when The Thunderbolt's guitarist went missing and Neil called me to sub, I ran to London.

In the autumn of 1962, Neil left The Thunderbolts and asked The Lonely Ones to join him. We became Neil Landon and the Burnettes. Privately we felt superior to Neil because he could 'only sing', but he'd been around London and had bookings, including a residency in Hugh O'Donnel's Kingston Jazz Cellar. Hugh became our first manager as we worked around England and, during the really hard times, slept on the tables in his club with sacks for bedding.

Boozing was cheaper than eating – though not in the long run. I started to get ill and by spring I was forced to resign. I went home to recover and set about forming The Lonely Ones (Take Two) to keep busy. Back in the Caprice, I heard Derek Knight *(aka* Des Kay) singing along with the jukebox, but better. I grabbed him, Andy for bass and Trevor Sutton joined on drums.

They had day jobs, but I was still young enough to have trouble finding one. I landed one in a factory. On the second day I discovered I was making tracheotomy tubes, and what they were used for, got sick thinking about it and quit. Next came a four-day job cutting grass for hay at Lympne Airport and dragging it to a barn. Only the damp and mould landed me with a throat infection and visions of the tubes again. Then I delivered vegetables for Mrs Clark's shop in Saltwood where Molly would tell my fortune in the tea leaves and assure me I'd travel far and be all right. Mrs Clark was extremely good-hearted and lent us the delivery van for gigs as long as we had it back on time and covered expenses.

Any help was appreciated. We needed gear desperately. I traded in the Burns guitar I'd bought to replace the Futurama for a Gibson SG – 110 guineas with eighteen months to pay. We got Shure mikes for £9.12s.8d, and identical light blue suits with trendy bum-freezer jackets and leather Beatle jackets. And bless Aunt Lil, who remembered me in her will with £100. I should have used it to pay off all my debts but instead bought my dream – a Fender Bandmaster amp. I still have it! Mum was the greatest help as usual. She lent us petrol money and later she chipped in her own small inheritance for the downpayment on a yellow Thames van and signed the guarantee so we could purchase it. The group made the payments, covered insurance, servicing, etc – and fixed a pair of bison horns over the windscreen.

Every penny counted, so when a police car in pursuit hit me and drove off, I chased it all across town, filed a report and hassled them till they paid up. We carefully kept written accounts – so much for each member and so much for the emergency kitty. We grumbled, but it came in handy. And we never went home out of pocket.

In November, we recorded – much easier – at Hayton Manor. The session cost us thirty bob. We pressed and sold a hundred EPs of *Money, Talkin' Bout You, Anna,* and *Some Other Guy.*

The Burnettes got a German club gig, but I didn't feel up to accepting Neil's offer. Leaving the country to play was a real bridge and I wasn't ready to cross it. Besides, if I had gone, I would have missed the night I was allowed to stay *all* night in Johnny Kidd's dressing room *and* watch the show from the wings. Gene Vincent was also hanging out that night, but in my ignorance I never got his autograph.

Trouble came when Trevor left to concentrate on school. It took months to replace him. Finally, we found NuNu (Lawrence Whiting). Not only could he play drums, but Trevor's suit fitted him!

We tried running our own gigs, hiring a hall, making posters and getting a support group but couldn't compete with the established venues. So we worked as support for groups like The Hollies, Manfred Mann, The Alex Harvey Soul Band, and The Fortunes.

I've recently met The Fortunes again and Barry Pritchard told me that he remembers the gig. What struck him was that I humped in all the gear, set it all up, played, dismantled it and lugged it all out again – by myself! Then I came in for a drink with them. I always was the keenest one in my groups. And since we didn't have a driveway where we lived, it also meant hauling all the gear out of the van every night and in again before heading off to each gig.

In autumn 1964, a family holiday in Spain was interrupted by a cable from Neil, 'Join us for a tour', and I suddenly knew my career was at stake, that it was time to jump in the deep end and stop messing around beside the pool. Mum turned into Stirling Moss and got me from Rosas to Barcelona in four and a half hours with just six minutes to spare. The pilot actually waited while I was cleared and boarded my first aeroplane. We started rehearsing the minute I landed – Pete, Neil, and Kevin Lang (whose brother was a Mindbender). Kevin had one of the first Marshall amps direct from Jim Marshall's little workroom near Manchester.

We toured some great places in Scotland like Lossiemouth, Aberdeen, Elgin (the week after the Beatles, I think), Nairn, Thurso, Wick, Craigellachie and the Orkney Islands. We stayed in B&Bs like Mrs McBean's, where the porridge was so thick it didn't need a bowl and would stick to your ribs all day.

We ran into Manfred Mann again and this time Paul Jones asked me to join them. I was amazed, and tempted, but stayed loyal to my group and refused. Immediately, they shot to the top of the charts with *54321* as I slogged on earning two quid a night.

I learned about dancehall violence in Scotland. At ten p.m. (pub closing time) the empty hall would fill to bursting and for two hours we would accompany swearing and fighting. On the stroke of midnight, the tide would go out and leave a floor strewn with bits of clothing, broken bottles of undiluted whisky, and blood. When The Pirates toured there, they regularly had to down instruments and beat up portions of the audience. Mick Green, who would be a good guy to have on your side in a fight, had this great one-pickup Gibson Les Paul Jr that I really fancied until it too got smashed in a brawl.

For protection, I wore my glasses constantly and stayed within grabbing distance of a mike stand. I'd previously learned the value of a good stand when I got very severely beaten in New Romney by three army squaddies for speaking to a girl I went to school with. I retaliated by gathering up a few big guys to hold the creeps while I landed a few strategically placed blows with the stand. I never saw them again. But the vibes of the Kent seaside changed completely after the army training camp was built. The fields we'd played in as kids were now forbidden and behind barbed wire. The area filled up with thugs, the air filled up with the sounds of shelling and shooting, and ultimately a bunch of squaddies murdered an Indian man. Suddenly the bands, who were always off limits in punch-ups before, had to have their own heavies for protection.

Different halls had different quirks. At the Beach Ballroom in Aberdeen *everyone* would constantly walk around the hall anticlockwise. When the music started, the dancers would stand in place and bounce up and down. In Glasgow there was a place so rough they actually put the group in a cage. In Elgin Saturday dances were held at a place called the Two Red Shoes, which could easily have been called the Two Black Eyes. Another place we called 'Half Way Up The Wall' because the stage was literally half way up a high wall for security purposes. I remember one girl there who would ask guys to dance and floor them with a punch if they dared say no.

It was while up that wall that we heard we had a chance to go to Germany. We played, packed up and drove to Doncaster, slept in the hall for one hour, did the gig, drove all night to London, picked up a guitar, drove to Kent, slept for two hours, drove to London for the audition, got it, and left for Germany the next day via the Dover-to-Ostend ferry, driving through Belgium, Aachen, and on to Cologne.

Before then I'd thought that Scotland was unique in its conservative attitude. If we stopped at a transport café after driving all night everyone would snigger at our three-inch-long hair. One guy really cackled and Pete, who was feeling defensive that day, said, 'Laying an egg?' The guy stood up and he was massive. In classic style he lifted Pete off the ground by the collar, bopped him, dropped him, and left. We melted into our seats as the waitress rambled on about his professional wrestling career.

But Germany was similar. If your hair was longer than an army crewcut, people stopped in the street to laugh. In Frankfurt, we lived pretty well due to the kindness of the American GI's, who would let us eat (and sometimes sleep) in the base café. We were allowed to take advantage of the Rhein-Main Air Base PX for cigarettes and booze.

The one thing that was pretty standard with German gigs was the club-supplied room: just one, unheated room with a handbasin and filthy sheets. First thing you'd have to wash the sheets. For a bath you could choose between a stand-up wash at the basin or a trip to the public baths where you were allowed twenty minutes – exactly – before the Hulk-like attendant of indeterminate sex began banging on the door shouting, 'Out'.

Duisburg, Cologne, and Marburg followed. Wuppertal's room was so horribly damp we'd wake with condensation on our foreheads. We picked up a hitchhiker called Tut who became our first roadie. Happy just to sleep on our floor, we paid him in eggs and chips. We met an Italian/American named Nino. If you didn't like the bar prices, he always had a bottle stashed in his inside pocket.

In order to keep up our reputation for having the latest sounds, we had to have discs sent from England if we couldn't buy them at the GI bases. The crowds were crazy, the hours were long. At Cologne's Storeyville Club we played from 7.30 to 1.00 a.m. on weeknights, except Friday when we finished at 2.00 a.m. Saturday was a gruelling 2.30 to 5.30 plus 7.00 to 3.00 a.m. And Sundays were not much better – 2.30 to 5.30 and 7.00 to 12.00. It's an effective way of getting past the bloody fingertip stage and growing proper fingertip callouses while having a chance to play everything you know and quite a bit you don't just to fill time. In other words, learning how to play, to get past that point when you feel you can't play another note even if you could think of one. You soon learn to pace yourself. I felt sorriest for Neil. My fingertips were swollen, bloody lumps, but they still moved. Vocalists worry about the inevitable moment when the throat just swells up and the voice simply disappears. When that happened (it would take about a week), Pete would be the first to take over singing, then Kevin, then Adge (later Norman), with me as a last resort, 'singing' my only vocal accomplishment, *Rockin' Robin*. I was also allowed to be John Lennon for any Beatles songs. (I continued doing John's vocals even later in my career.)

With the club owners you could test your crowd-drawing power by seeing how far you could go ignoring the rules. If the club said 'No beer on stage' – plonk! Beer on every amp. If they said, 'No jeans', we all wore jeans every night. You didn't have to do much to appear rebellious to German audiences. They loved it.

Neil was always doing solo auditions on the side, looking for his big chance. He was in his element singing songs like *Things* and *Red Roses*. Once Neil actually deserted us in Germany for a chance to do some recording in England. We were saved when Johnny Halliday, who happened to be in the audience, offered to sing a few songs with us. I felt great when he said there would be a gig for me if I ever came to Paris. I was even more surprised when I met him later and he remembered and repeated the offer.

The Burnettes did shows and interviews for the British Forces Network and were recorded by the German Recording Company, who paid us a hundred marks and promised us three per cent of all records sold. That was the last we heard from them.

One night Alan 'Adge' Dickenson, who had joined on piano, got carried away singing this rock and roll song and came up with the idea of sliding down the front of the big curved-glass jukebox cover. CRUNCH! Coolly and carefully he got out of the jukebox and carried on until we noticed that he was dripping blood everywhere. We had to use up a break to get him repaired. He couldn't sit down for the stitches in his ass, and we had to pay the club's bill for the glass.

I tended more towards slapstick comedy and waited till the moment when Neil closed his eyes for the high note at the end of *Running Scared* before I poured a pint of beer over his head. He went into shock. I can still see the look on his face! He stalked off, but the crowd loved it. Then I got Kevin by pouring beer into his boot while he played. He said nothing but the next night he set my leg hairs on fire when I leapt up on my amplifier during our 'act'.

Inevitably, fatigue took over and we discovered helpful additives. For a 'straight' country there were lots of chemical drugs around, mostly stimulants. We got our pill education there. Generally, you could buy Captogan uppers very easily from club lavatory attendants. They helped offset the long hours and the amount of drink we consumed, and vice versa. Soon we were never without a supply.

Cologne was known as 'Little Chicago'. One night a brawl started and we were debating whether it might be a good idea to take a break when the bouncer was stabbed in front of the stage. Quick as a wink, he pulled this huge .45 revolver from his pocket and fired. The attackers (and everyone else in the club) fled – saved only because the gun misfired! When Pete decided to break off with the lady he was seeing, her move was, 'I'll have you killed.' We ran to phone our GIs in Frankfurt. Three hours later, nine of the biggest guys I'd ever seen arrived to sit between us and the audience. Everyone was watching everyone watching everyone. Shooters everywhere. Finally, our lot went up to her heavies: 'Mess with the band and you're dead.' No more trouble but it was ages before Pete stopped looking over his shoulder.

The GIs were heavy in other ways, too. For New Year's Eve in Frankfurt, they showed up with bottles of bourbon (bourbon?), which they mixed into hot drinks. 'It's just whisky, drink it.' Three hours into the evening, Pete slid off his stool, sank behind the drums and disappeared. The Fortunes were on the same bill so their drummer sat in – but in vain. One by one the band dissolved till there were no replacements. Pete was missing for three days after that.

At the Star Club in Cologne bands like Derry Wilke played even later hours than us, giving us somewhere to hang out. Derry was a black Liverpudlian with the biggest hands I've ever seen in my life. I also met Phil Kenzie there, saxophonist extraordinaire, who went on to play with Al Stewart and Rod Stewart.

When we finally got back to England in May '65 we were exhausted. Hating my glasses, even if Buddy Holly did wear them, I'd got contact lenses and straight after our last gig we (I actually did ninety per cent of all the driving) had driven non-stop to Ostend for the ferry and conked out. I woke to discover the agonies of a corneal abrasion. The guys carried me screaming off the ferry. Customs let us straight through (thereby missing the bass drum packed with duty-free cigarettes) and I was delivered to Mum's in terrible pain. I never wore contact lenses again, but took my glasses off for photo sessions for ages.

Nearly instantly it was Scotland again – Oban, Nairn, Tain, and the Islands. The halls were mostly echoey barns and the more eccentrically wired halls would be shocking.

June found us back in Frankfurt. Now the girls were screaming at gigs. Whether it was us or the fashion, I neither knew nor cared. I loved the attention better than the Telecaster I was then playing. I'd fatally injured my Gibson Stereo during a Who number. Imagine my face when I shook the neck and it broke off in my hand! I'd picked the Telecaster because of Booker T and Mick Green. It was great for some songs, but it wasn't me.

I first met Denny Laine when I had to borrow his amp for a Cologne Stadthalle concert/TV show with the Moody Blues which drew a crowd of four thousand.

At the end of August, nerves and tempers thin, Kevin computed that Neil had been taking the lion's share of the earnings. He always considered himself the Star and even grabbed a room for himself if we were offered two. We were a good, tight band. We liked each other, and we'd worked just as hard as him to achieve our position. Pete and I were in charge of all the music – I did the chords and Pete the lyrics of any new song. We also played fifteen minutes of each set before Neil came on. We deserved as much reward as Neil. It blew up into a huge row. We left Germany and Kevin left us, partly because he'd married a posh chick who'd come with us to Germany and hated it. He left the band. Then she left him.

Pete and I took charge of band business and I phoned Jim Leverton instantly. He quit The Big Beats and I taught him thirty-eight songs in four hours. I knew Jim was a big asset to our sound, but Neil had the nerve to threaten imperiously to dump him. I replied, 'If you do you'll lose me as well.' Norman Hale replaced Adge on piano and a day later we were back, supporting big stars The Merseybeats in Cologne. I was impressed and awed by them until very late the first night when we were woken by heavy duty banging on the door. It was the Merseybeats. Ejected from their hotel for smashing the door down because their girls were refused entry, they were happy to kip on our floor.

By September '65 craziness was setting in, and the room-busting-up syndrome was beginning to be a standard part of a rock band's repertoire. Jim and I got riotously drunk and tried to push our bed out of a hotel window. It wouldn't fit and we were reduced to dumping water on passers-by.

Pete started to fade physically and The Mersey's John Banks (bless him) sat in. Pay? 'Nothing. Just keep me in vodka and pills.' Then Pete cut his finger on a rusty drum, it went septic and he was told if he played he'd lose his finger. Pete went home to recover and for a week we used any drummer we could drag in.

Jim faded next. A huge mysterious lump developed on his cheek. For the duration we transposed *Jump Back Baby* into *Bump Back* as Jim tried to sing out of one side of his mouth while giving the audience a profile.

The much more affluent Tony Cartwright came into our lives, so we ate more often. He was touring with Chris Sandford's Coronets (Chris having graduated from *Coronation Street*). Mitch Mitchell was their drummer until he left for an acting job. Eric Dillon replaced him, but Eric was only fifteen and had to be smuggled into Germany in a bass drum case.

Home in October, we toured as support for The Ivy League, The Hollies, The Nashville Teens. But we were pissed off with feeling like we were working *for* Neil, and in November we gave him notice. Derek Knight, Pete, Jim and I started rehearsing as The Loving Kind and set about looking for a manager. Tony Cartwright was getting into agenting and later worked with Engelbert Humperdinck and Freddie Starr. He introduced us to Gordon Mills, who'd been writing songs which needed a group like ours to play them. Mills had made his name as a harmonica player with The Viscounts in the '50s, but he'd been writing great hits with Johnny Kidd such as *Hungry For Love* and *I'll Never Get Over You*. With session drummer Clem Catini and an interested Ivy Leaguer for support, we auditioned for Mills and got signed up. We were a bit of a change from his other projects like Engelbert (still Jerry Dorsey) and Tom Jones.

Tony got us work as backing band on Freddy Lennon's (John's dad) single. And we got paid – £6.10s.

Gordon organized an audition for Pye Records and we were offered a singles contract. Because we were all under twenty-one, our parents had to confirm in writing Gordon's management of us and on 18 January 1966, we were signed up.

In anticipation of recording Gordon's songs, we rehearsed at his plush home in Shepperton. The only trouble with this arrangement was the long drive there. We were so desperate that even a quid for petrol was often too much to scrape together. Mum was able to help sometimes, but when we were really, really skint we would literally beg Gordon for two quid's worth of petrol which he would allow us to charge at the garage which serviced his Rolls Royce and Jaguar.

There was another alternative. 'You could always stay the night, Noel!' 'Uh, no thanks, Gordon.'

Now that we were managed, we weren't allowed to hustle our own gigs and had to rely on what Mills and the agent got us. We did some Humperdinck sessions, but rarely gigged. The few we did were great, especially the night Eric Burdon and Zoot Money sat in with us for several numbers at the Mayfair Room in London. But we were making less money than when were semi-pro. Most gigs ended up being 'cheque jobs', which meant our earnings would be posted back to the office while we had to somehow come up with money to cover our expenses.

We had some terrible nights. The van was disintegrating. Gordon rang at three one afternoon in snowy January: 'You're playing in Coventry tonight. Get on the road.' I had to push the van to start it. I picked everyone up. Teatime already. Coventry was a good four-hour drive and we arrived twenty minutes late by the contract – not late for the 8.30 show, but the contract said we'd arrive by 7.00. The management told us to fuck off. We begged and pleaded to be allowed to play for free. No! Sent to Coventry with no gig and no money. Luckily Cliff Bennett and the Rebel Rousers were on the bill and he kindly lent us a tenner. We couldn't thank him enough. We watched his great show and drove on to a cheap Birmingham hotel. In the morning, our van had a flat. Fixing it took most of our cash and our next gig was Elsicarr – five more hours of winding road. In Doncaster the tyre gave up again. Now we had no money left for food. We tried to forget by sleeping in the freezing van before the show, which earned us four quid each. We took out the petrol money and used the rest for a crate of beer.

Next day we had a lunchtime gig in a big Wolverhampton pub. 'Don't worry, lads, you'll make thirty-five at lunch and about ninety pounds at night.' Driving all night, we arrived at six in the morning and were forced to sleep in the van again. At lunchtime we took three pounds and no one even listened. We'd been away all weekend, and had three pounds and a tenner debt to show for it. So we told the guy what to do with the evening show and started back, only to have the silencer fall off on the M1.

The fatigue was showing. It was getting impossible to stay awake while driving, so I always insisted that one person stay awake to make sure I did. Everyone else would crash out and the co-pilot and I would set off on what was usually at least a six-hour drive. We'd share a joint or one beer between us and do our best to keep Luxembourg tuned in on the radio. The BBC didn't care about people who had to stay awake all night. Neil was the worst driver and involved us in several prangs. He once flopped the van over while cornering and I was very nearly killed. The Binson echo chamber walloped me on the head and I came so close to losing my arm that the sleeve was ripped off my shirt.

Meantime, Gordon had been organizing photo sessions and suits and sorting things out with Pye and Jonathan Rowlands, our publicist. On 11 February we heard our first single, *Accidental Love* (Mills)/ *Nothing Can Change This Love* (Piccadilly No. 7N 35299) on Radio London. Total sales: 899. It was so exciting that for a while all the aggravation was forgotten.

But why were we working so much less now that we had all this organisation behind us? It was depressing. Privately, we grumbled that we were better musicians than most of Tom Jones's backing group, and they were earning excellent wages with all expenses paid. We needed gigs and gear – especially a bass for Jim, and a gearbox, battery, starter, speedo, and brakes for the van. The Merseybeats' bassist Bill Kingsley remembers passing our broken-down van with us sitting miserably beside it on the road between Manchester and Liverpool. We'd probably still be there if they hadn't turned round, found us a garage and taken us to Liverpool. We spent the night at the Blue Angel, playing and getting pissed. Why didn't Gordon help us out and let us pay him back?

19 February, Cardiff – 'The Dark Side of the Moon' – reached after an eight-hour drive on unbelievable roads and a ferry trip across the River Severn. It's impossible to imagine those pre-bridge days. Only the nether regions of Scotland could compete for remoteness. We had

just enough money/petrol to get there, but after we'd played we were told it was a cheque job. The club manager was good enough to give us a fiver in cash to get home. We towed the van to start it and pulled the front bumper off, complete with the license plate. I tossed it in the back – at least the van was going. Hours later at eight in the morning, with everyone else dropped off and probably already in bed, the Kent police stopped and ticketed me for not having a license plate, and then discovered our expired road tax.

Another Humperdinck session earned us £2.10s – *each* this time. I felt ill – we never had enough money to eat – and we had to go to Cardiff again. The place was jinxed for us. We went all the way there only to be told, 'Sorry, lads, must be an agent error. You're next week.' We started back and the dynamo went. It was winter and night-time. No heater, sidelights only, and we couldn't stop for any reason. The worst drive I ever made.

Fuck this! I phoned Jack Fallon, the German agent. On 14 April we were back in Germany. But Derek was ill now and Jim's resistance was running low. One night Jim got unexpectedly drunk – not that he didn't mean to get drunk, he did – but he was suddenly legless and fell off stage during *Whole Lot Of Shakin' Goin' On.* But the audience caught him and passed him around overhead and he hardly missed a note. So we incorporated it into the act.

Back in England the PA broke down, Pete lost a cymbal and his drum skins began breaking one after another. We couldn't afford to fix or replace anything. We started getting desperate enough to begin to resent our treatment. When Neil phoned offering two weeks' work, we jumped at it. Gordon didn't approve of us working with Neil, but he had nothing for us. Showdown time. When he came up with an another last-minute, long-distance gig, we refused it. I think the van would have refused it too.

We still had our Pye contract to think of, and Derek surprised us all by writing songs. He had lots of ideas and an old piano at home. I'd translate his rough chords into music and help him structure it. It was the first time I'd ever been involved with writing and I found it fascinating. Derek eventually came up with a couple of great songs and Tom Jones recorded one as a b-side. We chose *I Love the Things You Do* as an a-side, b/w Mill's *Treat Me Nice* (Piccadilly No. 7N 35318, released 24 June 1966). Gordon arranged publicity in the *Musical Express,* but the single didn't take off – selling only 645. I still like the track, and Derek, with his Sam Cooke voice, sounded great.

Once Neil's gigs were finished, I went for a discussion with Gordon. It ended with me quitting and him swearing, 'You'll never work again!'

Our farewell single, *Ain't That Peculiar/Rhyme and Reason* (Mills – Piccadilly No. 7N 35342), was released on 16 September and sold 682 copies.

I was fed up, sick a lot, and tired all the time. Back in Kent, I messed around looking for something interesting to do. I built a 'fuzz box' to vary my sound. This wasn't yet a commercial device in those days. You'd take a standard guitar lead, splice a transistor into it, knock up a rough wooden frame to protect the circuit, and there you'd have it. No switch, just two leads – one normal and one 'fuzz'.

I joined a local group, The Concords, because I didn't have the energy to start from scratch again. The Concords, who had earned themselves a well-deserved negative reputation, soon took on the name of The Lonely Ones to get better gigs, but weren't really up to it. When we backed Neil for a short tour in Scotland, it was really terrible. Or perhaps I wasn't into it. It was too amateurish. I'd been away from Kent too long, working hard and long. I was twenty years old. I went to see what other groups were doing and saved the night at a Joe Brown concert by somehow finding the spring from his Bixby tremolo arm after it fell out on his way to the stage. When I met him ten years later, he remembered! I advertised for musicians, but only one bass player answered. I confessed to Mum that I was completely down and she suggested one last try.

On 28 September 1966, I got on the train to London. It wasn't being the best day of my life – the polar opposite to my early trips to 'Tawn' when I'd excitedly windowshopped for guitars and attempted to 'hang out'. I knew a great shop where professionals went. I'd be quiet and invisible in the corner, and I could pick up riffs and techniques by watching the pros try out guitars. After the owners got to know me and the pros accepted me as part of the furniture, I could hang out more visibly, ask questions and have chats.

That day, as I wearily dragged myself off the train into the rush at Charing Cross station, after what was both the longest and the shortest journey I'd ever taken, I wasn't even sure I'd be a guitarist much longer. I felt old. I toyed with the idea of trading my guitar in for drums, but I hated the idea of all that stuff to carry around, of being stuck packing up ages after the rest of the group had finished and were off getting high somewhere. But there is always a drummer shortage and guitarists are two-a-penny. I already hated the thought of a straight job with eternal early mornings. But lots of people hate it and do it anyway.

Melody Maker had the best 'Musicians Wanted' ads. One caught my eye. Eric Burdon was auditioning guitarists for the new Animals. I'd have a chance there. The address given was Harold Davidson's ultra plush offices near Regent Street. It was intimidating just to walk through the door of one of the biggest agencies in London. I caught the first person I saw (probably Dick Katz) and laid my hype on him – Johnny Kidd, Johnny Halliday, etc – trying to be impressive. He told me to go to Birdland – a downstairs nightclub off Jermyn Street – the next day.

One of the nicer clubs, Birdland was very weird during the day with all the lights on. I found Eric and we ran smoothly through a couple of blues-type numbers. Then, awkward silence. . . I had the feeling the spot was already filled.

I was hanging around hoping when Chas Chandler (bassist with the chart-topping Animals, TV star and all-round god) came over and asked if he'd heard me before. I reminded him of the night at John Bentley's club on Baker Street when Eric had sung with us. Chas asked if I could play bass and sit in with this other guy, gesturing to a bloke who was pacing uneasily in a distant corner. He was dressed in a horrible tan raincoat and grotty black winkle-picker boots with zips! Awful! In London in those days, we all wore Annello and David's (theatrical shoemakers) Cuban/Spanish short boots with *squared* toes. I said I'd have a go.

Chas introduced me. Jimi, his name was, and he seemed quite pleasant and friendly. He also introduced me to drummer Ainsley Dunbar and pianist (Vox Continental) Mike O'Neill/Nero of The Gladiators. Meeting Nero was a highlight of that day for me. Jimi mumbled the chords of a song called *Hey Joe* and we ran through it two or three times before briefly trying a couple of sequences in the same vein as *Have Mercy*. Jimi was amazed I remembered the chords so easily. But what's a blues progression when you've been in Germany learning new songs between sets? No one sang. It didn't seem like much of an audition. No talking, just this American guy playing nothing particularly special and the feeling that someone was planning a group.

We finished up and Jimi came over and said, 'Can I have a chat with you?' I made my favourite suggestion that we nip next door for a half of bitter. He hadn't tasted bitter yet, and found it strong compared to American beer. We chatted about nothing and about music. I wanted to know if he'd ever seen Booker T? Or Sam Cooke? He had! That improved him a lot in my estimation.

Jimi commented on my hair, which I'd begun to grow even though it was curly like his own and therefore not trendy. I told him his hair was a bit longer than my image of an American – which was based on the

GI look of short back, sides *and* top. He said I must be groovy to have hair like that and as we walked back he asked if I would come up to the audition room again the next day as he hoped I'd be in a new group with him. Chas then asked me to come back. I said I could if he'd give me ten shillings for the train fare.

Once home, I excitedly told Mum all about it. She was very happy for me. I thought it would be bloody great to be in a group with an American – someone who had grown up listening to all that exciting music on the radio. This was fantastic! He seemed a reasonable player and a nice guy, plus Chas Chandler's involvement gave Jimi a lot of credibility.

On the 30th, I turned up again as requested and no one was there. Panic! I'd been given the Anim Ltd office address on Gerard Street. I literally ran there, and did a quick hype on the first person I saw. It was Michael Jeffery, Chas's partner and The Animals' manager. He just said, 'It's OK. You got the audition. Move to London.' I nearly fainted with relief. I'd been too depressed to allow myself to get excited before then. Afraid of being let down, I didn't really relax until Chas phoned on 3 October to say, 'Come on up.' I borrowed a pound from Mum and took the next train to London.

Chapter Two

Managers, Money and Music

Experience is the name everyone gives to their mistakes.
OSCAR WILDE

Honest bread is very well –
it's the butter that makes the temptation.
DOUGLAS JERROLD

This is really a simple matter, and it would look very good
if you did it by just saying, 'Give it to me and
and I'll take care of it – don't worry.'
It is very important with the 'rock and roller'
to establish a close personal relationship
and a little gesture like this buys a lot of client confidence.
A LAWYER

MY NEW managers were not newcomers to The Scene. Newcastle group The Animals were Bryen J. 'Chas' Chandler's and Michael Frank Jeffery's initiation into the real business of music. By 1963, The Animals were going great in Jeffery's Club-a-GoGo and hoping for a chance to break big in London.

Jeffery approached agent Don Arden, then famous for getting records into the charts. Arden brought them to London, put them into The Scene Club at £10 per night and, once they were a sensation, agreed to co-manage them on two conditions: production by Mickey Most, and sole ownership of the rights to promote them throughout the world.

The release of the inspired *House of the Rising Sun* and *We Gotta Get*

Outta This Place triggered an explosion of worldwide popularity which would continue for two decades.

By 1964 Jeffery had expanded his business, signing up Derry Wilke and Goldie (Genya Raven) and The Gingerbreads – an all-girl band who were his first go at booking an American act into Europe. He started wearing a .32 Beretta in a stylish kidskin shoulder holster, but still had a hard time keeping track of the finances. It began to be rumoured that he was 'heavily into East End money'. Now London's East End was tough, but so was Newcastle.

In his specs, Jeffery looked the perennial student bookworm type. But his stories of his pre-music career made me wonder. He was terrified of flying, and once during an emergency landing he grabbed his passport and refused to come out of the toilet, no matter how the stewardess pleaded. In moments of panic he'd nervously babble about working undercover for British Army Intelligence – real spine-chilling tales about attacking a secret Russian/Egyptian base during the Suez raid, or about being used as bait in Greece to lure three men in for the kill, or about being imprisoned and tortured in a Balkan castle, or about a captured fellow agent who was thrown back across the border with a glass tube broken in his penis. Training is training, and Jeffery once attacked a friend when she forgot her key and came home via the window. So I never knew what to make of him.

Anyway, co-management relations broke down, and Arden sold his interest in The Animals, which avoided an awkward public dispute, and eventually moved his business to Los Angeles. Arden had also managed The Small Faces, who left him claiming owed royalties – though Arden steadfastly maintained that management fees and equipment costs due him balanced it out. He sold their recording contract to Andrew Loog Oldham's Immediate Records and their management to Harold Davidson.

The Animals' business affairs were a mess. Before they could figure out who to sue – or if they could sue – everything was gone. However, it was the band members who were being investigated by the taxman, of course. They still had an American tour to do and precautions would have to be taken. Tax avoidance through offshore tax schemes is an established and legal business. Tax consultant solicitors usually have expensive addresses and posh offices. For a fee, you can learn the banking quirks of islands in the Caribbean and off Central and South America, where creative minds can set up a plan of company transfers so complex that the funds in question simply vanish. To quote a London company registration office: 'It is a tax haven and it's probably not necessary to file particulars of the directors' names and addresses.

You could instruct a local firm of solicitors to inspect the Official Register of Companies for the information as one would expect them to have to keep them. However, local law may not provide for such inspections. It's not remarkable that you cannot get to the bottom of companies which are deliberately set up so that no one can find out anything about them.' Also interesting to note is the fact that many of these countries have no extradition, so you can fuck around and then fuck off.

Jeffery and Eric Burdon (the lead vocalist) met with John Hillman, a solicitor already familiar with tax schemes through some earlier work in Nassau. He suggested a Bahamian company: no tax on income, capital gains, estates, inheritances, or gifts, and bank details are confidential. This popular escape route had been sussed decades earlier by a group of lawyers and accountants who called themselves The Belongers and lined Bay Street with their offices.

Deciding that anything was better than the mess they'd sunk in before, Yameta Company Limited, Nassau, was formed on 21 January 1966. The directors included Hillman, and most notably Sir Guy Henderson, barrister, former Governor General of the Bahamas, and Chief Justice of the Bahamian Supreme Court. Shareholders come and go in these companies and sometimes they are owned at least in part by other companies. In the case of Yameta it was Hillman's Caicos (another island) Trust Company, *aka* Caicos Trust Group, Caicos Investments Ltd, etc. Leon Dicker, a distinguished New York attorney, would handle Yameta's dealings within the States. All perfectly above board.

Yameta signed up Jeffery as a manager of musical groups and he signed The Animals to his new Anim Ltd. For music publishing there was Anim Publishing, which was handled by Aaron Schroeder's in New York. Jeffery opened two accounts at the Bank of Nova Scotia, Nassau, Bahamas, one for himself and the other with Yameta.

Mickey Most and Jeffery did a recording deal with MGM, taking a nice advance. The Animals were advised about tax benefits available for recordings made outside the UK, so the Emerald Beach Hotel hall in Miami was hired. Unfortunately the acoustics were better in the toilet. The attempts to save money backfired and the group's financial difficulties remained as pressing as ever.

Nor did the tax plans keep an American tour agent from being caught with his hands deeply in the till. 'You've got to make a buck. You know how it is.' The funds were recouped and The Animals did receive a detailed accounting – though little else. The pressure and disillusionment of the financial maze combined with the knowledge that the group had passed it's peak resulted in The Animals' official break-up in July 1966 when the tour ended. Chas always said he just grabbed what he could and got out with about £1,000. Eric and Jeffery planned a fresh start with The New Animals.

Bands get headlines about million-dollar advances but few can touch the cash. Some managers and producers have access to ways of preventing anyone from knowing where it is and who can spend it. High taxes and large lump sums breed these pirhana companies which feed off innocents who think being a musician has to do solely with playing music. In reality, it's a business, and a pretty sharp one at that. If you're only interested in playing, get a 'straight' job to live and play for pleasure. Being a musician is dangerous. And worse, it can put you off music!

At twenty-eight, Chas was fed up with the discomfort and upset of being a touring musician. And being creative, he wanted to produce an artist himself. Luckily, while finishing his last Animals tour, Linda Keith found him Jimmy James of The Blue Flames. It must have felt weird when Chas walked into the Café Wha? on McDougal Street in New York's Greenwich Village and heard him playing a set which included Tim Rose's version of *Hey Joe* – the very song that had caught his own ear. This guy was tearing down musical fences, obviously liking rhythm and blues *and* Dylan. On the other side, Jimmy respected Chas's accomplishments, as I did. I shouldn't think he struggled very hard to resist Chas's offer to have a go for his dream in England. His career was lagging, he had plenty of time, and that was all Chas asked him to invest.

Chas suggested he alter his first name to Jimi; and in August 1966 an account was opened with $1,068.39 at the Bank of Nova Scotia, Nassau, in the name: Yameta Company Limited, 'Jimi Hendrix', P.O. Box 1241. Jimi was not a signatory.

I wish Chas could have been our sole manager/producer, but he was still signed to Jeffery. A group's manager has a direct effect on the group itself and upon how – or if – it is accepted in the business world. Groups who play amazing music can fold because their manager hasn't been around long enough to have good connections or because he has worn out his welcome in business circles. On the other side of it, think about the times you've said to yourself, 'How the fuck did they get into the charts?' Jeffery as an agent/manager was brilliant, but his 'sheer confusion is best' policy haunted us. A real charming wheeler-dealer, he rarely let his left hand even know he had a right hand. However, he was well established and Chas's calling was creative management/production rather than business.

Chas applied himself to the task of getting Jimi's passport together for entry into England. But there was much more to consider. For Jimi to be a viable proposition, he had to be free of contractual obligations. Chas knew Jimi must have signed some papers – he was too talented to have gotten by without a few signatures. A few obligations. A few mistakes. The problem was in remembering what and with whom.

Entertainment entrepreneurs are consummate adepts at sticking bits of paper in front of you for signatures at strategically planned awkward moments, such as just as you're walking on stage. Ask for a copy and, 'Whoops, sorry, I left your copy at the office. Get in touch with me, I'll be back from Hawaii in two months.' You'll forget. You're meant to. If you're not given time to think about it, don't sign it. Jimi'd gigged with and done sessions for many artists, including Little Richard, the Isley Brothers, Curtis Knight and Lonnie Youngblood. They spent days attempting to track down contracts and buy them back, if necessary. Feeling they'd tidied up the loose ends, Chas signed Jimi up and headed for London.

At twenty-three, Jimi had three to four years of living ahead on me. He'd done time in the Army after getting in a bit of minor trouble in his home town of Seattle. He left when a convenient parachute jumping accident offered the chance. He'd also done his time, paid his dues by travelling countless miles on the road, playing the club circuit with friends and in pick-up bands. ('Dues paying' is an ancient concept stemming from a fine, old tradition, not widely practiced today, of making music before you make money. If one more person/band who knows three chords and four songs – 'We only play original material' – says to me, 'I'm not going to work until I have a record deal,' I'll scream!) Using his head, he'd picked up riffs and performance techniques from some of the best frontmen in the business. Sometimes he succeeded in out-flashing the flashiest and sometimes he got in trouble for it, but did it just the same. That was the main difference between us. Jimi wanted to be a star. I wanted to be a musician. I always envied Jimi's musical background – wished I'd been the one slogging away with Little Richard or Sam and Dave.

In the early '60s, if you wanted to play music in America, you went to New York. Jimi settled there and spent a lot of time in Greenwich Village, *the* place to be, the swarming, vibrating centre of the highly political folk protest scene that gave birth to hippie rock. He had learned how to hustle his own gigs (and it's a terribly hard thing to do at the beginning), and had landed a regular one at the seedily trendy Café Wha? There the pressure of being a solo artist/frontman forced him to round the rough edges off his style, relax in front of an audience and get his act together. This takes time and effort, but it's necessary to discover what you do and don't like, what you can and can't do, and what you will and won't do. There is nothing like being alone in front of an audience for an hour or so. I can do it now, but I hate it. Jimi had watched, learned and worked hard perfecting show routines I'd only seen in films which were still virtually unknown to white audiences, especially in England. Eventually he'd built a personal reputation that brought musicians to him, and offers of better gigs . . . And Chas.

I worried because I was still signed to Gordon Mills and he may have meant what he said about me never working again. Chas sussed it with a simple telegram giving three months to object or forever hold his peace. No objections, and I was free.

Hendrix was born in Seattle, Washington, on 27 November 1942. I know he was black – and I learned that on his mother's side he was part Cherokee Indian and that his stepmother was of Japanese descent – but to me the important fact was that he was the one who played guitar in the Experience. I didn't know any more about his background than he knew about mine. It didn't matter. We hit it off because of something musical. Later, I met his family, he met mine, and we found out a bit more about each other. A lot has been written about the man, a lot of it true, as far as I know, and a lot of it crap. The Jimi Hendrix Experience happened fast, so fast that we didn't really know what was going on. As a result, Jimi-the-myth is hard to separate from James Marshall Hendrix/Jimmy James/Jimi Hendrix. So is the Experience-the-myth hard to separate from the Experience-the-reality.

My most urgent musical problem after Chas asked me to play with Jimi was getting a bass. To make adjusting from rhythm guitar easier, a Burns six-string was suggested. But the strings were too close together for my fingers. Chas lent me his Gibson, but it was too big in the body for me; and it didn't have that trebly sound I was subconsciously looking for. It had taken me years to realize that Gibsons were everything I craved in a rhythm guitar, so I was shocked to discover they didn't make a bass that suited me. The choice was very limited in those early days of the electric bass. I visited a lot of guitar shops over the next few months.

Suddenly, we had a gig. A tour even! When Johnny Halliday (France's Elvis) heard Jimi jamming at Blaises Club with Brian Auger, he offered Chas a support spot – and we didn't even have a drummer . . . We jammed drummerless for a few days while we checked out various drummers. This was good because we got to know each other a bit and learned to understand each other's guitar style without immediately having to incorporate a third musician. I was enjoying experimenting on bass. Never having played one before was very liberating in its way. Then, on 6 October, along came Mitch Mitchell, fresh from Georgie Fame and The Blue Flames. His flashy style was perfect for us. With my Mick Green-inspired days as a skiffle-steady rock'n'roll rhythm guitarist as the rock on which my bass style was built, Jimi and Mitch could – and would – be free to flip out on either side of me. Sometimes it would feel like walking a tightrope between two cyclones.

We had no set idea of what sound we were looking for, and so auditioned bassist Dave Knights of Procol Harum, with me back on rhythm guitar. But when Dave didn't fit in, Jimi admitted once and for all that he wanted freedom for his guitar and himself, needed to be able to just let go without worrying about arrangements or treading on other soloists. Why not just play as a three piece?

We rehearsed casually, never resorting to 'This riff goes like this' or 'Play these notes'. When Jimi had a new idea, he gave the basic chord structure and tempo and within that framework we each found our own parts and a song and arrangement emerged. Luckily our concepts meshed. What a relief from copy-learning songs I sometimes hated just because they were in the charts. We whipped through vague blues and songs Jimi remembered – *Land Of 1000 Dances*, *Have Mercy* and one of my all-time favourites, *Johnny B Goode* – just to get used to each other. Any chance to play this material was perfectly all right with me. Jimi brought tricks with him – tuning a half-step down from concert pitch so as to make playing with horn sections and bending strings for blues easier. If only I'd known that trick before! I still remember with horror my early dancehall days – everything was in A♭, E♭ and B♭, with bar chords everywhere. I also think the lower tuning subconsciously relaxed our feel, instrumentally and vocally.

Our main – and rather huge – problem was that nobody wanted to sing, not even at rehearsals. Even though he'd been singing in New York, Jimi was still nervous about being in England and got terribly embarrassed about singing. Me too. I had a squeak, not a voice. Mitch's voice was more trained and relaxed because of his stage schooling, but it wasn't what we needed, and besides, drummers weren't expected to sing. Out first gigs were virtually instrumentals with extremely minimal mumbles. Finally we broke down Jimi's shyness and persuaded him to sing. We needed him to sing. His voice had good bass fullness in it and his American accent would certainly catch the English ear. At first he'd crank his guitar up really loud to cover his singing, but gradually, he gained confidence and found the right balance between voice and guitar. He was very pleased and relieved that he could do it, and so were we.

We truly hated rehearsals. Without audience reactions (and girls), it was too much like work. Mitch sometimes didn't show up even when we started doing the odd recording session. Chas finally docked him a week's salary and he was never late again. Jimi and I worried that he didn't care and in November sneakily auditioned Merseybeats drummer John Banks (bless him). But John was tired of touring, and he was nervous. Mitch's brashness worked better.

Chas was very conscious of the artistic necessities – a good 'look' and a catchy name. Mitch would soon have a perm to standardise our curly-haired, skinny look. The fact that Jimi was black guaranteed him notice in England, even more so when he was playing next to two white guys. I can't think of any other mixed group in England at that point. Jimi wasn't tall, but when posed with us flanking him he photographed larger than life. The three of us looked really good together – symmetrical. Even on stage Jimi's left-handed technique against my right-handed one looked balanced. Jimi loved the English Carnaby Street fashions and in a few months we lost all vestiges of a traditional early sixties look. We began to realise how much we were itching to break out into something new. The possibilities excited me. We felt free.

It was Mike who came up with our name – The Experience.

11 October was contract time. We all felt embarrassed and shy about money. Surely it would be impolite to ask questions (even if you understood enough of the foreign language called legalese to be able to think of one) or even to appear to scrutinise the contract? It'd be like saying: 'I don't trust you.' Trust was everything for us. I knew they could trust me, and they were famous, respected professionals. What could go wrong? We knew about groups – you played, you hopefully earned money, and you shared the profits. What else could a contract say? In silence we listened to a quick rundown, hearing only that we'd be making records and getting money.

In our ignorance, we never realised how we were being tied up. The gist of the seven-year contract (six-month option and five-year extension available to the producers) was: We three, known together as the Jimi Hendrix Experience, signed as exclusive artists to Jeffery and Chandler, producers desirous of making and exploiting sound recordings and enhancing and promoting our professional reputations. As artists we agreed to create songs and perform them together or otherwise to the best of our skill for a minimum of ten single sides per year (more if the producers want and less only in the case of an act of government or God). If anyone left the group he left the name, remained contracted, and would have to get anybody he later joined with to sign up too. We couldn't record for others without permission, or record the same material for anyone else for five years, or grant any rights and licenses, or do anything which would impair our fulfillment of this agreement. We gave Jeffery and Chandler the worldwide rights to any copyrights (songs) and performance rights (radio, TV, film) of material recorded, the right to use our names, biographies and any other information useful for selling records, and the right to assign our rights to someone else.

We agreed not to get convicted of a criminal offence, behave badly in public, or get ill. We agreed to protect them against any breach of the contract when the producers interests had been granted to a third party, and against any lawsuits under UK law. We granted them power of attorney (the right to sign anything for you, including cheques, whether you've seen them or not) during the course of the agreement.

In exchange, the producers agreed to organise recordings, to pay all costs incurred, including royalties, and to try hard to exploit our records. After contract termination, they retained the right to sell stocks of our records (sell-off period) for five years. Then, if we notified them on time, the masters would be destroyed or delivered to us if the producer's (unspecified) costs were reimbursed.

The artists were to share a commission of 2½ per cent of the *net* retail price of our recordings, calculated on 90 per cent. The percentage dropped to 1¼ per cent for tapes, one-sided records, and records sold outside the UK, US, Canada, and Benelux. Half of these amounts would be paid for sales through records clubs, and one quarter if the records were given away to induce the public to join a record club. The group would share as little as 0.31 per cent in some cases. In two years our percentage was to double!

The producers were to account to us twice yearly within three months of the end of June and December (the first accounting was due before April 1967) and in a dispute the producer's auditor would decide. They could deduct all recording costs. They could pay one member of the group and be discharged from all further responsibility.

Jimi, Mitch and I eagerly put pen to paper and signed. We left the documents at the office. Where would I keep them anyway? In my suitcase beside my clap pills in the six-quid-a-week Madison Hotel? I should have. Never say, 'I needn't think about that, let them do it.' If you don't want to think about it, you shouldn't be doing it. Elvis's slogan became, 'Take care of business.' Memorise the following: *Get copies of everything you sign and save them.* Even if you just chuck the hieroglyphics in an old box and stash it in the closet. Of course, it's better to read and understand it all first – preferably before signing. But if you don't, at least you'll be able to dig it up and figure out why someone was able to stick that knife in your back.

That same day Chas brought Burns gear for us to check out. No chance. Too lightweight sounding. It even looked like cardboard. With that decided, Jimi and Mitch started kicking a combo around the room to see how long it would last. I was horrified! But I will say this for that Burns amp – it survived. Even the stairs! I rescued one PA column and when I got a record player I cut it in half for speakers. Jimi was all right, living with Chas first at the Hyde Park Towers, then in a Beatle's ex-flat in Montague Square. Mitch was living at home in Ealing, London. But I had the expense of the hotel room and eating out. I scraped by on Wimpy burgers and Indian curries. I couldn't have afforded one item of the gear that had just been rejected.

Next day at seven a.m., after being a group for only a week, it was Marshall gear we carted off to France – three amps, two speakers, two PA cabinets, three Shure mikes, three stands and strings for a total of £1066.7s. Add to that the cost of getting Jimi to England (£191.8s, including luggage, clothing, lawyers fees, passport, hotel, and airfare), and the £15 paid to each of us. Costs weren't too bad, but they were mounting.

At least we were working.

Chapter Three

Evreux to Monterey to The Monkees

Nothing great was ever achieved without enthusiasm.
RALPH WALDO EMERSON

Art is not a handicraft,
it is the transmission of feeling the artist has accumulated.
LEO TOLSTOY

OUR first tour started with a late plane, speakers missing on arrival, and a mad rush to get to rehearsals (press admitted) at the wonderful Paris Olympia. We all, including Chas, humped gear, counted pennies, fretted and prayed. We were so happy just to be playing *and* eating. The schedule was as follows:

October
13 Evreux
14 Nancy
15 An unknown venue near Luxembourg
18 Paris Olympia

The musician's coach took us to Evreux, where we were supporting Johnny Halliday, who travelled separately in his Aston Martin. Before the gig we sat quietly and had a couple of smokes – hash and tobacco combined European style in big multi-skinned joints – to calm the nerves. Jimi wasn't used to smoking in this way and he always asked 'Roll me one of those big English joints, Noel. I can't do it.' I don't think he ever sussed rolling those joints. We felt uncertain about how we'd be received, because we knew our sound was hard to categorise: a real mish-mash of influences, plus a few decibels thrown in for good measure. We needn't have worried. Our fifteen-minute, four-song set got a good reception, in spite of the blown bass speaker which forced me to plug directly into the PA. Good vibes for the best of beginnings. And more hash than I'd ever seen . . .

In Nancy we extended our pre-gig brain modifications. I introduced the band to the uppers Captogan and Preludin I knew so well by now. Europe's huge chemical drug companies had the continent swimming in pills. I rationed everyone to half a tablet, knowing that a whole one would keep us up all night. After that, before gigs, it was, 'Hey, Noel. Got any of those tablets?' And because I'd finished my course of clap pills and could drink again, it was up, down and sideways.

After our Luxembourg gig we had a day off to look forward to. We got drunk together after the show and at half-twelve we crawled into the coach, set off, and promptly ran out of petrol. Was it cold! This never would have happened in the summer. Mitch grabbed Chas's raincoat for himself and went to sleep. Chas, Jimi and I huddled together and tried to keep from freezing through the long, long night.

We were required to rehearse for the big Paris gig. This meant sitting around all day thinking too much, getting terrible nerves, and feeling ill. At least when roaming around outside our amazement at being in Paris kept out minds off the impending show. I spent some time with Brian Auger's Trinity, but was getting to know my nerves pretty well by the time we were due to play. As it turned out, our three numbers – *Everybody Needs Somebody to Love*, *Have Mercy* and *Hey Joe* – went down a bomb. Talk about relief. We got merry at the theatre, then headed off to a big party in a posh downstairs club and got drunker and more stoned, with the uppers keeping us raving. Suddenly it was six-thirty in the morning. We just managed to pack up the gear in time to drag it to the airport, complaining constantly and dreaming of a roadie. But we laughed and joked. High on our success (total earnings for the tour were an astronomical 3,375 francs) we could handle anything.

Back in England, though, we joined the multitude of unknown groups praying for a break. When Jimi had first arrived, Chas took him around to clubs such as Les Cousins to jam with established musicians like Alex Harvey, Hughie Flint, Alexis Korner, and Cliff Barton. But although there were great sessions, the general feeling was 'black people will not make it – not in the "stardom" sense of the word'. It was this narrow, conservative attitude of the older generation of musicians that forced the whole music scene to burst free.

But we were different from other bands waiting for the call, and fortunately, we had Chas's knowledge, connections, belief in us, and guitars he could sell to cover living expenses. He spent hours grooming and creating 'HENDRIX, the PR man's dream'. We all had to refine our roles. Jimi would be the macho man, Mitch the bouncy type, and I'd be the quiet one. From talent to gimmick to notice to success. Some things never change.

To get by, I sold my Fender Bandmaster amp (but bought it back as soon as I could), did demos and gigged with The Loving Kind – making as much with them as I was with the Experience. But The Loving Kind was on it's last legs. Pete went off to join Leapy Lee, then The Honeybus (*I Can't Let Maggie Go*), then did session work, then joined Shanghai with Mick Green, then The Liverpool Express and finally Status Quo. Neil joined The Ivy League, The Flowerpot Men (*Let's Go to San Francisco*), did sessions, then some solo work, went on to Fat Mattress and then moved to Germany where he is a solo artist. Jim joined Engelbert's band, then Fat Mattress, Juicy Lucy, Joe Brown, Steve Marriott, Marianne Faithful – to name a few. Adge became a session pianist. NuNu became the drum roadie for Yes. Derek, married and a father, retired to Folkestone and opened a book store.

On 23 October Chas took us into Kingsway Studios to demo *Hey Joe* and *Stonefree* for a single. *Hey Joe* is a very difficult song to do right and it took forever. The Marshalls were too much for the mikes and Chas and Jimi rowed over recording volume. That 'loud', full, live sound was nearly impossible to obtain (especially for the bass) without the distortion which funnily enough became part of our sound. No limiters, compressors or noise reduction units yet. I found the Marshalls fine (though for me nothing can better a Fender valve amp) for guitar but not solid enough sounding for the bass. Somehow the difficulties were ironed out, tempers subsided, and we finished off *Hey Joe* with background vocals by The Vernon Girls. Chas tried to interest Decca. No luck. But then they'd turned the Beatles down, too.

We pissed about rehearsing what we knew and jammed the loose chords that were to become the songs *Can You See Me* and *Fire*. No vocals. Each of us just imagined what the melody might be. Our schedule looked like this:

October

23	Recording at Kingsway Studios, *Hey Joe*.
24,26,28,31	Rehearsals.
25	Scotch of St James, London

November

1	Rehearsal.
2	Rehearsal at Averbach House. Saw Hank Marvin. Recording from 6-12. Three numbers.
3,4	Rehearsal
8-11	Munich, West Germany, Big Apple Club (£300)
25	Reception at the Bag O'Nails
26	Hounslow, Middlesex, Ricky Tick Club

The Scotch of St James was an original 'groove' club. Chas must have been on his knees using up favours to get past the problem of 'Who? Never heard of 'em!' but our half-hour set with terrible sound went down well, and the Harold Davidson Agency, a proper, respected booker, booked us into the Big Apple Club in Munich. A few weeks earlier, knowing (hoping) we'd need a road manager, I'd sent Gerry Stickells, a drinking mate, into the office with orders to 'hype' his way in. I knew that nothing was more important than having a mechanic with the group. Vans are always breaking down. And he was a good driver which would be helpful on those long hauls. He was hired. What luxury!

Our standard two forty-five-minute shows per night drove the Munich crowd wild. To them, we were real freaks, perhaps the first Anglo-American group to play there. There Jimi discovered demolition feedback during our bash-type last number. The crowd was going crazy and began to pull Jimi into the audience. He panicked, and to save his guitar, he threw it onto the stage. It exploded into amazing sounds in response to the impact. It startled Jimi, but the crowd went right over the top. New dimensions in sound, new dimensions in German audience freakout.

Back in no-gig London, Chas – with no help from Mike the Invisible Man(ager) – sold guitars and scratched together enough for a reception at the Bag O'Nails, John and Rik Gunnel's trendy Soho club. We did forty-five minutes for an audience that included the Beatles, The Who and Donovan. For only three people, the sheer volume was breathtaking. Some of the audience fled. Part of the problem was gear. Our future set-up hadn't even been invented yet, and pushing the current gear always resulted in a large volume of hiss, crackle, and sheer noise. Afterwards, the *Record Mirror* asked for an interview. We'd finally gotten the press's attention. Jimi, Chas and I got very drunk. We seemed to get drunk a lot, but our euphoria was just the aftermath of the pre-gig tension combined with the prospect of lovely ladies.

Kit Lambert and Chris Stamp attended that one and to impress us they took us round their studio to meet their group, The Who, who had just struck lucky. Previously stuck with Decca, then basically a classical label, they'd had little success breaking into the States (only the Beatles and the Stones had, so far). After Lambert and Stamp asked for a release, Decca offered them three times their current royalty rate, a £50,000 advance, and introduced them to the rest of the world. Polydor took over the rest of the world for a £30,000 advance, and agreed to distribute their new Track Records. Now they wanted The Experience.

Eventually Lambert and Stamp offered an irresistible deal, including a £1,000 promotional film for every record, a substantial advance, some recording costs, and an immediate appearance on *Ready, Steady, Go*. TV exposure was virtually impossible to get then, and promotional films were unheard of. We would never have believed then that television channels would one day put out music promo films twenty-four hours a day.

On 1 December, Jimi signed an exclusive four-year management contract with Yameta Company Limited who would try to promote and further the career of Hendrix the Performer for 40 per cent (down from 45 per cent) of all gross payments, excluding gross payments for recording and publishing. If Yameta terminated, Jeffery could claim Jimi for ten shillings. Yameta hired the agent, and our earnings would go directly to Yameta, who would then return the agent's fee. Jimi guaranteed that he had no outstanding contractual obligations, and promised to be good and send every penny to Yameta. Anything Jimi did during the contract period would earn 40 per cent of any subsequent income for the management forever.

Our improved position inspired us to work harder. We spent hours with Chas in post-mortems of our gigs and in working out the finer points of the act. The best part of these meetings was visiting Chas's comfy flat for some wine. My grotty hotel room was for sleeping only. I actually lived in the (now gone) George pub on Charing Cross Road.

Then Jimi's guitar got nicked and Chas's last guitar went to replace it. In those days, the price of a guitar in England could easily be the equivalent of a half-year's wages. Our December went like this:

December
10 London, Brixton, Ram Jam Club.
13 TV: *Ready, Steady, Go* (£100). Dave Clarke (of the Five) later bought the tapes and released them on video.

Recording at CBS. Three songs in three hours.
15   Recording session turned into rehearsal because Mitch didn't
      show.
16   Photo session. Radio Caroline interview.
      London, Chislehurst Caves.
21   London, Blaises Club (£28.10s).
22   Southampton, Guildhall – two shows.
26   London, Forest Gate, Upper Cut Club (£40).
29   BBC TV, *Top of the Pops* (£78.15s).
31   Folkestone, Kent, Stan's Hillside Club (£50).

We totally freaked the regulars at the Ram Jam – an all reggae, black, smokers' pub – who had no idea what to make of us.

On 2 December *Hey Joe/Stonefree* was released on a Polydor one-off deal because Track wasn't functioning yet. Then on 13 December, only two months to the day since our first gig, we filmed our first TV, the last *Ready, Steady, Go* show. It featured the Mersey's (two original Merseybeats, Tony Crane and Billy Kingsley), the Troggs and Keith Relf (lead singer of the original Yardbirds). Mitch had acted on telly before, but Jimi had only limited TV experience and I had none. We were extremely nervous, and in those days you played LIVE. You arrived at ten in the morning and rehearsed, returned at three for another run-through and did it live at seven. The hard part was staying sober all the boring day. Once, ITV goofed and put on a Who backing track as we went out live on *Top of the Pops*. It took Jimi aback but he calmly announced, 'I don't know the words to that one,' and by that time they'd switched tapes.

I think we just played *Hey Joe*. Right before the show my stage clothes were nicked from the van. Chas was probably happy. He hated my pink jeans. We dashed out and he bought me trousers and a terribly conservative striped jumper, for which he then billed me. We often finished off the night in the Bag O'Nails because we could get in free. The £1.00 admission price would have been hard to come by.

We met at Chas's on the 16th to watch ourselves on TV. It was just as nerve-wracking watching it as doing it. Jimi and I had never seen ourselves on telly before. Chas was well used to it, but we were his baby and this show could make or break us. It certainly went down well enough to pack the Chislehurst Caves gig. Chas was so jumpy about carrying our fee that when a guy suddenly appeared to say he'd liked the gig, Chas thought he was a robber and flattened him with a punch.

The tide started to turn. The BBC being the BBC, we got no airplay. Selling in spite of them (or perhaps because of them), after three months as a group, we were thirty-eight in the national charts and eighteenth in London. Then suddenly we jumped to six. Track were working hard and spent money on advertising: 'Our policy is to promote more than EMI and pay more than Decca.' And within nine months they had seven records in the Top Ten, including ours which stayed in for four months.

This was our break. Chas's intuition had been right and his determination had paid off. Now we could actually afford the capable Gerry Stickells. Since we were soon using two tons of gear, we needed him. And he organised us too: 'I have to get them to the right airport, then the right continent, the right venue, on time, and put them on stage. Then see that they sleep as well as checking to see that they don't go to bed with the wrong girls.'

What more do you need as a twenty-first birthday present than to know that the Beatles came to your gigs? Money worries loomed less large as our successes piled up. We were so gratefully amazed to be doing *Top of the Pops* with Wayne Fontana that we never considered we should be paid for it. Our fees were duly passed on to Nassau, unless the management drew them from the agency account. Idly discussing our circumstances, we assumed that we still had debts and when there was something extra it would go into a kitty and be divided. In the meantime, we supplemented our income in any way possible.

I figured I'd rather eat by playing music with the Experience and organised a New Year's Eve gig for the band at Stan's Hillside Club in Folkestone – fifty whole pounds! I was the only one he'd ever heard of, and Stan worried about booking an unknown band for such an important night. I had to sell hard to convince him that we were worth it. Then the management and agent contacted Stan and bang went our pocket money.

It was a great night – amazing warmth and acceptance from the regular Folkestone crowd, which included Doug and Joan the Bone, Charlie Brown, and Maggie. But English licensing laws madly insist on throwing you into the street just before midnight even on New Year's Eve, so we stopped at eleven-thirty and ran to the van. Gerry floored it and raced like a madman along the dark, marsh roads, but we didn't make it to Mum's till half-twelve. We, including Cathy Etchingham who'd come down from London with Jimi, were dying to get sloppy and sentimental, sing *Auld Lang Syne* and drink in our New Year – our new life – with Mum and Gran. I loved sharing my family with Jimi. I knew he felt lonely and strange at times. They hit it off great! Mum had a blazing fire going. First thing that Jimi asked was, 'May I stand in front of your fire?' He said he found it great to stand with his back to the warmth of the fire during the cold and damp English nights. Mum always felt that the words to *Fire* came from that night. Mum loved Jimi's reserved, polite and shy manner. And Jimi took to Mum, later signing a photo for her with 'From Your Son, Jimi'. It's one of her most precious possessions. Jimi was like that. When asked to sign an autograph he usually tried to add a personal touch. When Jimi and Cathy retired, I donated my bed. I was too excited to sleep. Everything was starting to accelerate. We could feel our momentum building. I stayed up drinking in 1967. A most amazing year it turned out to be.

Just to keep things in perspective, not everyone loved us. We still had wretched nights when the audience hated us and every note we played. There were also personal bad moments. In Manchester, we borrowed the van to go to the Twisted Wheel Club. They refused us entry and then the plainclothes police showed up. I was nervous because of driving without proper insurance. They started searching me and found an anti-smoking (cigarettes) pill in my wallet. I tried to tell them what it was, but they were looking for the Bust of the Century so they hit me in the face and knocked my glasses off. They left Jimi alone because he was a foreigner and, in those days, exempt from police harassment. Very educational, but from now on I had little spare time to dwell on anything good or bad. If I had an afternoon off, I escaped to the fantasy world of the cinema.

The new year began:

January

1   Rehearsal at Stan's.
4   Bromley, Kent, Bromel Club (long, hour-and-a-quarter set).
5,6 Interviews. Photos for *Fabulous* magazine.
7   Manchester, New Century Hall (£38).
8   Sheffield, Mojo Club.
9   Photos at 7½ Club. Record is twenty-five in *NME*, fifteen in *Disc* and twenty-six in *MM* charts.
11   Recording at CBS (*Purple Haze*, I think). John Mayall at session. Sound bad.
     London, Bag O'Nails. Two half-hour shows. Packed!
12   Personal appearance at Race Car Show for Radio London. London 7½ Club (£35).
13   London, 7½ Club.
14   Nottingham, Beachcomber.
15   Yorkshire, Kirk Levington Country Club.

16	London, 7½ Club. Seven in *NME* chart.
17	Radio: *Ready, Steady*.
	7½ Club.
18	Interview, probably only Jimi, with David Frost.
	London, BBC TV, *Top of the Pops* (£75.15s)
	London, 7½ Club.
19	London, Speakeasy Club (£47.10s).
20	London, Haverstock Hill Country Club. Jimi's amp blew.
21	London, Golders Green.
22	Oldham, Lancashire, The Astoria.
24	Photo session. Rehearsal.
	London, Marquee. Broke the crowd record and still hold it.
25	Norwich, Oxford Cellar. Smallest, hottest place I've ever played in. Terrible sound.
27	London, Chislehurst Caves. Crowd of 2,000! (£50).
28	London, Forest Gate, Upper Cut Club. 5,000 tonight!
29	London, Saville Theatre (with The Who) – two half-hour shows with bad amps.
30	Radio, *Pop North*. Terrible sound.
31	Filming from early till five-thirty at the Saville for Kit Lambert. Possibly a promo film. Heard our French EP. Got 200-watt Marshalls today.

Things changed fast and our days settled into a routine: up late, travel, gig, get pissed, crawl into bed between four and eight in the morning. Most of our days were spent in brain-and-body-numbing travel covering every corner of England and much of the middle. It was like being with the Burnettes all over again. Usually Stickells drove the van and we'd pack ourselves in with the gear. I'd squeeze in between the roof and equipment because there weren't enough seats. Sometimes we had the luxury of Neil and his car and we'd share the driving. We avoided asking Mitch to drive. Jimi and I got into a car with Mitch driving once and swore we'd never make that mistake again! And Jimi couldn't get used to driving on the left in England. The roads were cowpaths compared to what they are now. We'd get back at some God-forsaken time of the morning and drag ourselves up to my place where we would sit, each in a corner with a beer and a hash joint, relaxing in silent thoughts we were often too tired to share. It was during these moments that I turned Jimi on to my small record collection – the Kinks, the Small Faces and, most enjoyably, the Goons.

We were constantly skint. Even Jimi, who had no immediate accommodation problems, borrowed a few shillings here and there.

There were so many more expenses, especially the fancy (and expensive) stage clothes. Our accelerating popularity increased the number of hangers-on, and the pressure accelerated our drinking. It was difficult to leave anywhere without at least two girls on each arm. I was seeing about a dozen birds regularly. I think I spent most of January in bed. After a radio appearance on 17 January, we ran up a huge bar bill of over two quid. Even pooling our money, we couldn't cover it.

On 11 January producers Jeffery and Chas, owners of 'the sole and exclusive services of JAMES MARSHALL HENDRIX', and Chris Stamp signed the New Action Production Limited (Track Records) contract for all territories, excluding the United States and Canada, France, Belgium, Luxembourg and Switzerland, two months before the company was actually set up. The three-year (plus two-year sell-off period giving the outside expiry date as 10 January 1972) contract called for four singles and two LPS per year. If sales were good, the second advance would increase. Recently I wrote for information about this, but unfortunately all the Experience files had been 'lost in a fire at the home of one of the directors'.

Had we realised how our lives and creative efforts were being manipulated, the Experience might have ended right then. We hadn't an inkling of the multitude of contracts being signed. Even Jimi's signature didn't do him any good since his given address was usually the office address. (Always use your own address on contracts.) I assumed that if there were other contracts, we'd be asked to sign. After all, I'd had to sign my Pye recording contract, as had my mother, since I was underage. I was still under twenty-one when I signed with Jeffery and Chas. We'd not been signed to Jimi. There was never any inference that we were less than a group, sharing everything, or that business was being done on a different basis. But we'd signed an 'everything contract' with Mike and Chas which gave them the right to proceed on our behalf without consultation. Since our office was the Anim office, I'd been hanging out with Eric Burdon, Terry McVey, Tony Garland, and the office staff, who had seen the Animals' troubles go down. They tried to warn me to be careful, but I didn't really understand what they meant.

February

  1 South Shields, New Cellar Club (£71.5s). Jimi's 200-watt amp blew. Terrible PA.
  2 Darlington, Imperial Club. Two amps broke down. Mains fused. Crowd fantastic.
      Club-a-GoGo. Party with the Moody Blues.

3 Recording new single at Olympic Studios, London.
Hounslow, Ricky Tick Club.

4 London, Ram Jam.
London, Flamingo Club.

6 Croydon, Surrey, Star Hotel.

7 Recording. Three tracks.

8 Recording.
Bromley, London, Bromel Club.

9 Recording.
Bristol, Locarno (£260).

10 Newbury, Ricky Tick (£50).

11 Cheltenham, Blue Moon. I used my new Fender Jazz Bass for
the first time (£40).

12 Stockport, Sinking Ship.

13 Radio: *Saturday Club*. Did *Stonefree, Love or Confusion, Hey Joe,
Foxy Lady*, and one more.

14 Photo session.
Tilbury, Essex, Gray's Club (£90).

15 Cambridge, Dorothy Ballroom (£75). Lost two plectrums –
bass eating picks. I could have used some Jim Dunlops.

17 Windsor, Ricky Tick (£50).

18 Photo session.
York, University of York, Art College (£150).

19 London, Brady's Club (£75).

20 Recording.
Bath, The Pavilion (£192).

21 Rehearsal of four new numbers.

22 London, BBC radio, *Parade of the Pops*.
Press reception at Speakeasy for the Soft Machine.
London, Roundhouse. Awful – died a death. Horrible place.
Jimi had his white guitar stolen (paid £100, unpaid £50).

23 Photo session. No one there.
Recording at Kingsway.
Worthing, Surrey, Pier Pavilion. Not very good (£189).

24 Leicester, University of Leicester. Good gig, bad sound (£75).

25 Chelmsford, Corn Exchange (£220).

26 Rehearsal
Southend-on-Sea, Essex, St Mary Cray, with Koobas, Dave
Dee, Nashville Teens. Two twenty-five-minute shows (£250).

27 Photo session.

We were running late on 1 February and jumped on the revolving stage just as it began to swing round. Jimi's amp instantly blew up. He plugged into mine and I grabbed the other group's tiny amp – about a five-watter. The bass was buzzing like mad (and I imagine the amp owner was praying like mad) as Gerry rushed up and plugged me into the PA which obliterated the vocals except for a whisper in the backing breaks. As we finished the stage began to revolve away. The audience just reached out and grabbed us. I clung to Jimi and he held fast to Mitch and we JUST escaped getting crushed against the wall as we spun. A couple of nights later, Jimi broke his guitar and I had to borrow my old Telecaster from Trevor Williams.

Costs were forever escalating, so it was no big deal when we got a £20 bonus and a raise to £25 from £15 per week in mid-January, and then up to £30 in mid-February. Like most musicians, we hated to speak up, preferring to avoid any form of upset and concentrate on making music. We'd mumble and complain to each other and hustle on the side until we felt desperate enough for a confrontation. Slowly it began to sink in that unless we worked ourselves into a lather and complained, nothing would happen. Thinking of my earlier bands that had made less and taken home more, I started to write down the gig fee whenever I could discover it.

The matter of a bass rumbled on. In January I borrowed a Fender Mustang for a few gigs, but to me the short-scale neck didn't feel like a real bass. In the back of my mind I'd already fallen in love with the Fender Jazz Bass, even though the Precisions were all the rage. On 7 February, I found my bass in Sound City. When you find a guitar that's 'yours', you know it. If you're worried, it's the wrong one. The right one will have that 'at home' feeling. However, it's always the one you can't afford. I'd previously swopped my Telecaster with Trevor Williams for a Gibson two-pick-up. So I used the Gibson as part payment on 'my bass', which was costing well over £200. I tried to take it away to use but they wouldn't let me. So Chas loaned me the balance and I had my Fender Jazz Bass. I loved it.

Musically, we picked up steam daily, and press cuttings piled up hourly. Even if you didn't like us, at least you could be sure of seeing someone – Keith Moon, a Beatle or a Stone, Liza Minelli, Eric Clapton, Jane Asher, Marianne Faithful – at our gigs. Last month we'd played to hundreds. This month, thousands. The demands on the gear were incredible. We needed to be loud – and I mean deafening – to deliver our concept of a complete orchestra in three pieces. We blew amps left, right, and centre as we pumped up and up, trying to fill the whole hall and any gaps between us and the audience with sound. In order to hear me, Jimi liked one of my speakers on his side. I had no trouble hearing Jimi. Poor Mitch, who at times couldn't even hear us (no monitors) but could follow by watching the rhythm of my fingers, was left in the middle to beat his brains out electronically unassisted, trying to compete with hundreds of watts full up with nothing but sheer energy. The miking of drumkits was unheard of, and our electrical demands were already terrorising clubs.

It cost more, in every way, to hang out every night, but we just had to relax and unwind from the shows. However, the unwinding soon became a wind-up as more and more people gravitated towards our aura of success. We had party invites every night – more drinking, more smoking, and more pills for energy. Sleep was now reduced to two to six hours per night – *if* you went home, or home alone. The star treatment was overwhelming. No matter how much I'd dreamed about being 'a star', I'd never appreciated what a mixed blessing it would be. I loved being recognised, but hated being unable to claim a bit of privacy when I needed it. And I needed it more and more. Star dreams created in pissed-off, impatient moods are just that. You never put bad bits in your dreams, only a life of total happiness surrounded by adoring fans. Slowly, I began to realise just how much was expected of me and my time, just when I thought I'd paid my dues and could have some fun.

You can try to maintain two lives until you look for a focal point for your private self, then the realisation hits that your previous life has been demolished. Everything has changed. Even friends. Simple pleasures – a quiet pint and chat, a good night's sleep – were gone. If I tried to go ice-skating, I'd be pulled apart by schoolgirls (another lovely fantasy that's better in the head). If I went to a club, they'd announce my presence – applause, people rushing up for autographs, free drinks, fucks. Getting a bag of chips became a production. My most wonderful dream was becoming the most nightmarish imposition. I was the lucky one, but I survived only because, for a quid a week, wonderful Margaret and Rose fed me.

March
1   Rehearsal.
    Recording at Kingsway: *Like A Rolling Stone*. Difficult to get a good bass sound.
    Purley, Orchid Ballroom (£154.14s.4d).
2   German TV (*Beat Club*) filmed two numbers in the Marquee (£185).
4   Paris, two radio shows. *Hey Joe* released in France.
    Gig – in the club of a hotel, I think.

Concert at Faculté de Droit D'Assas Graduation Ball with Pretty Things.
5 Belgium, Mouscron.
Lille, France (French gigs – £300).
6 Brussels, mimed *Hey Joe* for TV.
7 Waterloo, Belgium: mimed two songs for Brussels TV.
9 Hull, England, Skyline Hotel (£200).
10 Newcastle-upon-Tyne, Club-a-GoGo (£250).
11 Leeds, International Club (£51).
12 Ilkley, Gyro Club. Gig stopped – fire regulations (£60).
13 Amsterdam, session for Dutch TV.
14 Amsterdam, TV and press reception. Mimed *Hey Joe* and *Stonefree* (Dutch sessions £140).
15 Photos before flying back.
London, interviews and photos.
16 Three interviews, press reception.
17 Hamburg, press reception.
17 Star Club, two shows (£200).
18 Radio show, five-song session.
Interviews.
Star Club, two shows (£200).
19 Photo session, interview for *Bravo* magazine.
Star Club, two shows (£200).
20 Photo session. Fly to Frankfurt, then Luxembourg.
21 Radio Luxembourg. On to Brussels then London.
23 Photo session.
Southampton, Guildhall (£175).
25 Boston, Lincoln, Gliderdrome (£300). Roger Taylor of Queen first saw us here. The loudest band he'd ever heard.
26 Stockport, Tabernacle Club (£100).
27 Manchester, BBC TV, *Simon Dee Show* with Kiki Dee, Lance Percival, Cat Stevens (£95.4s).
28 Aylesbury, Market Hall (£175).
Radio, *Saturday Club* – *Killing Floor, Fire, Purple Haze* (£34).
29 Recorded three songs at Kingsway.
30 London, BBC TV, *Top of the Pops* (£21).
Recording. Walker Brothers Tour starts, two shows per night (£100 per show).
31 London, the Finsbury Park Astoria. Jimi set fire to his guitar for the first time.
Press reception at the China Gardens.

The pressure created personality problems. I was drinking too much and Jimi started getting what I called 'moodies', having a terrible one on 13 March while doing a session for Dutch TV. He insisted on playing at the volume he wanted, and it literally brought the ceiling down in the studio below us. Then they made us mime and we always felt stupid miming.

Purple Haze/51st Anniversary (Track/Published and Produced by Yameta) came out as we left for Germany, where I put my German to good use, scoring the leapers, doing the interviews, and announcing. I'd picked up German very quickly when I'd worked there – if you didn't, you didn't get laid.

Up to this time, Jimi's sound had been a combination of impeccable playing of the Stratocaster and VOLUME. He had this inimitable ability to incorporate even the minutest sound coming from his guitar into the tune. He used no electrical effects besides feedback, nor was he pushed to adopt any. It had been *Satisfaction*, in 1965, that had prompted my experimentation with my home-made fuzz unit, but *Purple Haze* was The Experience's first recording to use the effect. There are no effects at all other than basic distortions on our first recordings.

I still loved to hang out in London guitar shops, where I'd finally earned myself a bit of credibility. Now I was a working London musician, I'd be shown all the latest gear. When I first heard the Vox CryBaby pedal (later called a WhaWha), I knew Jimi would love it, so I persuaded him to come down to the Vox shop on Charing Cross Road and have a go. I was right – Jimi and WhaWha struck up a serious relationship. It opened up new avenues of sound for him. In fact it was a surprisingly similar box of tricks to the diArmand Tone and Volume Pedal I'd been using for guitar since The Lonely Ones. The Wildcats had recorded *Trambone* using one. The diArmand pedal differed in that you had to move your foot up, down and sideways for different tones, and perhaps this awkward design drove it from the market, though I'd love to find one again. When Jimi showed interest, the shop made him a gift of the CryBaby. He didn't use it right away, but it was to have a remarkable effect on our second album.

Later this year, Jimi met Roger Meyer in England. I wondered about this strange guy on the edge of the stage during the 1968 tour. Roger started by modifying the pedals Jimi already had, then there came what turned out to be the Octavia. Eventually, Roger married and disappeared from the scene, though he continues to market effects.

Jeffery, who had disappeared from our scene as soon as the contracts were signed, was in the States, and on 21 March 1967, a Reprise Records (Frank Sinatra's hitless label distributed by Warner

Brothers) contract was signed: a five-year, million-dollar one. I can't get a copy, but the advance was reported to be $120,000 with an 8 per cent royalty for the artists and 2 per cent for Jeffery/Yameta Productions.

Chas asked me to set up his new £330 stereo in his new flat. Mitch and I joined forces and managed to find an upstairs flat in Bayswater to call home – until Jimmy Leverton came over for a bath. The tap came off in his hand and he flooded the place with scalding hot water. Our downstairs neighbours had just redecorated, so we were flat-hunting again.

Pye contacted me about extending the Loving Kind contract. I wrote to Mills hoping there were royalties due. No reply.

Now it began to get crazy. We'd get ambushed and mauled going to gigs. Girls in the audience would scream our names louder than we could play our songs. The management were allowing the group to be billed as 'Jimi Hendrix' and that lack of 'Experience' created a resentful division. I began to feel we were being put down by our own management, even though we were playing well as a unit and all working like slaves. It was also difficult not to take personally Chas's subtle reminders that my role was to be quietly supportive so as not to detract from Jimi onstage, 'Why don't you just lay back and cool it, Noel. Just sway.' This actually made it difficult to relax because if the music took off, I felt restricted. I suppose Jimi was the same but in reverse. If he felt like standing and playing seriously, the little voice in his head would go, 'Mad. Sexy. Wildman'. We began to vent our annoyance and resentment on each other. It was hard on Jimi, even though he was being groomed as the star. He began to feel the pressure of taking it all on his own and sometimes lost the lighthearted approach which was such a big part of his appeal.

We headed to the studio every free moment we had. There, Chas and Jimi would quarrel over how high to mix the voice or how much volume distortion was acceptable. Jimi, still shy, wanted to bury his singing. I actually played a guitar on the original Polydor recording of *Red House*. Jimi said, 'Blues in B.' I had borrowed a terrible old hollow-body electric guitar from someone at the studio – it might have been Alan Freeman – because I liked to play along on rhythm to familiarise myself with a sequence, not being quite at home on the bass yet. We ended up just recording it – first take, I think.

April went like this:

1 Ipswich, Odeon. First show filmed for Paris TV, who still hold the film.

 2 Worcester, Gaumont.
 3 Photo session for *Daily Mirror*.
   Recording at Olympic Studios.
 4 Recording.
 5 Leeds, Odeon.
 6 Glasgow, Odeon.
 7 Carlisle, ABC.
 8 Chesterfield, ABC.
 9 Liverpool, Empire Theatre.
10 London, radio show.
11 Photo session.
   Bedford, Granada.
12 Interviews.
   Southampton, Gaumont.
13 Wolverhampton, Gaumont.
14 Bolton, Odeon.
15 Blackpool, Odeon. Bad crowd.
16 Leicester, DeMontfort Hall.
17 Kingsway Studio, London. BBC TV, *Late Night Line-up*.
   BBC interview.
19 Birmingham, Odeon.
20 Lincoln, ABC, accompanied by the girls from *Fabulous* magazine.
21 Newcastle-upon-Tyne, City Hall.
22 Manchester, Odeon, Mobbed! Jimi lost hair and Mitch nearly lost his leg.
23 Hanley, Gaumont.
24 Interviews.
25 Bristol, Colston Hall.
26 Cardiff, Capitol.
27 Aldershot, ABC.
28 Slough, Adelphi.
28 Bournemouth, Winter Gardens.
30 Tooting, London, Granada.

The month-long Walkers Brothers farewell tour which began in late March was our real turning point. It featured The Quotations, Nick Jones, The Californians, Engelbert Humperdinck (still with Gordon Mills), Cat Stevens and us. We had to crack England now or never, as Jimi's work permit was running out. We paid for it. It was hell.

Mickey Keane, Engelbert's guitarist, left after a few gigs. I was hired as guitarist for his pre-intermission set, which followed ours. But I couldn't join his band on stage, so there I sat, all alone in the darkened wings, just a long lead trailing out to the amp on stage. I wonder if anyone in the audience ever guessed where the lead guitar was coming from? For this honour, I received two quid a night. It felt like I was being bounced back and forth in a time warp. Their set couldn't have been more of a contrast to ours.

On the first night, Keith Altham had the idea of setting Jimi's guitar alight during *Fire*. It was the most dramatic moment of the night. Even the Walkers, who were England's biggest sex symbols, paled by comparison. It was more than just drama for us, though. Jimi had a terrible time getting the lighter fluid to catch. Tour manager Tito Burns freaked. Screaming, he grabbed the guitar and hid it under his coat to be used as evidence against us. Having got the public's and the press's attention, we really began to push that flash act we had been working on. The other groups began to notice Jimi's amazing stage presence and bizarre antics like rolling around on the floor, which knocked out audience after audience and made the rest of the show seem if not forgettable, then certainly nothing you'd discuss on the way home. If Jimi did a sexy bit one night, Tito would be tackled by the theatre managers and we'd be told, 'Clean it up, or else.' Petty things began to happen – the house lights would be turned up full in mid-set, or Jimi's guitar would be found untuned just before we walked on stage.

In Bolton Jimi was in bad form. He messed through only three of our four numbers. If you play Bolton and don't deliver, you don't hang around after the show. We were advised to take the next train to Blackpool. Stopping in a club, we saw Jayne Mansfield. This cheered us up, until she left with Engelbert. We took a couple of pills and headed for the hotel. But we couldn't remember which one the tour was booked into, and no other hotel would take us. At five in the morning we gave up and crashed in a B&B. Next day we discovered everyone else just around the corner. Was it the banana skins we'd smoked? I sort of doubt it.

By now the crowds were making it tough to escape from the theatre. In Liverpool we had to wait nervously backstage while someone found a cabbie willing to force his way through the mob to collect us. Dying for a pint, we headed for the sanctuary of the nearby pub, pursued all the way. The screaming fans surrounded the premises, hammering on the fancy glass doors while inside the clientele began to realise who we were and move in on us aggressively. The manager pushed us, frantically protesting and genuinely terrified, out into the mob. We could only hold on to each other and run, praying for our lives. By the time we found a taxi who would take us, we had been stripped of everything loose, our pockets emptied so we couldn't even pay the cabbie. It was getting too frightening to be fun.

As the hysteria built up, the 'Wildman' image Jimi and Chas had carefully cultivated began to pay off. England (which really didn't swing like a pendulum, despite claims to the contrary) was so conservative. Headlines appeared playing up to Jimi's 'threatening' image, his impassioned vocals, back-to-the-jungle rhythms, and freaky and funky guitar. The crowd climbed on stage during some shows, which gave the press something to write about – the music hardly interested them. Jimi could get away with this crazy image because he wasn't British. Americans could be forgiven for such behaviour.

Once the media picked up on the image, Jimi and our 'look' became fashionable (except in Spain, where a TV show was cancelled due to our long hair). Between our popularity and the Walkers', the tour sold out. It began to dawn on Jimi that he *could* be personally successful, that his dreams *could* come true, and that boosted his confidence tremendously. Our egos grew and sometimes clashed. But our conflicts, mostly over women, were short-lived. After I went home with a girl he fancied, Jimi freaked and hit *her*. Next day, all was forgotten – except by the poor girl, I guess.

A much bigger problem was boredom. Since we could no longer go out and cool off between shows, we had no option but to sit around in dressing rooms with nothing to do but get smashed. In Dunstable, you weren't even allowed to drink. Just what was one supposed to do, sitting on a wooden bench breathing the stale air in an eight-by-ten-foot windowless box with wall-to-wall hangers-on? You *might* have one horrid toilet and/or basin with a *cold* tap (dripping). You'd certainly have peeling paint speckled with graffiti and who knows what else, cracked concrete floors with antique cigarette butts, and a ceiling cascading with condensation.

I began to come to terms with the kind of gear required by our breakneck tour. I gave up my favoured tortoiseshell picks, which the bass ate alive, for some new German experimental plastic ones. Over the years, I went through hundreds of different types of picks before settling forever on Jim Dunlop's standard picks, starting with a grip surface of .73mm for electric guitar and .88mm for banjo, bass, and acoustic, and ending up using 1mm for everything. The lovely thin neck of my Fender Jazz felt great. I settled on wire-wound Rotosound strings (which I still swear by today) because they cut through no matter how loudly we played – a good, clear, trebly zing. And Rotosound actually *gave* me a present of some strings.

May looked like this:

1,2   Interviews.
4   Recording, *She's So Fine*.
      London, BBC TV, *Top of the Pops* (£78.15s). We're Number 4 this week.
5   Rehearsal/photo session.
      Recording – two numbers.
6   Nelson, Imperial Ballroom (£378.18s).
7   London, Saville Theatre – two shows (£200).
9   Recording.
10   London, BBC TV, *Top of the Pops* (£78.15s).
      Photo session.
11   Paris, TV show. (5,000 francs).
12   London, Bluesville Club in the Manor House.
13   London, Imperial College (£300).
14   Photo session.
      Manchester, Bellevue. (£222.12s.6d).
15   Berlin, two shows (£314).
16   Munich, two shows (DM 3,500).
17   Photo session.
18   Frankfurt, TV show with Dave Dee and Sandie Shaw: *Beat, Beat, Beat*. Played *Stonefree*, *Hey Joe* and *Purple Haze* (£324.19s).
19   Gothenburg, Sweden, two shows.
20   Karlstaad, Sweden. (Not only were we on after the trained seals, but we shared a dressing room with them, complete with buckets of fish!)
21   Copenhagen, Denmark, Sports Arena.
22   Helsinki, Finland, TV with Cat Stevens. Press reception. The Concert Hall, one show.
23   Malmo, Sweden, Bongo Club/New Orleans – two shows.
24   Stockholm, Sweden, TV show, *Popside*. Played *Wind Cried Mary* and *Purple Haze*.
      Stora Scenen/Grona Lund/Tivoli Gardens (7,000 people). Jump In/Tivoli Gardens. We broke the Beach Boys' attendance record.
      Radio Interviews.
25   Interviews. Photo sessions.
27   Kiel, West Germany, Star Palace, two shows.
28   Herford, Germany.
29   Spalding, England, Blue Action Hall (4,000 people).

Jimi's songwriting inspired me. My only attempt so far had been with Derek in The Loving Kind. Since *Top of the Pops* still demanded a crack-of-dawn arrival for a seven p.m. live broadcast – as alive as possible after trying to waste a day away without passing out – I brought an acoustic guitar along and had a go at writing to while away the time. My efforts that day became *She's So Fine (She's In With Time)* which to everyone's surprise, including mine, sounded good when we demoed it. Jimi played bass, as he usually did when I introduced a song.

Track released *The Wind Cries Mary/Highway Chile* on 4 May. The reviewers were relieved to have a more sedate sound to analyse along with Frank and Nancy Sinatra's *Something Stupid*. Having more trouble with our electric sounds than our audience ever did, they hailed it as 'a good indication (hopefully) of how the Experience will expand musically'.

On our so-called days off we managed to finish our first solo LP, *Are You Experienced?*, which Track released on 12 May with 25,000 advance orders. We had a bill-topping appearance at the Saville Theatre scheduled for 4 June, and it would certainly be necessary to have an Experience LP out in the States before the recently booked Monterey Pop Festival on 18 June.

There was a furore in the press. Traditionally, a single (let alone an LP) wasn't released until sales of the previous offering had completely died down. Chas was quoted as saying 'This LP may damage the sales of the two singles. People judge an artist on his success in the singles charts and *not* on LP sales.' But the acceptance of the LP was part of a new trend in buying habits away from singles in favour of LPs. Reviewers were also at a loss to describe our enthusiastic but drug-assisted energy, calling us a musical nightmare, raw nerves recorded, and electrical neurosis.

Impervious to all this analysis, we bounced back and forth between some semblance of normality and life on the road. We *were* getting rather raw and neurotic. I borrowed a pound from Kit Lambert before our flight to Paris on 11 May. For the first time, I collected our pay and saw the contract. A TV rep advised me, 'You should collect the money all the time.' But the implications eluded me.

Immediately after our Paris TV appearance, Jeffery nipped over and negotiated a contract with Barclay Records, The 15 May 1967 contract was for 10 per cent royalties, with no points to the group, and an advance of $35,000.

While Jeffery was lining his pockets, we were rushing for a flight to Berlin and the show that would begin our European tour – seventeen dates in fifteen days. We all insisted on seeing the Wall, with grey East Berlin trapped behind it. What a contrast, we thought, to our lives. But touring was a trap, too. The only distractions were reading music papers like *Beat Instrumental* (in which I was proud to see myself elected Player of the Month) and the competitions for girls we'd use to while away the time otherwise spent fidgeting and getting terminally smashed in interminable terminals while worrying about our two or even three flights per day. We'd laugh and say we'd sell more records by taking fans to bed. As if we needed an excuse. Back at my empty flat, girls moved in till I had no bed to come home to.

Travelling also gave us time to talk about this creepy sensation that things were not well back at the office. Mitch and I were cheesed off about the new single's cover shot of Jimi alone. Jimi took some stick, though he wasn't to blame; but he didn't complain either. We tried to escape these feelings by getting more stoned.

One night in Germany Jimi was totally out of his head for the gig. I apologised to the huge audience and, hoping no one would notice, casually strolled over to tune his guitar – backwards! Jimi sat on his amp swinging his legs and giggling his head off. Every time we tried to play he'd collapse laughing, till eventually I said some hasty goodbyes and we fucked off, pulling Jimi along with us. It was then I learned he'd taken acid before the show. It angered me to think he'd do that and risk everything we'd worked for. I considered it highly selfish. He could just as easily have taken it after the gig.

It brought on a serious discussion about the group, and we discovered we were making over £300 per night – a fortune then, when flights were as cheap as our shared hotel rooms. And yet I was living on the same income as in my Burnettes days. This was a sobering thought. We'd had no account at all to date, though we were due one. I was assigned the task of writing to Chas. We all signed the letter (no copy, of course), the gist of which was: 'We know what we're making. We have nothing. We want to part company.' The result was a meeting at which Jeffery agreed to a 50/25/25 split (Jimi/Mitch/me), with the management percentage coming off the top. There was never any mention of any of us being employed, and foolishly we never discussed what we were splitting. We just assumed it was everything. It was agreed orally, and confirmed to the office lawyers and accountants, but never documented. £500 was deposited into each of our accounts for expenses on our US tour, and our weekly wage was raised to £45. We were happy – it didn't take much. This pattern continued. We'd get upset and instantly some cash would appear. I tried to think about business, but I was all questions and no answers.

Jimi's work permit was on its last legs as we geared up for the States. The farewell show at the Saville was preceded by a special photo session, and even a rehearsal! Two nights before I had watched one of my all-time favourites perform on that very stage – Spike Milligan in *The Bed Sitting Room*. Denny Laine and I went to meet him backstage and were honoured with an invitation into his dressing room. He sat there on the floor, wearing a sack, and gestured for us to join him. The first thing he asked me was, 'Have you got any smoke?' I apologised. I hadn't. I could have kicked myself. He offered us some wine and organised seats in the front row. Throughout the show, he directed all the jokes at us. I'll never forget it.

The Saville show, run by Beatles' manager Brian Epstein, was huge. Hundreds were turned away at the door. It opened with the Stormsville Shakers, chart-topping Procol Harum, The Chiffons, Denny Laine and his Electric String Band . . . and we closed it! In spite of amp trouble (as usual) it was a really good, loose show. Jimi liked rolling around on the stage, and kept nudging me and shouting at me to do the same. I'm not athletic, and in my shyness I hesitated. But he went on bumping me until I gave in. We wrestled together, then fell over and tumbled round the stage. Once down, I felt freer than I had since my carefree days in Germany. The Saville booked us for whenever we were in town.

The speed of our progress made it difficult for us to adjust to our new status. Invited to an after-gig party, I was overwhelmed when Paul McCartney opened the door of Epstein's star-filled home. I spent most of the night just watching people and marvelling that I was there. As we became famous, people began to hassle me, sometimes heavily, for money. I was regularly asked to guarantee loans, make investments, give handouts. Sometimes I was able to help friends, but mostly I didn't have what was wanted, and I was glad to escape the viciousness that followed some refusals.

The show at the Saville really capped things off. We'd got the music together, got the recording together, got the audience together, and now it was time to get America together. We shot a cover photo for the American release of *Are you Experienced?* at Kew Gardens with photographer Karl Ferris, did a lot of press, and hired Neville Chesters (previously with The Who, the Bee Gees and the Merseybeats) as road manager. Jeffery, of course, beat us to America. He had rushed over to negotiate a publishing deal (something which I had never realised existed). Through Yameta he signed the Soft Machine, Jimi Hendrix, and any artist introduced during the agreement term by Chandler, Jeffery, and their various business associates. Administration rights were assigned to SeaLark (A. Schroeder International – Jeffery had already signed Anim Music and Em-Jay Music to Schroeder's). If a record were to make the Top Ten, Yameta and SeaLark would become joint publishers. While Jeffery was taking care of business, we were being injected, stamped, inspected and prepared to take a plane to a different planet.

Things weren't coming in half-measures. I was flying first class to New York, seated next to Brian Jones, who had taken me under his wing, and cruising on a tab of purple Owsley. I was floating and swearing it hadn't affected me at all. What could be trippier than real life? Arriving in New York, I went for a sail on some bloke's yacht and had some more acid. I caught a plane early the next morning, chatted up a stewardess and arrived in San Francisco at 9 o'clock.

I had rushed from New York to San Francisco nervous that I'd miss something. Everyone was convinced that the three-day Monterey Pop Festival marked the beginning of a new era, somewhere – according to historians – between the Age of Aquarius and the Age of Asparagus. We'd been recommended to the festival committee by Paul McCartney, Andrew Oldham, and Derek Taylor, and our US debut was to be on the final day of the festival. The excitement was almost unbearable. Artists included Simon and Garfunkel, The Byrds, Booker T and the MGs, and many, many more. The exotic crowd ranged from madras to velvet. You only had to breathe the air filled with incense and marijuana to be high. Everyone believed something awesome was happening, that some amazing vibration was breaking out. The whole concept of this stupendous concert made everything previous pale into insignificance.

On our day we went to the gig early with The Who for a run-through. Just the fact that we had to follow them filled us with apprehension. Nobody knew how we'd come off. The Who's 'smashing' act had taken America by storm, but we were coming to the audience as total unknowns. Whereas in England Jimi's being American had helped us get noticed, it was the Englishness of the group that was being stressed in America. The press played up to our 'black English guitarist who could play with his teeth'. Suddenly it didn't seem like much. Joe Brown could play *Hava Nagila* with his guitar behind his head.

That night Brian Jones (blissed out) introduced us to America. Thanks to The Who, the audience was already in a frenzy. We were in fine form. The rapport was perfect and we flew through a great set. Jimi finished by burning his guitar. The lighter fuel was being stubborn again, but once it did finally flare up, the audience exploded. Jimi whipped the flames through the air, demolishing the guitar. (Later, when Jimi started smashing guitars more often because the sound effects were better than burning, he'd use the same reglued 'break-away' guitar.) It took ages for the crowd to settle for the next act. We'd gone down a bomb!

Chandler made it to the dressing room after a half-hour struggle through the crowd, getting there just in time to rescue us from – preposterous as it seems – a tongue-lashing from Jeffery. Tut-tut, we'd damaged a mike stand. Brushing such major crimes aside, we talked with Bill Graham about doing a gig with the Jefferson Airplane at the Fillmore. Then we plunged into the tons of drink and smoke laid on for the post-gig party.

The rest of the tour was scheduled:

June

20-24	Fillmore West – two shows a night.
25	Golden Gate Park.
	Fillmore West – two shows.
26	Photo session.
27	Screening of Monterey Film in LA.
28-30	Recording.

The day after our US debut we all felt frazzled by the adrenalin overdose and jet-lag, but there was still so much excitement in the air. We'd sneaked into America and found all the doors were ready to be opened. We agreed to do six nights at the Fillmore, two shows per night, and though we should have been catching some sleep, the streets of San Francisco were too tempting. Mitch and I went out to see 'hippies'. England was never like this. I came back from a stroll through Haight-Ashbury, smashed on wine, smoke and acid. I was *stoned*.

Jeffery remained true to form. He hadn't the faintest idea where our destiny lay, but went on hustling work. He flew to New York and rang us up to announce proudly that, 'I've got a great deal for a summer tour of America.' Punchline: 'You'll support the Monkees. They're where it's at.' Chandler was no more enamoured of the prospect than the others were and Jeffery had clearly not consulted him when arranging this unpromising marriage of ultra-hip band and four mop-topped cardboard cut-outs. I personally thought it was wonderful. They were big and we'd get their audience. In addition, we got to fly on their plane and stay in posh hotels. What's the problem?

There could be no more dramatic contrast to life in Monkees-land than our last day in San Francisco, where we played a free show from the back of a sun-drenched lorry in Golden Gate Park. Thousands of the most unusual and colourful people danced in the open air and they inspired us to play a really strenuous set. As a result, we put on a weak show that night, but got our energy up to finish with a good one – all of us being out of our brains. Even Stickells, our one link with sanity, got out of it. In mid-set, Chas found him lost in contemplation of the valves of Jimi's amplifier. When Jimi handed him his guitar for a string replacement, he just gazed at it. Chas finally changed the string. I was still getting acid buzzes two days later.

San Francisco provided a relief from the boxed-in mood that had taken us over in England. At last we were having fun together; we laughed a lot and felt great. Everything seemed fresh and friendly and exciting – and part of the thrill was watching Jimi enjoy his return to America as an 'English pop star'. For his part, Jimi grabbed me and took me off to experience his America through my stomach – barbecued spare ribs were a new one on me.

Our gigs were a huge success, so Bill Graham gave Chas a $2,000 bonus. We were put on wages of $200 a week. If I spent $100 on stage clothes, it was a serious investment. I never got new guitars, but discovered thrift shops and the miracles you sometimes find in them.

On the 26th, we were off to tackle Los Angeles and see a private showing of D. A. Pennebaker's film of Monterey, which Festival heads Lou Adler and John Phillips had commissioned with funds from ABC-TV, who later rejected it. We'd been given a flat fee for our performance, but we didn't stop to worry about that. We were so high and happy. Sam and Dave at the Whisky-a-GoGo suited us better.

We started our second LP with three days at T.T.G. Studios, LA. The sleeve artwork was already commissioned in London, so all we needed was something to put inside it. I became intrigued by the idea of playing a twelve-string through a Wha-Wha pedal, and the idea became the intro to *Burning of the Midnight Lamp*. Jimi got totally caught up in the production side of things, but the technical end of music never appealed to me. I'd get bored with the repetition and the whiling away of hours while they niggled over details. I felt in the way, hovering over the tiny desk. There were no pushbutton sound effects. If a phase effect was wanted the engineer, Eddie Kramer (at Olympic) or Gary Kellgren (in the US), would send us to the pub for an hour while they set up the slightly out-of-sync interaction between two recorders which resulted in the effect. A more positive use of time was messing around with my new Gibson guitar. I also worked on my bass technique and style.

June went and July opened, as frenetic as ever:

July

1   Earl Warren Showgrounds, Santa Barbara ($1,400).
2   Whisky-a-GoGo.
3,4 New York, Scene Club – supporting The Seeds and Tiny
     Tim.
5   Interviews and photo session.
     Rheingold Festival, Central Park, with Young Rascals, 18,000
     people came.
6,7 Recording, Mayfair Studios, New York – *Burning of the
     Midnight Lamp* (vocals by Sweet Inspiration).
     Interviews.

Our debut in Los Angeles at the Whisky was a flop. We were too tired
and too stoned. We could hardly stand up, much less play. The gig was
so bad that I broke my own rule and got pissed off on stage when Jimi
pulled a moody. Getting back to the hotel, I telephoned a friend only to
hear that she had cut her wrists (we had parted). There was nothing I
could do about it there and then, though, as we had to fly to New York
the next morning.

Sometimes attitudes in the States took me completely by surprise.
Coming from uptight England, I was convinced that America *had* to be
more groovy and hip. At the airport in New York I was shocked when a
terminally obese, balding man dressed in a gaping, gaudily-patterned
shirt, plaid bermudas and flapping sandals stood pointing and laughing
at *me*. What is this? Where's the mirror? Give this man some acid. His
brother must have been a desk clerk because when we arrived at the
hotel we were turned away.

Jeffery had already sorted us out in New York, working on the dream
in which we joined the Monkees on the twin altars of success and
exploitation. He had a lot of people in his corner. Our English agency,
Harold Davidson, was represented in the States by Steven Weiss of
Steingarten, Wedeen and Weiss of New York. Using Weiss as adviser,
Harold Davidson had booked the Dave Clark Five, Herman and the
Hermits, the Yardbirds, Jeff Beck and Led Zeppelin (and he was later
president of their Swansong Records). Weiss featured prominently in
the experience of The Experience. While Jeffery was creaming his
pants over the teenybopper landscape, Chandler thought the Monkees
tour a disastrous plot, far removed from his plan to break us through
groovy, underground-type gigs such as Steve Paul's The Scene. As we
were not consulted anyway, we spent time checking out Tiny Tim and

the Mothers of Invention. But pretty soon the next dates were upon us:

July

8	Jacksonville.
9	Miami.
	Photo sessions and radio interviews.
11	Charlotte, NC.
12	Greensboro, NC.
14,16	Forest Hills, NYC.
	Interviews.
17	Interviews.
18	Recording (B side).
	Interviews.
19	Interviews.
20	Recording (finishing *Midnight Lamp*)
	Salvation club, NYC.
21-23	Café-a-GoGo, NYC. Two shows.
26	Photo sessions, interviews.
29	Recording.

We picked up Jeffery and joined the Monkees in Florida. Our first show was twenty-five minutes long, playing to a strange audience for us – mostly girls aged seven to twelve – but we went down surprisingly well. Then we went out to watch the Monkees. It was awful to watch. Not that they weren't good, but they had a 'spare' group backing their set from behind the stage curtain. I couldn't believe what I was seeing. There was something embarrassing about it for both groups.

In Charlotte, we died a death. Jimi pulled a moody. Translation: turned his back on the audience and got unreasonably pissed off when his guitar went out of tune or an amp began to hum. He'd get flash and say, 'I can't play with this,' and then slop through the show. Mitch and I carried on and pulled it through – difficult when you're not the lead singer. The next night, we bounced up again.

There were plenty of ups and downs on this tour, but mainly the latter. Climbing on a plane nearly every night after the gig meant another excuse to drink and smoke too much. This led to some awkward moments as the tour was very straight. Amyl nitrites (poppers) – a vapour used in angina cases to lower the blood pressure in the heart – were legal and growing in popularity. You broke a capsule under your nose and every peripheral blood vessel in your body dilated. The rush turned you red, white, red, and was over in a couple of minutes. It was pretty overpowering, and I didn't really like them, sometimes thinking, 'Mistake. Too high.' I got the Monkees good once. Just before takeoff, I snapped one under their noses, 'Smell this!' A takeoff never to be forgotten. Another time I didn't count on the wonders of the automatic extractor fans in American loos, and my sneaky joint got sucked out and blown all over. Suss!

The tour manager nagged Jimi to tone down the act. Jimi acquiesced at the Forest Hills gig by turning off completely. Usually intolerant of his on-stage moodies, this time I agreed with his tactic. We were told to get off the tour, or else . . . Or else what? Get thrown off the tour? Second prize was being asked to stay on. Our publicists made up a classic press release to the effect that the Daughters of the American Revolution had demanded our withdrawal to save their daughters from ruin. Couldn't have put it better myself. We knew for certain that we were off the tour when we were moved from a posh hotel to a crappy hotel. Jeffery was livid, and stomped off in a huff to work on his Spanish clubs, boutiques, real estate, tax plans. Publicity-wise, getting off the tour did us a lot of good. Getting thrown off the Monkees tour was as good as not being invited to the White House as far as credibility went.

For us, exile to New York was a relief. Audiences there inspired us to get stoned and belt it out. Forget the Monkees. We could jam with Spencer Davis and The Who, play strip poker with Keith Moon and his assorted ladies. Finally, under pressure, we finished recording *Burning of the Midnight Lamp* and *The Stars that Play with Laughing Sam's Dice*, which were scheduled for English release on 19 August. It was a sign of the times that it took forty-two hours to record *Burning of the Midnight Lamp* while *The Wind Cries Mary* had taken six minutes. We saw less and less of Chandler. He was scheduled to marry a Swedish lady, Lotta Lexon, and honeymoon in Nassau. Off the sleepers and back on the leapers, Mitch and I did our best to make it a memorable occasion with lots of flowers and photographers. Jimi couldn't be bothered to attend. We were all entering what we described as the 'clenched-teeth era', in which everything became too much, man.

I, for one, had overdosed on sex. Not bad enough to say 'no' but still . . . so much and so easy. No fun. No chase. After the shows, we'd scan the crowd of girls, 'OK, you and you (and you?) come with me.' I didn't think it'd ever be possible, but I just got fed up with girls trying to pull me, with twosomes, threesomes, and group efforts. Every part of my body was showing signs of wear and tear. I'd met a few lovely ladies and I preferred to see them regularly instead of a series of one-night stands.

We'd spent ten months living in each other's pockets and out of suitcases. The fatigue, the ceaseless round of drugs, the fans who followed us everywhere, and the creeps who stole from our hotel rooms made us feel on the edge of screaming. Our conversations centered more often on money because we felt money would make us free. I hated to, but asked Eric Clapton to repay a $20 loan. Slowly it dawned on me that songwriting could bring in extra income, which spurred me on. I started, nervous but determined, recording the roots of *Little Miss Strange*.

Jimi lost a lot of drive once we broke in the States. He seemed content enough to have conquered the place where he had struggled so hard. But I found the complete lack of English publicity upsetting. When the press did start again, it made matters worse by dropping 'Experience' and using only Jimi's picture. After all, I too wanted to be successful where I'd struggled so hard. We'd left England as The Experience, but American success had promoted Jimi and left Mitch and me in deep background. After a while in America, what had seemed noisy and exciting became normal and we had to escape it. Jimi crept into the studio where he could control the sounds. Mitch and I heard police sirens and scanned the sky in search of spaceships. I hankered for a bit of quiet English countryside and stars at night. The closest I could come was a locked, darkened hotel room where I could repair my fan-ripped stage gear. August saw another exhausting round of gigs:

August

3-8	Salvation Club, NYC, Interviews.
9-12	Washington DC, Ambassador Theatre, two shows.
13	Ditto. Two shows plus 'Keep The Faith For Washington Youth Fund Benefit'.
15	Detroit, Michigan, Fifth Dimension Club. Interviews.
16,17	Los Angeles for some filming.
18	Interviews. Hollywood Bowl, backing The Mamas and the Papas.
19	Interviews.

Still, the music was getting good again, and the New York pack followed us to Washington. When Mitch missed the first gig due to a bad gut, the English papers ran the story, 'Mitch Miller collapsed on stage and was rushed to hospital.' Miller became a pet name for Mitch.

As we relaxed, Mitch and I began to do our show bits – changing instruments and bashing away. As a frustrated drummer, I loved this. Our gigs were very serious attempts to create a fun atmosphere. If we started in a good, positive daze, we could feed off each other's highs and get higher still.

As our popularity increased and sales of *Are You Experienced?* went up and up, others who had odd tapes with Jimi playing started trying to cash in on his reputation. In August, Ed Chalpin and Curtis Knight released *How Would You Feel* from Jimi's days with Curtis's Squires, who were signed to Chalpin. Jimi felt embarrassed, angered, and horrified – especially by the relaxed jam style of *Hush Now*, on which his guitar obviously needed tuning. He swore it wasn't him singing, but Curtis. It was so obviously a casual demo, but the cover played up Jimi's participation to the hilt.

Unfortunately, they were completely within their rights. A contract between Jimi and Ed Chalpin's PPX Enterprises Inc ('Master Producers and Agents') dated 15 October 1965 materialised to haunt us all. In a simple, one-page document, for an advance of one whole dollar, Jimi promised to produce (for a 1 per cent royalty), arrange (for minimum scale), sing and play (for free) exclusively for PPX for three years. Jimi agreed to be available to produce a minimum of three sessions per year (four titles a go) paid for by PPX, who would be reimbursed from the first profits and have the exclusive rights to assign all masters. Jimi said he wanted it stopped. A million lawyers went on the payroll and everything got nasty.

As we tripped more and more, we felt that acid was the great cure-all for any upset – past, present and future. Chas, who disapproved, hoped it might at least inspire Jimi's lyrics, which did get spacier and spacier. But you can rely too much on grinding up your brain for emotional fodder to drive the song machine.

If acid wrote the lyrics, speed played the music, and the combination exacerbated tensions and amplified the annoyances inherent in a scene plagued by hangers-on and career parasites. We all had tempers and they had surfaced throughout our career, but now they were right up front. Only a year earlier, we were all together pushing for success, but now we were falling apart and getting reassembled by forces we neither understood nor controlled. We didn't have the time or the heads to suss it and, not knowing what else to do, we kept going.

Los Angeles was hard on us. We died a death in the Bowl. The Mamas and the Papas' folk-type crowd were the very opposite of our own followers. Jimi hated being distanced from the audience's emotions, and at the Bowl there is an ocean of a pool separating the stage from the people, and no roof to create the close, intimate atmosphere we fed on and which enabled us to take the crowd out of themselves.

We needed to film a short to accompany our single, but I was so tired no one could wake me. Next day we travelled to a groovy old house in Watts, dropped some acid and filmed with GTO member Pamela Miller. Zappa's GTOs didn't last long, but Pamela survived and now has her own book out, entitled *I'm With the Band*.

In LA I met Murray Roman, comedian extraordinaire, who was to be a true friend. I loved his crazy sense of humour. He could actually laugh at doing time in jail for non-payment of alimony. And it was in LA that I was heartened by a chance meeting at a party. I went to have a beer and Steve McQueen was pulling the pints! I invited him outside for a smoke and we ended up having a great, stoned chat. It was one of the nicest, most relaxed escapes I can remember. It made me realise how infrequently I got the chance these days to simply sit and chat idly, person-to-person. Steve was also plagued by the necessity to be 'Steve McQueen' twenty-four hours a day. I felt better when he said it drove him crazy, too.

Life rushed by like the psychedelic scene in *2001*. The States always made me think: 'They don't call it the human *race* for nothing.' It became difficult to attend to living a life. Spending most of my day killing the time around the gig, I began to lose touch in the whirl. So I jumped on a plane and escaped to London, where I could feel I was slowing down for a minute. Getting out of America, even for a day, somehow meant I could take a deep breath – even if I did have to score sleepers to counteract the leapers and acid enough to sleep on the flight. Once there, another leaper and I was ready to set about picking up the fraying threads of my English life.

We had conquered America, but at high cost. We had our act worked out, but we were doing it night after night and unsure about where it was getting us. The finances were a mess, personal relations were nothing to write home about, and our lifestyle was taking an obvious toll. Every night we opened with *Killing Floor* and took it from there. The audiences were obviously waiting for Jimi to do his leaping-about bit, bashing the amps and setting fire to his guitar, but you can't do that every night. We were very pissed. Very stoned. Very shattered.

Michael Goldstein joined us as publicity agent. If he was the one who said it was time for us to refresh European memories, then bless him.

Chapter Four

Round Two

*Experience is never limited, and it is never complete;
it is an immense sensibility, a kind of spider-web of
silken threads suspended in the chamber of consciousness,
catching every air-borne particle in its tissue.*
HENRY JAMES

*To travel hopefully is better than to arrive,
and the true success is the labour.
Is there anything in life so disenchanting as attainme.it?*
ROBERT LOUIS STEVENSON

COMING home was never like this before. With press at the airport
and a European tour awaiting us, it felt good to be back. The leaper
soon overtook the sleeper as I nipped up to the flat, went over to the
office where a pile of fan letters awaited, then met friends Pete and Jan
Kircher, Cathy Etchingham, Denny Laine and Tony at the George,
and finally flopped into bed for a few hours before the flight to
Manchester to film for Simon Dee. A *Top of the Pops* appearance with
Jeff Beck lead us back into a typical period in the life of The
Experience:

August
22 BBC TV, Simon Dee's *Dee Time* (£102.9s).
23 Interviews.
24 BBC TV, *Top of the Pops* – two shows (£157.10s).
27 Saville Theatre with Arthur Brown and Tomorrow (£250).
28 Photo sessions and interviews.
29 Nottingham.
31 London, photo session.

Berlin, photo sessions.
Radio Show with The Caravelles.

September

1   *Are You Experienced?* released in US by Warner/Reprise with
    slightly different tracks to UK version.
    Berlin, West Germany. Press reception with the Manfreds and
    Dave Dee.

2   Berlin. Colour TV show with Small Faces, Bee Gees.

3   Gothenburg, Sweden, two shows.

4   Stockholm, Stora Scene, Dans In.

5   Stockholm. Interview, then Radiohuset show with live
    audience: *Sergeant Pepper, Wind Cried Mary, Foxy Lady, Fire,
    Hey Joe, I Don't Live Today, Burning Of The Midnight Lamp,
    Purple Haze.* Bootlegged several times.

6   Vasteras, Sweden, two shows.

8   Stockholm TV show – mimed 5 numbers.
    Hogbo, Sandviken, Sweden, Hogbo Bruk. Two shows with
    The Outsiders, Interview between shows.

9   Karlstad, Sweden, interviews and two shows.

10 Malmo (Sweden), two shows.

11 Stockholm, Frona Lund. Interviews for Swedish radio
    (£12.10s).

12 Gothenburg, interviews.
    Liseberg, two shows (£540).

25 Rehearsals in London. Film and photo session. Royal Festival
    Hall, Liberal International Party's 'Guitar-In' (£350).

26 Interviews and photo session for *Newsweek.*

27 Recording at Rye Muse Sound Studios without Jimi, *She's So
    Fine.*

29 Interviews and the David Frost show (£60 and £29).

Our first Saville set went great but then we heard the sad news of Brian
Epstein's death. The second was cancelled out of respect, but I felt he
would have preferred the show to go on.

Jimi didn't bother to attend the German press reception in preparation for the Berlin TV show that would launch our tour with Traffic,
so I got stuck doing all the talking in my pidgin German. I wondered if
Jimi's heart was still in the States and he'd lost interest in Europe. But
if Jimi was impatient with the tour, there was no escape in Berlin. We
went to the Playboy Club with the Small Faces and the Bee Gees, but
the atmosphere was heavy and our energetic attempts to party fell flat.

The pace was so gruelling that the memory of fatigue colours all my recollections of that time. We sometimes felt incapable of facing another bunch of journalistic brain-pickers and trying yet again to come up with something fresh, witty, incisive, clever and intelligent. Jimi tended to play the spaced-out refugee from Planet X, leaving the interviewers to interpret it as they wished.

Worst of all, I started to hate flying, and reckoned my odds of survival were getting grim. I'd sit at the back, hopefully next to a priest or nun but usually next to a screaming baby. Once our scheduling really freaked us. We were to be on Flight 13, Gate 13, on Friday the 13th.

While we'd been in the States, our financial arrangements had changed. We were now allowed to draw money as needed from the office, but not real money – just small bits I'd piss away hanging out – the Ship for daytime pints, the Speakeasy for after hours. Because we now played huge and therefore fewer venues, the lack of a daily gig to dictate the hours gave a strange sense of purposelessness to the day. It wasn't so much a life of leisure as a life of suspended animation. Not to say there weren't moments of great satisfaction and pride and fun, but I felt like an interim person. My only goal in life – success – had been fulfilled a millionfold, and it would take some serious soul-searching to find another. To avoid that I occupied my mind with short-term aims: Can I score? Will I get laid tonight? Where's the nearest pub? I wasn't alone. Speakeasy regulars included Chris Wood, Steve Marriot, Entwhistle, Moon, Trevor Burton, Brian Jones, and wall-to-wall willing women.

We actually rehearsed for the Royal Festival Hall show featuring Bert Jansch, Paco Pena, Sebastian Jorgensen and Tim Walker. The acoustics were so good we could speak on stage in a normal voice and be heard throughout the hall. We used one cabinet each instead of our usual wall of sound and we were still loud. Afterwards, Liberal MP Jeremy Thorpe, trailing a million photographers plus entourage, came backstage for a press chat. The resulting photo had Jimi ruffling Jeremy's (sparse) hair while I waved our large post-gig joint around behind his head.

October

1 Recording. Graham Nash dropped in.
2 Recording. Peddlars next door.
3 Recording. The Move's Trevor and Ace sang on *Got Me Floatin'*.
4 Interviews and photo sessions.
  Recording. The Stones came to the session. They were

recording next door to us most of the month.

5 Recording.

6 BBC Radio, *Top Gear – Catfish Blues, Drivin' South, Hound Dog, Midnight Lamp*, plus one more. Also, a jam with Stevie Wonder.

7 Dereham, Norfolk, Wellington Club (£550).

8 Saville Theatre, London, two shows (£450).

9 Rehearsal in Paris.
   Paris Olympia with Faces and Pat Arnold (£441).

11 Paris TV show – two numbers mimed (500 francs).
    Radio show (150 francs).

12 France, two TV shows (950 francs).

13 England, ATV 1, *Jonathan King Show* (£350).

16 Crawley, Sussex, used Haagstrom 8-string (£625 or 60%).

17 Interviews and photos for American magazine.
    BBC Radio – *Rhythm and Blues* with Alexis Korner, who jammed on *Hootchie Coochie Man* with us, playing brilliant slide guitar. (£34.5s).

18 Photo session.

19 Demo session of my songs at Regent Sound with Pete Kircher on drums.

22 Hastings (£600).

23 Rehearsal and Eire Apparent session.

24 Marquee Club, London. New amps, record crowd.

25 Rehearsal at Regent Sound.
    Recording at Olympic.

26 Rehearsed at Regent Sound. Thrown out after two songs for being too loud!
    Recording at Olympic – one song and vocals.

27 Recording – night session. Used Haagstrom 8-string.

28 Dunstable, California Ballroom (£750).
    Recording – two tracks.

29 Recording – two new tracks.

30 Recording – *She's So Fine*, with harmonies.

While at the BBC studios, we were introduced to Stevie Wonder. When Mitch nipped off to the loo, some enterprising person suggested an 'informal jam' between Jimi and myself, with Stevie on drums. We jammed two segments, then Stevie sang an old R&B song called *Not Too Proud To Beg* (or something like that). Of course, they forgot to turn the tape machines off. This jam was aired a couple of times and then bootlegged. I feel a jam is an impromptu musical creation and is therefore co-written, but when the songs were registered after Jimi's death, my part in them (surprise, surprise) wasn't.

Only I managed the Paris flight – everyone else *just* squeaked in, minutes before the Olympia show. It was a fabulous show – the French always understood us and responded. I got to play guitar on *Red House*, using an instrument borrowed from Keith Richards, who'd been hanging around backstage. I cranked up the guitar's bass and went through my bass amp. Guitar was my first love and I kept telling myself that bass was just for the time being. But the more I played with The Experience the less I was considered a guitarist, as I so rarely played guitar on stage now. The era demanded flamboyant, loose and soaring melodic lead guitar lines – not my style at all. To me, rhythm is everything. Drummers are the heart of a group – a good one is worth his weight in gold and deserves to be looked after (and they usually need it). No amount of guitar playing can overcome a boring drummer (or a drum machine). Mitch was never boring.

We partied at Rosko's with the Faces and did Paris TV – for which in the absence of a manager, I was paid. So I divided it up and when Chas asked where the money was, I gave him 20 per cent. We found it highly elating to have our earned money in our pockets and went shopping. This time I missed the plane and Jimi and Mitch left my luggage behind, revenge for my having rubbed it in so thoroughly about their late arrival. I only just made it back to London before the Speakeasy closed.

We worked hard and *Axis: Bold As Love* was finished on 30 October. I really enjoyed the creation of *Axis* – it's my favourite Experience album. We felt positive and reasonably relaxed during the sessions, trying to take our own time, even though it was made plain that at least three record companies were drumming their fingers anxiously awaiting the product. We'd slipped into the routine of doing a gig and then heading to the studio for a midnight to early morning session. I was chuffed beyond belief that *She's So Fine*, my first attempt at writing, producing and singing, was included. I'd made lots of arrangement and riff suggestions (as in *Remember*) prior to this, but with no credit. Seeing my name after my song was thrilling, though I never got production credit. And I discovered I'd already signed my publishing away.

Our outlook on music, drugs and women was highly experimental at that point. In the studio we started playing around with electronic noise. While Jimi and Mitch, his voice speeded up, did weird voice-overs, we'd set up a couple of guitars, turn the volume up full and smash them against the amps for the background. Other groups relied on using a variety of instruments to keep new, but we relied on Jimi's irrepressible urge to experiment with new guitar sounds – which he did with a vengeance, especially now that he had embraced pedals. With my bass turned up to full treble, we got a tremendous variety of effects both on stage and in the studio. The only new instrument was my Haagstrom 8-string bass, which gave the rich, full sound on *Spanish Castle Magic* (though this was a song I never liked playing), *Little Miss Lover* and *You Got Me Floatin'*. I didn't use it much live – I don't know why, but I never got into changing bass for different songs on stage.

The new eight-track machines now available made experimenting easier and more rewarding. In the early days we'd wait until some ideas got semi-worked out before booking studio time. Now Jimi got into the habit of hanging out in the studio, taping everything, and hoping for inspiration. You never know what will come out of a jam that is flowing well from several musicians' input. Despite this, ideas were coming more slowly. I was concerned that the lyrics weren't as together as they had been. There were good ideas, but the word substitutes for the oral noises with which Jimi would accompany his guitar playing were awkward and sometimes vague. Record companies put a terrible strain on the gigging/composing artist who couldn't or wouldn't just cover an oldie or choose from a selection of songs written for him, expecting two or three LPS a year.

I tried to keep writing, too. When I had worked out an idea, I'd demo it playing guitar, with Jimi on bass and Mitch on drums. Dave Mason sometimes helped and Chas would suggest a mix. For all the good it did me . . . Jimi pinched my guitar riff from one of our co-written demos, *Dance*, to form the basis of *Ezy Rider*. My 'Booker T riff', as I called it, showed up as *Midnight*, written by Jimi, on the *War Heroes* LP. I could never get Jimi, who disliked musical retrospection, to play bits like that. I could understand that to a certain extent. Personally, I'd refuse to play *Twist and Shout* ever again, but I'd have a go at The Shadow's 'steps' any time. When I was introduced to The Shadows at a Talk of the Town show, I was thrilled! I'd memorised many of Hank Marvin's guitar lines, and trained my feet likewise. When we were doing a really relaxed show Jimi would sometimes slip gracefully into the 'steps' he'd done for so long. He'd startle himself and I could see him think, 'I shouldn't do this any more.' Why not?

Much recording delay was caused by the hangers-on who infested the studio, making it nearly impossible to accomplish anything. If the studio followers had just got us high and split, we could have concentrated. But they wanted to be there. Soon, out of boredom, they'd start to party amongst themselves. Without meaning to they became a barrier between our good intentions and any potential output. 'Here! Take (snort, smoke, swallow) this!' Zap! Suddenly everything was forgotten, and there we were getting high on studio time at $80 per hour. We'd end up pissed, and pissed off, blaming each other and feeling guilty because none of us had pulled the wasted session together to get the pressure off us. Thankfully, when we sat down at Chas's on 7 November to hear the test pressing, it sounded good. The next day the pressure started to begin the next LP. Each new LP may have meant new advances, but it also meant fresh material, which we could no longer polish live in front of an audience before recording. The crowds now demanded the tried, tested (and now boring for us) hits. And there was no let-up on the touring front:

November

7   Photo session.

8   Manchester, photo session.
       Manchester University (£500).

10   Amsterdam, TV show – three songs. (£165).
       Rotterdam, Holland. Ahoy Hallen – Hippy, Happy
       Beurs Voor Tieners En Twens (£374).

11   Brighton, Sussex University. One of the worst gigs we ever did. Should have missed it. Everyone was terrible. Left town immediately.

12,13   Rehearsals.

14   Rehearsals.
       London, Albert Hall.

15   Interviews.
       Jonathan King Show – on BBC TV
       Bournemouth, Winter Gardens – two shows.

16   Photo session at the Roundhouse.

17   Sheffield, City Hall – two shows.

18   Liverpool, Empire Theatre – two shows. (Chas there!)

19   Coventry, Coventry Theatre – two shows. (Chas there!)

22   Portsmouth, Guild Hall – two shows.

23   Cardiff, Sophia Gardens – two shows.

24   Bristol, Colston Hall – two shows.

25   Blackpool, Opera House – two shows (filmed). *Catfish Blues, Foxy Lady, Purple Haze* and *Wild Thing*, now bootlegged.

26   Manchester, Palace Theatre – two shows.

27   Belfast, Queens College – two shows.

December

1   Chatham, Town Hall – two shows.
      Axis released in England.

2   Brighton, The Dome – two shows.

3   Nottingham, Theatre Royal – two shows.

4   Newcastle-upon-Tyne – two shows.

5   Glasgow, Greens Playhouse – two shows.

6   Saw run of BBC2 film *Colour Me Pop* featuring The Experience. The first colour test recording – never aired.

7   Photo session.

8   TV show: *Good Evening* (with Jonathan King) (£150).

13   Recording.

14   Photo session.

15   Radio show: *Top Gear – Radio One Theme, Day Tripper* (with me being John Lennon!), *Wait Until Tomorrow, Hear My Train A-Comin', Spanish Castle Magic*, now on *Radio One* album (£34.5s).

16   BBC-TV, *Top of the Pops*.

19   Photo session and filming (with Bruce Fleming).

20   Interviews for an American magazine.
      Recording demos: *Touch You, Dream* (my song), maybe *Cross Town Traffic*. I played guitar on all three, Jimi played bass.

21   Interviews.
      Recording demos – two tracks. I sang on one and wrote both lyrics. Probably *Dream* and *Dance* again, but I'm not sure, since I haven't been able to listen to any of the tapes we made.

22   Rehearsals.
      Photo session for *Daily Sketch*.
      London, Olympia Theatre: 'Christmas on Earth, Continued' (£1,000).

30   Demo session.

In Manchester, a thin three-fan welcoming committee presented me with the gift of 'Please' written 50,000 times. These days the bands weren't the only ones sniffing pure methedrine crystal and living off a rainbow of diet pills. We rarely ate. Fashion-wise, if your cheekbones didn't jut out over your sunken cheeks, if your thighs weren't as thin as your arms, you just couldn't be trendy. When I felt really bad I'd have a multi-vitamin or B12 jab. Nor were the bands the only ones dropping acid regularly. It became a matter of status – either you had taken LSD, or . . . There was no denying that it broadened your outlook, giving you the sense that life really was beautiful if only you could see it that way.

I fully admit that drugs influenced our music. Whether it was true or not, we felt we had to be properly stoned to play properly. Good dope equalled good music – music to get spaced to, music that gave our audience the freedom to let go, to fuse, to be part of something bigger than the band. This is what our audiences craved, not just good music but a good buzz, too, a chance to travel elsewhere on the vibrations of our sounds. Music is a bridge or it's nothing. The swirling lightshows made it impossible to use your eyes in the usual way, and helped create the sense of the band operating in a different dimension. Our listeners wanted to hear us use our high to extend their high, to use our energy as a catalyst . . .

Until eventually we had no energy left to give. The nightly demands to push ourselves to the limit of our creative feelings and unleash a torrent of music to sweep everyone away drained us no matter what we took to help keep us going.

In spite of the leapers (which at the beginning, when you're healthy, make you feel brimful of confidence and energy), I felt depressed and gave in to one of the constant stream of insurance brokers pushing life policies. To maintain human contact, I hung out with journalists – a measure of my alienation from the 'real' world. But they knew plenty of after-hours drinking clubs – which I went to but never really relaxed in. I just consumed till I passed out – in trains, cars, friends' flats, wherever sleep overtook me.

We were warming up for a big tour, with us headlining for the first time. The Move, Amen Corner, The Nice, Pink Floyd, and Eire Apparent (signed to Mike and Chas and road-managed by Dave Robinson, later of Stiff Records) were also in the bill. Standing in the Albert Hall for the first gig, it hit us like a ton of bricks just how big we were after only fourteen months. A Rolls Royce had delivered us to the gig. The dressing rooms were ultra plush. Chas offered his stage-fright cure of whisky and coke (the liquid kind) to anyone who looked vaguely worried. We weren't nervous, just sobered by the thought of the venue. We played at being a bit blasé. Albert Hall? Oh yeah. Nice enough gig.

As guaranteed earners, our fees were now on a percentage basis; and we could pull up-and-coming groups along with us. Chas and Jeffery pooled efforts with Robert Stigwood and Rik Gunnell for tour purposes – the rock tour was now big business. Group discounts for travel and hotels, shared advertising and publicity expenses – all this meant less trouble and more profit. And it was fun for us to be travelling with a whole gang of raving loonies.

Desperate to have somewhere to call home, Trevor Burton of The Move and I rented a house near Wandsworth Prison, but we had weeks of touring before we could move in. For a while I was mobile in a second-hand Ford Executive, but I soon crashed it while trying to drive on the newly trendy Mandrax sleeping pills. The trick with sleeping pills was to take one and *stay awake* so you could walk around with rubber knees talking funny. Getting high had become a new competition: a game of Russian roulette. Only instead of holding a gun to your head, you boasted: 'I can take more than you.' Mitch and Trev wrote in my diary: 'Redding at death's door. Near spewing (couldn't). Trev and Mitch still going strong. Did spew and flaked at four a.m.'

Jimi seemed to have higher tolerances than me. We always took the purest we could find – the acid always purple Owsley, or liquid or crystal Sandoz. Know your source was the rule. If I took two tabs, Jimi took four. We got crazy on pills and got thrown out of hotels. After consuming a half-bottle each of Collis Brown's cough mixture (an over-the-counter remedy containing opiates) Phil Robertson and I thought it terribly funny to put an ashtray in Gerry's suitcase. He got arrested for nicking it. All that mattered was: tour, hang out, be a 'lad', get laid, get pissed, get stoned . . .

It was about this time I was offered a snort of coke which turned out to be heroin. I knew it wasn't for me and never knowingly touched it again. I don't like getting sick to get high and heroin made me deathly ill. People who like the same highs hang out together. Musicians who liked heroin formed groups together, but I never could relate to having a basin in the middle of the studio for spewing up. This distanced me from Jimi, who was always longing for an escape, even for a few hours of 'the next best thing to being dead'. It wasn't a West Coast drug, but in New York smack was trendy among the 'intellectual' set. I find junkies boring, but many people are perfectly happy doing nothing, drifting into blackness, playing with shades of grey.

The tour had it's memorable moments. Sheffield was terribly enthusiastic and we got torn apart coming out of the hall, losing clothes, glasses, hair. I always wondered what would happen if the detachables and semi-detachables (like hair) ran out. Chatham was terrible, but the girls in Nottingham . . . In Newcastle we met pleasantly intelligent but coldly determined people like bouncer Dave, who beat up eight guys after they'd axed his head in and before he walked to hospital. During the show, one guy jumped twenty feet from the balcony to the stage only to be lobbed off by a roadie wielding a mike stand. The audience was wonderful in Glasgow, but the vibes were heavy. This huge bouncer was staggering about nearly legless shouting for the bands' autographs. 'Where are ye?' We hid. Afterwards, while trying to get the crowds out, he got his finger cut off in the door. He never missed it, only wouldn't you know it was one of the musicians who eventually said 'What's this? Aaauugh!' At the London Olympia, a prestige gig, I encountered strobe lights for the first time. I got lost in them, feeling far too detached, but knew I had to play. I was caught in a slow-motion, black and white time warp. All I could see were old-time movie flickers of Jimi laughing at me as I tried to keep in touch with the tempo. I still can't handle strobes. Everything was designed to let it 'flow', but it was sometimes hard not to just melt away.

Dropping acid on my twenty-second birthday and again on New Year's Eve, I found my trips were changing. First I lost my memory while up, and then the bad trips started. I couldn't forget these, no matter how hard I tried. Gone were the days when we would play around, tossing energy and thoughts to each other like kids having a pillow fight. It was hard to even get coherent, because we weren't leaving any time between trips to sort ourselves out. Only when we were working did I feel whole.

January 1968

1 BBC interview.
2 Photo session.
4 Gothenburg, Sweden, Lorensberg Cirkus – two shows (£578.10s.4d).
5 Sandviken, Sweden, Jernvallen Sports Hall (£500).
6 Interviews for Danish TV.
7 Copenhagen, Falkoner Hall – two shows (£527.8s).
8 Stockholm, Konserthus – two shows (£578.10s.5d).
19 London, interview for the *London Herald*.
20 Photo session for *Top Pops* magazine.
23 Interviews.
24 Interviews.
25 Interviews. Rehearsal.
26 Recording.
29 Paris, Olympia – two shows with The Animals (£616.9s.2d).
30 New York via London.

1968 wasn't a good year for the group. It wasn't too smooth for Chas and Jeffery either, but it didn't seem to wear them out like it did us. We were starting our downhill slide as a group even while sales were accelerating. It's hard to imagine three people with less in common – a country boy, a theatre school suburbanite, and a city kid. It made for good music but we were spending more time together than a married couple. We all coped in different ways. I'd go to a bar. Jimi'd retreat to his room, sitting with the shades drawn and a scarf over the light, storing up energy. So we called him 'The Bat'. I also called him 'Henpecked'. He called me 'Bob Dylan's Grandmother'. Besides 'Mitch Miller', Mitch was 'Julie Andrews' or 'Queen Bee'.

Gothenburg has burnt a horrible memory in my mind. After the show, we went off to do the club round. Jimi didn't usually come drinking with us seasoned English drinkers as he couldn't handle booze very well, but in Scandinavia it was alcohol or nothing. That night we all got rotten drunk. Jimi'd been hanging out with this gay Swedish journalist. Perhaps he was putting ideas in Jimi's head, but Jimi suggested we should have a foursome. The Swede was really pushing it, and the vibes got stronger and stranger. Jimi made an advance to me – I passed on it. The tension built up until Jimi started dashing about smashing everything in his room. It was terrifying to see. And very sobering. I hate violence of any kind. The journalist split. I was frightened. Mitch and I knew if we didn't stop him soon we'd all be in trouble. Jimi outweighed me, but I managed to wrestle him to the floor where I sat on him until he calmed down and promised to behave. I let him up and he started again. After going through this routine three times, I gave up and went to my room. You could hear the noise all over the hotel and at about six in the morning someone called the police. Jimi was taken away and charged with disturbing the peace. Luckily we had the gig to do, and Chas had good Swedish connections, so he was released after agreeing to return to face charges.

The gig went very well despite the unpromising entry into Scandinavian life. Perhaps the scene had cleared out whatever was bothering Jimi because we did two excellent one-hour sets to a very appreciative audience, but it was clear that things were drifting apart. Mitch and I talked about how shaky things were getting before the gig the following night and Jimi confirmed our doubts by begging off with a sore throat after only thirty-five minutes. He, like the rest of us, had reasons for being depressed and upset, but his periods of moodiness were stretching out. We were all pissed off and worked our frustrations out on each other because we had no one else close at hand. Management was remote, to say the least, so who better to scream at than each other? Friends and fans couldn't understand. To them, everything was going great, and our complaints were simply crazy. The only relief from loneliness came in the form of girls and dissolution. My diary entries from the period are virtually the same day-to-day: get up, go to the bar, get pissed, feel rough, bathe, get stoned, gig, get drunk, get smashed, collapse shattered.

We had a gig in Sandviken before having to return to Gothenburg to see what the law had planned for Jimi. Returning to Gothenburg, no hotel would have us, but there were no serious charges, just a demand to pay damages to the hotel and a £475 fine. We were on the first boat home.

Back in London, not much had changed except for the fact that everyone seemed to be dropping acid. We happily joined in. I wasn't in the best mood for tripping, still paranoid about what was happening on the business front. I wrote to Chas again to arrange a business meeting, and after seeing Mitch and me, he promised to 'sort things out', whatever that was supposed to mean. There was still nothing in writing. I bought a gun. Is this what being a musician had come to? I spent my free time going to clubs and hanging out more than usual with Mitch. Jimi was living with Chas, and the distance between us was growing. Recording sessions were not happy affairs. None of us was very good at verbalising problems and the studio was as usual cluttered with hangers-on. Too often it was pointless to try to work amid all the distractions of liggers and I simply didn't show up.

A date in France – two shows with The Animals at Olympia – was a welcome break and we were received with warmth and enthusiasm. We brought some of the latter ourselves in the form of methedrine, which gave an energetic and sociable high that helped pull the group together (temporarily). Spiking our morning orange juice with some liquid meth, we set off to reconquer America.

Our brief return to England and Europe hardly provided enough time to recover our balance, much less prepare us for the rigours which awaited us. The flight from London to New York was delayed for one and a half hours and the helicopter which was to have taken us to a big press reception atop the mid-Manhattan Pan Am Building was held up by fog. By the time we had arranged alternative ground transport and made our appearance, we were methed to the gills, anxious, and ready to party, but the press had decided not to wait. They were well into their cups and hardly noticed our arrival. Even the canapés were gone. We split.

Not only were we well and truly back in the USA, we were also well and truly back in Jeffery-land. He was hustling so fast, setting up his New York base, that he appeared to be twins. Steingarten, Wedeen and Weiss (Steve Weiss in particular had a lot of experience getting English bands established Stateside) were now heavily involved on a

$1,000 per month retainer. At our first meeting I was struck by how little Weiss resembled a lawyer. He was wearing red flares, a leather jacket and shades, far from the English model of three-piece suit and school tie. In spite of his appearance, however, he was from the business-as-usual school. The guy even had a TV in his limo.

Jeffery and Chandler Incorporated was officially opened for business on 21 February 1968. Part of the reason for establishing themselves as a US business was to avoid problems with English currency regulations. Jeffery had by this time a lot of experience with the problems of running English bands in the States, and knew what was required. This tour was with the Alan Price set, Soft Machine, Eire Apparent, and The New Animals. Bob Levine, a former road manager, was put in charge of the office, Weiss looked after work permits, and Michael and Donald Hecht were in charge of the books.

Until Jeffery and Chandler had sorted out their American operation, Harold Davidson (of MAM) had booked us in England (and some parts of Europe), Fritz Row had handled Germany, and General Artists Corporation (GAC), Premiere Talent and Al Grossman had handled the States. Davidson's instructions had been to send gig income directly to Yameta, but Jeffery had some new ideas: first, to sidestep Yameta whenever possible; and second, following Weiss's advice, to self-promote and save the agent's percentage. Instead of doing tours, we were performing a series of huge one-off concerts. From the band's point of view, it really didn't make any difference who was doing the booking: our earnings still disappeared.

While the business operation was being streamlined, other efforts were being made to ensure our high profile. The Experience, despite its dramatic entry into the American consciousness via the Monterey Pop Festival and despite good record sales and well-received gigs, was not a guaranteed, spontaneous success. It depended heavily on hyper-activity in the press-agent department and the two full-time operatives, Tony Garland (Madeline Bell's manager and co-Yameta-ite) and Mike Goldstein (then owner of the *Village Voice*), made sure that our non-gigging days were taken up by photo sessions and interviews. Off-days may have meant no walking the boards, but we still had to work, and in its own way, doing press is just as gruelling as being 'up' for a gig. As time wore on, Mitch and I were left on the sidelines and Jimi grew larger than life. And larger-than-life demands were made of him. I usually made a point of attending all the publicity sessions in order to keep track of what was going on. It was strange, however, to be in attendance as an observer of 'The Experience'.

We were now seriously at work. In February 1968 we played thirty-two shows and did many interviews. It was impossible to stay straight. We would awake stoned after a short nights' sleep and begin the cycle again. Everywhere we went we were given handfuls of various substances which, due to our sociable natures, we did our best to consume. The chemists' labs must have been working overtime because there was an endless stream of new highs. The latest was DMT – a foul-tasting white crystal – which gave a detached high I didn't much like. We wisely invested in a reassuring amount of lovely Colombian grass which we carried in an airline bag. Before each landing, I'd be passed the satchel. Placing it on the floor between my legs, I'd skin up. The second we were in the limo, we lit up a joint each. This saved us the aggravation and danger of trying to score in unfamiliar territory. The accelerating pharmaceutical generosity was matched by a change in our sex partners. Before, the girls had been companionable, whole people who liked hanging out with us, but gradually they become women whose presence was strictly sexual and we too became less men than famous fucks, another notch in the knickers. I met some really lovely, nice ladies, but what did I have on offer other than a famous dick? The thrill of unlimited sexual access was gone and all that could interest our increasingly jaded members was novelty entertainment, group sessions and weirdness, paying off hotel detectives to connive in elaborate scams. In retrospect, what I really needed then was a massage, a proper meal and a reassuring chat.

I did make a good friend of a lady named Linda Eastman. She interviewed me, did several photo sessions with the group, and was responsible for the *Life* magazine centerfold of Jimi and me. She's never stopped taking great photos, but now works under the name of McCartney.

The shows were flying it. At one point Bill Graham gave each of us a wristwatch. (Jimi lost his instantly, so I gave him mine.) What was he trying to tell us? That it was time to retire? Should I take some acid to cheer me up? Well, sure. But even acid was succumbing to commercial pressures which drove out fellow freaks and opened things up to dealers with an eye on the methedrine content. So, to the confidence-withering, endless blah blah blah of life in public could be added the bone-tiring, teeth-grinding, nerve-unravelling paranoia of crummy acid. With pure acid you could eat and sleep to rest the body if not the brain. Not any more. And we mixed chemicals so badly, too. Mostly from necessity. Just how do you get down after the show so you can sleep? If it was a good one, you'd feel all energetic, happy and up. If it was bad, you'd be too pissed off to sleep. Knowing that there were only two or three hours to squeeze a night's sleep into didn't help either, so a few stiff drinks and a sleeper sped you on your way. But plane time would come long before the sleeper wore off, hence the leapers. But the flights are terribly boring when you're up, so a creeper rounds off the edges and a lot of drink takes a bit of the cotton wool out of your mouth. But booze (well over a bottle of Vodka a day now) makes life a bit grim, so 'just a bit' of acid makes you feel all tingly and good. But it's hard to concentrate on acid, so a quick sniff of coke (just becoming trendy for the richer set who could also afford massive pieces of Indian jewellery and designer leathers) brings the brain briefly to attention while you smoke some grass or hash to take the nerviness out of the coke. Then, as you're beginning to feel a bit tacky by the time the flight's over, the hotel is found, and it's gig time: a bath, a snort of methedrine and a big tobacco joint puts you on stage. Repeat as necessary. As a result, I was a bit tired most of the time. I wouldn't (couldn't) do it again in a fit!

The drink (vodka and beer), smoke (grass, hash and opium), psychedelics (acid, mescalin), leapers (amphetamines, methedrine, dexydrine, etc.), sleepers (barbiturates, etc.), and creepers (miscellaneous tranquilisers) and other various pills made me feel constantly flu-ish as I got more rundown. Drugs are one way to grow up, though I can't totally recommend it. Everyone tempts death and toys with mortality in their own way. Some find their Meaning of Life, some fuck up, some get addicted to adrenalin or pain. Some stick to toying with their own bodies, others more selfishly experiment with someone else's. Some war with others and some war within themselves. There are positive and negative ways to expand your consciousness; but if life is an educational exercise to raise our consciousness, I try to stick with the 'All You Need Is Love' method these days.

The 1968 American tour was the one that did us in. We stopped making music and started doing time. In the confusion we lost sight of what we wanted to do and started coping (badly) with what we were doing. We were the centre of something, but it was unclear what it was. Gerry Stickells, the tour manager, started borrowing money off us, the band, to pay for tour expenses. Jimi starting pissing me off more and more as he became chronically temperamental. He fucked up a show in Anaheim by only half-heartedly singing the occasional word. Even the reviewers noted his changed attitude. I was wholly unsympathetic to his 'star' attitude and I deeply resented his refusal to play my song, *She's So Fine*, when audiences shouted for it. He kept saying: 'We never do anything new,' but refused to rehearse.

There were good moments, though. In San Francisco, where everyone was as stoned as us and very receptive, we just jammed all night. One night Mitch tried to do a Keith Moon trick – jumping on to his floor tomtom. Only Mitch was getting rather thin (his arms looked more like matchsticks flailing, half-hidden, behind his kit) and when he jumped upon it, the drum bounced him right off. At The Shrine in Los Angeles, we had massive and beautiful new Sunn amps (broken in by professional amp-sitters Mickey Dolenz and David Crosby). On stage we looked like three midgets against the wall of speakers, dwarfed but reassured at the same time by the black and silver tube-lit jungle which pounded the body. The otherworldliness was exaggerated by the police calls and radio signals which the circuitry picked up.

In Seattle, Jimi's family was waiting for us at the airport. It was a triumphal return. Jimi received a Key to the City, and Mitch and I were made to feel at home in a warm, happy family reunion. I got stoned with Jimi's brother Leon, and caught the odd moment with my new super-eight camera. It was a brief hiatus, however, and once back on the road the routine of star moodiness was back to the fore.

In Denver Jimi was feeling bad, but instead of talking it out, he took it out on the audience. I kept telling him to share his problems, but it rubbed him the wrong way to admit he was troubled. During one show he freaked, smashing his equipment and shouting, 'I don't need ANYONE to talk to!' This hurt, because Jimi was obviously in pain and I only wanted to help. But it was more than Jimi bringing us down. It was the management. We *never* saw them. I was dying to get us all together for a good, long, air-clearing talk. I'd had three or four good chats with Chas and a couple with Mike. But nothing had changed.

In my mind, Fort Worth, Texas, was the beginning of the end of the band. It was the first time we'd been assigned separate dressing rooms. When I chanced to go into Jimi's room to see how he was doing, I was met with: 'What are you doing in here?' This separatism guaranteed we went on stage cold as ice. Jimi and I argued openly and bitterly during the show till Mitch said something so funny that we had to relax. But the feeling persisted. There was plenty of time to chat because the state seemed full of girls who didn't fuck. Instead, with so much building up inside, we hit the booze to avoid conversing. It was hard to know how to start communicating.

I did better communicating with the locals. My Englishness in America also gave me a certain license, a certain protection. If I went to the hotel bar in places like Texas, the minute I walked in all these big, dangerously drunk guys would start in with the usual, 'Who's the fag?' (Fag is a word that brought many awkward moments until I figured out that in America it meant homosexual, not cigarette.) Having hair was still risky in some places. In my most English accent – which saved my ass as many times as Jimi's American accent had saved him in England – I'd order, 'Give us a beer, mate.' And the barrier would be broken. 'Say, you ain't from here. You sound English. What you here for?' 'I'm playing at the Stadium tonight.' At which point we'd start talking about the gig, then music or whatever, and someone would buy me the beer.

Another time, ignoring the usual remarks, I started talking to this nice black guy at the bar. The heckling increased and they started moving in. My new friend rescued me, loudly telling them to fuck off. They did and I discovered my guardian was a championship boxer. He also got aggro all the time and blamed it on people having a go at your success, at your visibility. He said if he walked into a bar, five guys would instantly want to beat the shit out of him. He had to be really cool as it didn't do for pro boxers to get into brawls, besides which he was strong enough to kill someone by mistake. As Hendrix was the most visible of our group, he was hit with the most aggro. Sometimes, I'd walk into his room and he'd be sitting in the middle of a bunch of creeps, going 'Duh' and trying to be invisible.

Jimi had a lot of unresolved troubles in his private life, too – paternity claims, for instance – while the PPX mess prevented any Reprise royalties from being paid. Not having an ounce of business know-how between us, we relied on our feelings to make all our decisions. We knew that this was no way to do business, but we didn't know what else to do.

Instead of trying again to talk to Jimi in his brick-wall mood, I tried talking to Chas. My body and brain were so continually upset that I'd forgotten what feeling good felt like. When I'd been happy, the highs would let me be free. Now everything was a burden. I wanted to get away. He agreed that Jimi was getting unreasonably hard to work with and tried to relieve my mind. 'Wait a while, then start your own band.' But this attitude of Jimi's was very draining. To perform we were dependent on finding a spontaneous feeling and 'playing it'. Some-times it translated into notes, sometimes into leaping about. But once the crowd expected us to be spontaneous every night, for Jimi to perform oral sex on his guitar and pretend it was a big dick every night, to freak out on feedback and destruction every night, it became impossible. The gimmick became a chain and the fun died.

Still this rather sad winding down was punctuated by moments of fun. In Chicago the Plaster Casters, a couple of girls dedicated to the creation of casts of erect penises, literally descended on us in order to add our organs to their bizarre collection. My offering was unusual – a corkscrewed rendition – the result of a combination of bad timing of the rate the plaster would set at and Stickells' surprise entry into my room at the crucial moment. Then again, it was difficult to feel sexually attracted to a container of plaster.

Aside from such rare diversions, I depended on writing letters and postcards to everyone I could think of in an attempt to maintain contact with a world outside the increasingly oppressive Experience, a bitter collection of mind games and minor cruelties. An acid diet provides ideal conditions for sustained freakiness. Whenever Jeffery was around, Jimi moved to the front in the freaked, tense, and nervy stakes. Jeffery always made sure that Jimi was not short of drugs. Whether this was in the name of wrong-footing Jimi or keeping him relaxed and 'groovy', I don't know, but the effect was one of the victimisation. I reacted to Jeffery's presence and my bitterness over the business scene by getting him as wrecked as possible, hoping to bum him out, thinking – mistakenly as it turned out – that he was an unlikely candidate for a career in substance abuse (he got heavily into acid).

Running parallel to on-the-road confusion was the business drama. The management was doing good business with several touring and recording bands, but the hidey-hole in the Bahamas was looking more and more like a swamp. Among the London, New York and Nassau branches of the operation worked ranks of lawyers and accountants supervising a vast income derived from many sources. In late 1967 a general accounting was called for (perhaps prompted particularly by the negotiations with PPX concerning Hendrix's earlier contractual obligations) and the accountancy firm Price Waterhouse was called in for this mission impossible. Sums were known to have left London with open tickets; the New Animals' New York accounts didn't tally with the bank statements; there were subsidiary accounts popping up; in spite of all the LP advances and tour earnings for the Experience, Jeffery's account was overdrawn by $27,000. Nassau operatives complained that they had no way of knowing what the artists' revenues should be. Where were the receipts? Were there any receipts, or was there just money? Don't ask me!

Jeffery acted like a member of the Nassau tourist board, talking up all the great opportunities awaiting the sharp investor (me?). What did I want with a piece of unoccupied Caribbean land? Jeffery made it sound like heaven, so Mitch and I relented and flew down to have a look. Heaven it wasn't. One look at us and the hotel lost our reservations and we were shunted off to $100-a-day rooms in another hostelry designed to separate the tourist from his money as quickly as possible. The weather was relaxing, but we were constantly hassled by idiots about our long hair. Nassau . . . the heat was nice, but in the long run a sauna would have been better.

It was, none the less, a welcome break from touring. February and March had been killers:

February 1968

1   Fillmore West, San Francisco. With The New Animals, Alan Price, Soft Machine.

2   Interviews.
       Winterland, San Francisco – two packed shows.

3   Fillmore West.
       Interviews.

4   Fillmore West – two shows
       Interviews.

5   Arizona State University.

6   Tucson, Arizona.

8   Sacramento State College, Sacramento, California.

9   Anaheim Convention Center, Los Angeles. Two shows with Eire Apparent and The New Animals.

10   Shrine Auditorium, Los Angeles – sold out ($10,000).

11   Earl Warren Showgrounds, Santa Barbara ($4,000).

12   Center Arena, Seattle, Washington.

13   University of California, Los Angeles. Audience stormed the stage.

14   Denver, Colorado.
       TV interviews.

15   San Antonio, Texas ($5,000).

16   Auditorium, Dallas, Texas ($5,000).

17   Will Rogers Auditorium, Fort Worth, Texas ($25,000).

18   Music Hall, Houston, Texas – two shows.

20   Interviews, New York City.

21   Electric Factory, Philadelphia, Pennsylvania – two shows.

22   Electric Factory, Philadelphia, Pennsylvania – two shows.

23   Detroit, Michigan.

24   Coliseum, Toronto, Canada.

25   Civic Opera House, Chicago, Illinois – two shows.

27   The Factory, Madison, Wisconsin – two shows.

28   Milwaukee, Wisconsin – two shows.

29   Milwaukee, Wisconsin – two shows.

March 1968

2   Hunter College, New York City – two shows.

3	Veterans' Memorial Auditorium, Columbus, Ohio.
4,5,6	Nassau with Mitch.
8	Brown University, Providence, Rhode Island.
9	Stoney Brook, Long Island, New York.
10	International Ballrooms, Washington DC – two shows.
13	Interviews, photo session.
	Recording. My song *My Friend* tried with Steve Stills on bass, Buddy Miles on drums, me on rhythm and Jimi as engineer.
14	Reception for Soft Machine with Mike and Chas.
15	Clark University, Worcester, Massachusetts. Two shows filmed by BBC.
16	Lewiston Armory, Lewiston, Maine.
19	Capitol Theatre, Ottawa, Canada – two shows (now bootlegged).
21	Community War Memorial, Rochester, New York.
22	Busnell Memorial, Hartford, Connecticut.
23	Memorial Auditorium, Buffalo, New York.
24	IMA Auditorium, Flint, Michigan.
26	Public Music Hall, Cleveland, Ohio – two shows.
27	Teen American Building, Muncie, Indiana.
28	Cincinnati, Ohio – two shows.
29	University of Illinois – cancelled due to electrical fault.
30	University of Toledo Fieldhouse, Toledo, Ohio.
31	The Arena, Philadelphia, Pennsylvania.

In Worcester we were filmed by the BBC, an inhibiting intrusion. Self-consciousness crept in when we were being filmed or recorded, a stiffness that kept us restrained musically and physically. In Cleveland there was a press party which neither Jimi nor Mitch attended. Bored, I wandered into another of the hotel's 'function' rooms and found Leonard Nimoy having a press party for his new LP. I hate to admit it, but I hardly recognised the star of my favourite television show without his Mr Spock ears. We snuck up to my room for a joint and commiserated over the utter boredom generated by press affairs.

We went down a bomb that night – in spite of a very real bomb scare at the hall. Big deal. We could take anything in our stride. Any hitch and we'd simply retire to our rooms and play records on our new portable players to stay sane. Or we went out window shopping for flash cars. American sports cars were all the rage in England and I fancied a Cougar. Jimi favoured Corvettes. We were told, 'Forget it, no money.'

Ottawa in March, Montreal in April: You'd think we could have done Canada in one go, especially as we always had trouble at customs, but the logic of touring by plane meant that geographical proximity was unimportant. In Canada we'd get pulled by a French official every time, and being English, frizzy-haired and wearing paisley shirts, we'd get the full treatment. Once into Canada, though, things were good. There were lots of American draft dodgers hanging out, and we took in a concert of Irish groups in Montreal, followed by Chubby Checker and Bobby Bland at a club and a singsong with the Irish bands.

Plane travel could get quite silly. We flew into Virginia Beach one day only to be told that the gig was held up for a day, so it was back on a plane to New York for a night of partying at Salvation and the Scene Clubs with Roger Daltrey. Jimi disappeared and we were late getting to the airport the next day. Arriving with minutes to spare, we were told we could still make the plane if we ran. I ran and got on board. Jimi and Mitch were too groovy to run and ended up in Virginia Beach only after changing planes five times. Good gig.

Our gig in Newark brought home to me how little I understood about America. We got into the limo and drove from Manhattan and as soon as we crossed into Newark we were somewhere weird, a place with tanks in the streets, but no people. I didn't know what was going on. At the hall we were met by police. We freaked. What had we done? Then we heard that Martin Luther King had been assassinated and Newark was under siege. This was beyond my experience. The cops told us that there might be a riot and that we should do one show, do it quick and fuck off. The hall was huge – a several-thousand-seater – but contained at most two hundred people. We did the show for the deserving few who had braved the streets and escaped as quickly as possible.

This was an occasion when the whole black thing hit Jimi in the face. He couldn't turn away. Jimi was never heavy about being black. He was into being *Jimi* – human being, pop superstar. When his blackness became an issue, he dealt with it, but he never put it out front. Once, touring in the South, we missed the plane and had to drive to Shreveport or some other Louisiana town. Normally when we travelled by car we'd stop on the road and buy a lump of cheese, crackers and some beer. This time, when the car stopped, Jimi stayed put and wouldn't come into the store with us. I asked what was up but he simply said, 'No, man. You go in. I'll wait here.' I didn't know about any of this stuff. I knew America from aeroplane seat, hotel room and stage. It never occurred to me that two foreign white guys and a black guy dressed in pink suits, fruit boots and scarves would be a shock to the redneck system. We did manage to coax Jimi in, but once through the door it hit us like a wave. The entire café turned to stare at us. Mitch and I ordered loudly in our politest, best English accents and we threw the food down our throats as invisibly as we could. It was scary. I wondered that people could hate so blindly and still live with themselves. It made our petty irritations seem so trivial that the incident drew us together again.

In my experience, Jimi had blackness thrust upon him in certain respects. In the midst of rising racial tensions, Jimi was an obvious focus of attention and political activists would seek him out for various kinds of support they felt his celebrity would lend. Jimi distrusted people approaching him from this angle and he did his best to avoid such attachments. He was disillusioned enough to be cynical and he was no more keen on letting black people use him than he was willing to be exploited by white people. If he felt a cause was his, he reacted without prompting: giving $5,000 to the Martin Luther King Memorial Fund, for example. He didn't appreciate the fact that the press emphasised his unusual position as a 'black rock star', as though this were some kind of freakish thing. Jimi liked to stand out. He was a flashy dresser. He liked the high profile. He would have welcomed a black audience, but was seized upon by a primarily white one. For him (and us), the 1960s was a period of mixing and sharing. One tried to be open and open-minded.

In April, I escaped to England for a breather, undergoing the by now usual excess-baggage charges as well as a detailed examination by customs. My flat was occupied by two Danish girls who had – uninvited – taken up residence. I cleared them out. My mother, chronically hounded by the press, had taken up with and married a Spanish sponge whose cross-border activities of a smokeable nature had, unsurprisingly, attracted the attention of the police. He was in my bad books anyway for having sold me a dud E-Type which, in my absence, he totalled. My telephone had been cut off after a huge bill was run up by 'friends' unknown. The American Embassy wouldn't renew my visa without verification that I wasn't a certified bum. Welcome home.

My pile of songs had grown and although Chandler's suggestion that I look for something beyond the Experience sounded good, I had lost touch with local musicians and was reluctant to leap right in. I wanted to make sure that if I started up another group, it would be a group of friends I could relax with. We could do what I had done before The Experience: be working musicians, make a bit of money, get on with it. The Experience had a nice financial exterior, but the gloss disguised a major mess. My circle of acquaintances included plenty of lawyers and accountants, but they were weekend hippies in wigs, swingers in false moustaches and carefully pressed bellbottoms, 'groovy guys' looking for a bit of 'free love'.

My sister worked as an auditor and she introduced me to her accountant boss. I signed up my own professionals and found out how naïve I had been. Television fees, record percentages, merchandising cuts, film rights were among the various sources of income to which I had remained oblivious – dozens of pieces of action to which a successful band has access. I was bass player in blunderland. I had been out there working and knew that despite the protests of management we must at least have been breaking even, but the reality was that my business days were not unlike my working days: get up, get smashed, collapse, and have Jeffery hand me a piece of paper to sign.

My accountant looked around and returned to report that he could not find any contracts which I had signed. He couldn't even trace the companies with which I had signed contracts. As far as anyone could tell I had not signed any contracts at all.

I was not in a great position to pursue such matters. It was difficult to keep any inquiries going on when I was spending only a couple of days in any one place. Jimi must have known more about what was going on than he let on and I know that he worried about coming out of The Experience broke, but like me he was put off by the business world. Keeping the group going was work enough without the added burden of taking care of the business of taking care of business. We pursued our own private, misguided strategies, signing contracts outside the presence of others, figuring that everyone was getting the same bits of paper to sign. One night in a back room at the Scene we were offered $1 million each to sign with a prominent, allegedly mob-orientated organisation. Did anyone give in?

In this climate of mistrust and doubt, we started to record *Electric Ladyland* at the Record Plant in New York. Recording technology was moving on and the tape machines were up to twelve-track. We still played well together although it was difficult to get over the high level of tension which kept us apart off stage. The approach we had used for *Are You Experienced?* and *Axis: Bold as Love* was still preferred: work from the format of knowing the basic chords, get a rough tempo, and agree the break positions. After that we would run through a couple of times to get the feel and get our individual contributions sorted out. With twelve tracks, however, mixing became a bigger part of the process, and Jimi and Chas tended to get carried away. Jimi in particular was entranced by new electronic effects as well as the possibilities afforded by complicated overdubbing, and the lovely simplicity of our earlier recordings got lost. Instead of just playing the songs through a couple of times and then going to a take, Jimi began trying to function as a director. This might have worked, but his attempts to verbalise his ideas just didn't. He'd lose his train of thought, skip to something else, fail to convey to us what he was up to. We'd do four basic tracks of drums, rough vocals, rhythm guitar and bass, but when it got to the thirty-sixth guitar overdub it was all systems stop. I could nip out to a club and pull a chick and return only to find Jimi still hadn't finished tuning his guitar. I told him he was being silly to try to do so much at once – writer, producer, singer, guitarist, arranger – but he took no notice. Things had to be done Jimi's way or no way, and Jimi's way was getting more and more unproductive. Nothing was happening, or if it was happening it took so long that you couldn't tell it was happening. As the recording process got stretched out into marathon twiddling sessions, an audience grew in the studio, legions of hangers-on who contributed nothing to the music but were there solely for the trip. Chas, who had nurtured The Experience from the beginning, was getting fed up. He had successfully produced the first two albums, but now found himself stymied by Jimi's demands for control.

It was not only The Experience and Chas who were exploring new dimensions in frustration, but the record companies as well. It had been five months since the previous album, and demand for a new product was heavy. Track Records compiled *Smash Hits* – a collection of singles – to fill the gap, but it was a holding action. In desperation, Chas put pressure on Jimi to cut down on the studio crowd scenes as well as the drug diet. He risked a lot of bad feeling, but Jimi did promise to shape up, a promise which lasted as long as it took for a scenemaker – there was no shortage – to show up with something to smoke/snort/swallow.

There was pressure from another, and up to this point, more or less remote source: Jeffery. With The Animals now consigned to the bin of defunctness and few of his other groups having made it past the starting-gate advances, Jeffery had reason to get The Experience back into a serious money-earning position. I could tell what he was thinking as we both watched the studio clock ticking away the dollars, and the result was Electric Lady Studios. Before that, however, we still had to get through this patch and finish *Electric Ladyland*, an album marred by – among many other things – the 'nude' cover.

I took advantage of unused studio time to work on demos of my own material, helped out by – among others – Steve Winwood and Chris

Wood of Traffic. It was awkward for me. I was shy, and new to the production booth, but certainly too impatient to learn by watching Chas and Jimi mix the millionth guitar overdub. I dreamt big – orchestras – but settled for a good sound organised by engineer Gary Kellgren, and in late April, *Little Miss Strange* was recorded. Mitch and I (playing various guitar parts) did the basic track and vocals, and Jimi came in to put the lead guitar on. He was very nice about it, making sure I was there when he overdubbed and checking that I approved of his contribution. I did, and was very pleased with the result. My publishing from *Little Miss Strange* and *She's So Fine* (from *Axis*) remain my only sources of income from the Experience.

We recorded and gigged during early May, two activities which kept us unhappily together and further removed from others. I needed something to do musically outside The Experience and wanted to produce a Canadian group I'd heard, The Churls, but was told that The Experience organisation didn't have enough funds for such sideline activities. On 2 May I took it out on Jimi, letting him know what I thought of the scene he was building around himself. There were tons of people in the studio, you couldn't even move. It was a party, not a session. He just said, 'Relax man . . . ' I'd been relaxing for months, so I relaxed my way right out of the place, not really caring if I ever saw him again.

I returned the next day because the session was being filmed. We played the same number all day long (*Stonefree*). I showed up the next day as well, but no one else did. At least there were no crowds. So I redid some bass lines in peace and quiet and later had a fantastic blow with jazzer Larry Coryell, who turned out to be an adept rock'n'roller. I moaned to Chas, who was sympathetic but had a different – if equally depressing – angle on the whole affair. To him, it was a matter of seeing how long The Experience could be kept going, how long the product could be sustained. He and Jeffery were on the downhill run and live gigs were being recorded to ensure that there was enough material in the can to spin things out (a policy which paid benefits in the distant future when patchy albums were strengthened by judicious use of gig recordings). Despite what seemed a hopeless set of circumstances, the Miami Pop Festival gig we did that month was excellent, and when the second day's show was rained out, Jimi and I headed to the hotel for a jam and general craziness with Arthur Brown, Steve Paul, the Mothers of Invention and Blue Cheer. That was coming to be the pattern – fight, get smashed and make up and be friends – but that's a kind of relationship which can't go on for ever.

May

23   Milan.

24,25   Brancaccio Theatre/Piper Club, Rome – two shows each night (£3747.8s).

26   A 3,500-seat sports hall in Bologna – 2 shows.

30   Zurich.
       Press reception: Animals, Traffic, Move, Koobas, John Mayall
       Hallenstadion, Beat Monster Concert. (£1350).

31   Photo session.
       Hallenstadion. (Both concerts were attended by over 200 police.)

June

4   Rehearsal for Dusty Springfield at Elstree Studios.

5   Dusty Springfield Show.

10   Interview.

12   Majorca.

27   Interview and Photos.

Setting out from London, English customs, always attentive, pulled a new one: they searched me as I was *leaving* the country. This treatment was no doubt prompted by Mitch's mouth ('I suppose you want to search us for drugs?') I was left with a mouthful of melting Black Bomber. On the way back, Mitch got his mouth searched – poetic justice.

I took my sister, Vicki, on this European tour. I think she found it educational. I also proposed who should work with us on the road because I kept in touch with 'normal' people. Mitch and Jimi preferred to hang out in exclusive clubs while I continued to drink in the Ship on Wardour Street. The amount of gear grew on each tour, amps fried regularly, speakers fluttered and died. Roadies came and went. Stickells was in for the whole run. 'H' (ex-Pretty Things) joined, then Neville Chesters (ex-Who, Bee Gees, Merseybeats). Neville left and Eric Barrett joined for this tour. H left and Upsey joined. (Both H and Upsey are now dead. Upsey got on the ferry at Ostend and never got off at Dover. H, a strong swimmer, went swimming and was never seen again.) To give them their full due, they handled things very smoothly. Our gear was so huge and heavy I could barely lift any of it. One of my amp and speaker setups weighed about a hundred and sixty pounds and was about six feet high. To give the airlines credit too, little got

I got my first guitar aged thirteen – it was love at first sight. Before long I'd formed The Lonely Ones (BELOW auditioning for the Southern TV show *Home Grown* in 1961): left to right, me, Mick Whibley, John 'Andy' Andrews and Bob Hiscox. I then joined Neil Landon and The Burnettes (ABOVE, at Folkestone Town Hall in 1962): left to right, me, Neil Landon, Peter Kircher and Bob Hiscox.

My next band was The Jimi Hendrix Experience! TOP: me, Jimi and Mitch in Germany in the early days. BELOW: Jimi shows how happy and relaxed he could be on stage.

Spring 1967: the three of us plan world domination over a game of *Risk*. To begin with none of us wanted to sing, but I always felt Jimi's deep, laid-back vocals were an important complement to his guitar.

Jimi – a portrait by Linda McCartney.

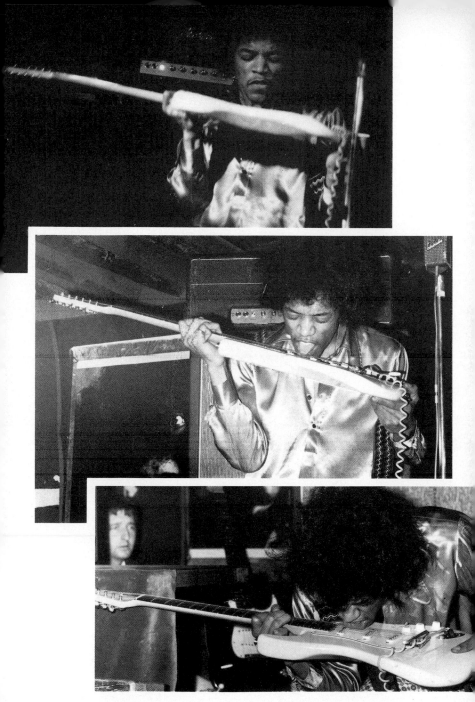

Jimi on his way to becoming a legend. Nobody did it better . . .

If Jimi could play behind his back, so could I!

ABOVE: backstage on the 1967 tour with The Monkees. (The gorilla is not a Monkee . . .) RIGHT: Jimi and I prove that – in 1967 at least – we still had a sense of humour. BELOW: in Majorca in 1968 – left to right: Eric Barrett, Cathy Etchingham, Angie Burdon, Neil Landon, me, Gerry Stickells and Sue.

FROM LEFT TO RIGHT: Jimi Hendrix, Mitch Mitchell, Jack Casady, Noel Redding
at a gig in Berkeley in 1969.

The band at the Ambassador Theatre, Washington DC, in August 1967 – rapidly getting Experienced.

Linda McCartney took this shot of me on stage in Miami in 1968.

Jimi, by Linda McCartney.

The band in Minneapolis in November 1968 – even more Experienced . . .

ABOVE: me and Keith Moon after a recording session in London in 1974. LEFT: with my lawyer Mickey Shapiro in 1972 – we look pretty determined here, but it wasn't enough.

TOP: the authors with Bob Dylan. BELOW: myself . . . and Carol, singing at a festival in Clonakilty, Ireland in June 1990 – one of our last gigs together before her tragic death.

Caught with my trousers down . . . A publicity shot taken in 1975.

damaged. This was all a big change from carrying my guitar in one hand and my Fender Bandmaster amp in the other.

In Italy, we were mobbed at the airport while waiting for the gear, which was in bits from the US tour, to arrive. The amp tubes were shot, the power went up and down like a yoyo, and Jimi screamed constantly. Since we played everything at a volume of ten with bass and treble full up, the amps lasted about one show. My Sunns were wonderful, though. Jimi, who'd started with 75 watts, now had six Marshall four-by-twelve speaker cabinets (we tried one on my side but I couldn't stick the volume) and four Marshall 100-watt amps and more and more gadgets like fuzz, WahWah, Univibe, and Octavia.

The audience in Rome couldn't believe what they were seeing. Italy wasn't on the main circuit for pop groups then. Everyone was chattering like crazy to their friends as they tried to comprehend what they were hearing. They nearly drowned us out and Jimi got fed up: 'If you don't stop talking, I'll stop playing.' I came to the mike and translated it into simpler English: 'Shut up!'

We were warned not to go to the Coliseum because it was 'dangerous' (frequented by homosexuals), so we snuck out between shows and went anyway. It was open all night then, so we sat and smoked a huge joint while soaking up the atmosphere. We just made it back for the second show and saved Stickells from having a heart attack. Our great driver, Tony, made sure we got around and would take me to the Titan Club after our shows so I could jam on guitar. We tried to take girls into the posh hotel. No way. So we walked up a nearby hill and got stoned until six in the morning, arriving back when the doormen were changing guard and slipping in with the ladies.

Zurich anticipated our arrival by laying on 200 extra police, some of whom, friendly lads, followed us everywhere we went. When they complained that our rehearsal was too loud, official earplugs were issued. The prim and proper hotel staff hated us when we arrived, trailing hordes of press in various stages of inebriation. Whether the police presence sparked the crowds or not, there were incidents both shows. First night, the police linked arms and marched the length of the stadium cracking anyone who got in the way. The next night, the audience showed their appreciation (or perhaps their retaliation) by breaking up the chairs. Even the hangers-on were strange. The hotel was raided and guests thrown out. It was a relief to leave. I plugged a mike into the plane PA system and interspersed the rock music with comments. 'Will the bearded man with the harp please keep away from the windows?' And, 'Will Buddy Holly please report to the rear of the plane.' And we drank the bar dry.

Back in London, there was little scheduled except the Dusty Springfield show. It was a warm, relaxed show, but Jimi insisted on playing with his teeth. I hated it when he did that. It put my teeth on edge. Even the producer wasn't too aloof to get mangled with us afterwards. Then we went to a party at some Sir's house where there were all kinds of weird scenes going on.

At a loose end, I became a fixture at the office, the last person they wanted around, 'How about a holiday in Majorca? We'll hire a villa!' This would keep me from being underfoot while Jimi was off with Jeffery. With the office staff it was often impossible to tell where friendship ended and politics began. Well, why not? Neil, Eric, Cathy Etchingham, Angie Burdon, Mitch, Gerry, Chas and Lottie (who was living in Jeffery's apartment) and I headed off. Jeffery's Spanish interests were widespread. I could go to any club for free, jam wherever and whenever I felt like it (especially in the Haima Club), and even draw money from his tills. George Best was there with a gang of English footballers. It was a mad whirl of booze and girls. When Keith Altham came down to organise PR for Jeffery's newest club, we went to see the famous Cordobes fight a bull. It was easy to see the grace of a master fighter, though I couldn't stomach the brutality of baiting and mutilating animals for fun. When one fighter was gored, I cheered the bull and nearly ended up as steak myself. At the club restaurant I took the opportunity to do a quick takeoff of Mitch. I bounced up the steps, boinging about; 'Oh, sorry I'm late. What's going on? Can I have some of that?'

On 24 June 1968, the curtain had gone up on a major financial drama. PPX (Ed Chalpin's record company) had been energetically trying to reclaim rights to Jimi's output. Hendrix had resisted, but there was no point in carrying on. When Chandler had come along with his offer, Jimi was a year into his PPX contract and he must have hoped that he could somehow keep Chalpin locked away in a closet. When The Experience hit the charts full force with *Are You Experienced?*, Chalpin was armed, ready and dangerous, and he booked a first-class seat on the bandwagon. The case had almost come to court when Warner Brothers/Reprise offered to step in and settle the mess. The could sort out Chalpin and Jeffery in one fell swoop by negotiating for some of Jimi's rights in exchange for paying off Chalpin. The result was the signing of three documents on 24 June 1968:

1) Settlement agreement between PPX *et al* and Jeffery/Chandler.
2) Sale agreement: Jeffery/Chandler sold Jimi to Warner Brothers/Reprise.

3) Warner Brothers/Reprise recording/production contract with Jimi which superseded the original contract of March 1967.

In exchange for PPX's contract with Jimi, Warners offered Chalpin a two-point royalty on *Are You Experienced* and *Axis: Bold as Love* as well as the as yet to be released (or even fully recorded) *Electric Ladyland*. The guaranteed income on these three albums was $200,000 (or $1,000,000, according to your source), although estimates of its eventual value are as high as $4,000,000. In addition, Chalpin was given the rights to another album by Jimi (which turned out to be *Band of Gypsies* on Capitol). Despite these rather generous blandishments, Chalpin in addition packaged, released, repackaged, and rereleased some fourteen albums consisting of pre-Experience, Hendrix recordings.

Warner Brothers also purchased 'certain rights' of Jimi's (whose address for these purposes was Nassau) from Yameta/Jeffery/Chandler for $450,000 ($250,000 initial payment and the balance in six-monthly payments over four years). Chas was leaving the partnership ('I just got out and left all my papers with Jeffery.') while Jeffery was staying on as agent/manager. Yameta – Jeffery's offshore company – retained the right to have the buyout and royalty payments channelled through its Nassau operation at a fee of five per cent. According to the terms of the four-year recording/production agreement between Warner Brothers and Jimi – effective 10 July 1968 – the record company retained the rights to all previously recorded Experience material as well as any material Jimi might produce for others – such as the albums he did for Cat Mother and the All Night Newsboys, the Buddy Miles Express and Eire Apparent – for five years. Jimi would be responsible for any and all royalties payable to sub-producers, musicians, vocalists, etc. That took care of that.

Although the relationship between Jimi and Warner Brothers was straightforward, Jeffery and Chandler still had to sort out Yameta. They felt that Yameta's administration charges were too costly, that the accounts were poorly kept, and that until the Yameta operation was reorganised no money could flow from the Warner Brothers agreement. In early July, an agreement was reached between Hillman (Yameta) and Jeffery. Yameta agreed to account for everything to date, compensation would be based on the gross earnings of the Yameta artists, everyone would furnish receipts, documents, etc, and Price Waterhouse would act for Yameta, Michael and Donald Hecht for Jeffery and Chandler. Any agreement would be final and in the case of a dispute, it would be settled by Henry Steingarten. Jimi was released from his December 1966 employment agreement with Yameta as of 31 December 1967 and in return, Jeffery agreed to supply Yameta with the same agreement signed by Mitch and me – backdated to 1 December 1966 – and running seven years. Neither Yameta nor Hillman would act any longer as personal managers or business agents; they would deal only with taxes and banking.

A new procedure was to be adopted for handling the income and expenses of tours, and Jeffery and Chandler engaged the legal services of Steingarten, Wedeen and Weiss while Yameta signed Leon Dicker. Jeffery was still managing Eric Burdon (until 1970) at twenty per cent subject to the outcome of ongoing litigation. Twenty per cent of The Animal's income was held in escrow pending the outcome of The Animal's lawsuit against Jeffery.

The relevant clause from my point of view read: 'Yameta shall in the future receive its commission on the share (fifty per cent) of Warners royalties applicable to the two English members of The Jimi Hendrix Experience.' Jeffery signed on Chandler's behalf.

Apparently, an artist's management company which pays and receives in $US can maintain a dollar account in a Nassau bank as long as the authorities are apprised of the payments' destinations. The bank was informed that forty per cent of the income would always be converted to sterling. On 11 July 1968, $250,000 was transferred from Warner Brothers' New York office to the Bank of Nova Scotia, Jamaica.

After dues had been settled, a grand total of $148.10 remained in the account. In addition, Dicker was sent $100,000 for US obligations relating to agency fees, promotional expenses, recording expenses, studio rentals, advertising, and so on.

Business is a world demanding time and concentration – nasty but necessary if you want to play music and not starve. Most entertainers have a certain disregard for money, but business is business. You will meet good people, but there will also be very likeable chancers, cheaters, and conmen. It's not good enough to be a shit-hot guitarist. Still in school and dreaming of music? Use your time to study basic business skills and be prepared to spend time regularly keeping up with what is happening in your life. It'll take much longer afterwards – going backwards to go forwards – and be much more painful. You have to like music to do it, but you can't live doing it for fun. Gigging is called playing, but it's no game. You can't even call in sick!

The July gig list was very sparse:

6   Woburn Abbey with Geno Washington, T Rex, Family, New

Formula, Little Women.
Photo session.

11 Filming.

12 Recording at Southern Recording with Pete Kircher for Fat
Mattress: *Petrol Pump Assistant, She Came In The Morning,* and
Sitting at the Lights.

15 Palma, Majorca, Sergeant Pepper's Club.

18 Photo session.
Jam at the club.

27 Back to the States.

Woburn Abbey was a huge outdoor gig, including a photo session with
Roscoe and Francis, the Duke of Bedford. As we were leaping, we
followed it by hitting Blaises followed by several parties in town. Then
American-in-London Tim Rose organised a game of star baseball.
Team members included Rod Stewart and Ron Wood, and the venue
was the green near Olympic Studios in Barnes.

The Experience was scheduled to open Chas and Jeffery's latest
venture – Sergeant Pepper's, a London-style nightclub off the Plaza
Gomilla (known to us as the Plastic Gorilla). It was a posh, air-
conditioned job with a lighting man, PA, restaurant, the works. Jimi
and Mitch flew in at the last minute, and we went straight to the club
and started – not an Experience set, but a good, loose night of great
rock'n'roll, jamming on *Lucille* and *Johnny B Goode*. Neil Landon
joined in and I think it was the only time anyone ever did vocals with
us. Jimi and I swopped instruments. At the end of *Wild Thing*, Jimi
raised his guitar towards the dropped ceiling and it went straight
through the flimsy material. So he left it swinging there and the crowd
roared.

Gig over, business started again. Jeffery started on about getting
Jimi back to the States to 'sign some papers'. But Jimi was in no hurry.
We sunned, go-karted, swam (proof on film), smoked dope and
clubbed around before we split. I felt very insecure and started a long
relationship with Mandrax sleeping pills. Walking sideways, I kept
bumping into the English taxman who was hounding me. After all, the
press were always on about the millions we were making. Chas
recommended accountants. Can I claim for clothes that are stolen as
fast as I buy them? And my glasses?

Jeffery and Chas seemed very blasé. With Chas more or less out of
our lives (though Jeffery and Chandler Inc. was still undissolved in
1979), the new Michael Jeffery Management, Inc. of 27 East 37th
Street went into action. With the power to negotiate and sign for us,

Jeffery's idea seemed to be to work The Experience and/or Jimi as hard as possible until either we burnt out or the audience got bored. Following the summer's Yameta negotiations, Mitch and I signed the requested backdated contracts. My diary reads: 'Went to office. Talked business all afternoon. Went to Weiss's office. Talked to accountant. Signed some papers.'

Jeffery was making a big show of 'putting everything right'. An impossible task – the proverbial shutting of the barn door after the horse had gone. The group would now have a company of it's own through which all group income would pass, including royalties being held up by lawsuits and past and future gig earnings. Taking 20 per cent off the top for management, and after meeting all the expenses, the group would divide the balance as per our early 1967 50/25/25 agreement, with Jimi getting the lion's share, plus his own publishing and production income. On 18 July 1968, 'our' company, Are You Experienced, Inc. was formed. We were really pleased with ourselves, but failed to realise that we should have been assigned shares and issued with stock certificates.

When Jeffery tried to slip in a document saying I'd pay $15,000 toward Jimi's legal fees I refused to sign. They included fees for the PPX case – $35,000; legal fees for the Betty Sperber case – $2,500; and a $37,500 settlement to Betty Sperber. I knew who and what the PPX case was all about, and that was far beyond my responsibility, but who was Betty Sperber and why did I owe her money? Although I didn't sign, the funds were removed from 'my' account anyway, helping considerably to reduce management's cut of the costs. I figured that if Gordon Mills had sued me you could bet that Jimi or Chandler or Jeffery or Mitch was unlikely to have chipped in. Luckily he was decent enough not to. In any case, if Jimi was having trouble he could certainly afford to handle it. In exchange for the eventual release from Chalpin, The Experience, not Jimi, paid. The lawyers made a fortune, Chalpin got his due, and The Experience was ruined.

Once Are You Experienced Inc. was incorporated the only difference from our informal arrangement was that we could see more clearly how our money was being spent despite our wishes. Jimi always spent money like there was no tomorrow. He'd overdraw his account, and funds would be transferred from either Mitch's account or mine to cover him. It was a great arrangement: what's mine is The Experience's and what is The Experience's is whatever anyone spends. We should have been drowning in earnings, but even Jimi – who had more access to Experience funds than Mitch or I did – regularly went begging for cash from our agent, Dick Katz.

We were being taken to the cleaners by our own outfit, by us. Nevertheless, the shows were very good at this time, something to do with serious dues-paying, I suspect. It was tough. On the one hand we were going down well, we were doing a good, professional job, we were doing what musicians were supposed to do, and the audience reaction showed us we were on the right track. On the other hand we were bored brainless, churning out The Experience Show, churning out the hits and Jeffery (still true to Monkees form) was there to remind us that what the growing (and younger) audience wanted was what we did so well.

Among the three of us a plan was hatched for each of us to form his own band and regroup twice a year for an Experience tour with our solo bands serving as opening acts. Mitch's band was to be the Mind Octopus, mine was to be Fat Mattress, and Jimi's was to be the Band of Gypsies (a name originally given to a proposed Experience jam-type album). Everyone liked the idea and – innocently – it cheered us up to have something cooking for the future. There might, after all, be some way to salvage The Experience.

Jimi's stable base in Chas's home disappeared with the business shake-up and Chas's desire for some privacy for his marriage. He moved into a hotel, then got a flat and began to spend more time 'at home'. To maintain our sanity, we rarely saw each other when we weren't working. Which didn't last long. We were waiting for a flight to the States when we met one of the original rock'n'roll idols. We could hardly wait to shake hands. Only when Jimi offered his hand, the (white) idol declined to notice it. That moment horrified me! Wasn't life hard enough?

Chapter Five

Round Three

How can you hang on to a dream?
How can it really be the way it seems?
TIM HARDIN

Suddenly, as rare things will, it vanished.
ROBERT BROWNING

THE New York office presented me with my first Gold Disc award:
'Uh, Noel, Warners sent this over. Shall I ship it to England for you?'
Touring resumed with no messing.

July
30   Baton Rouge, Louisiana, Independence Hall, Lakeshore
      Auditorium.
31   Shreveport, Louisiana, Municipal Auditorium.

August
1   Reception in Park.
      New Orleans, Louisiana, Stadium.
2   San Antonio, Texas.
3   Dallas, Texas. Moody Coliseum/Southern Methodist
      University.
4   Houston, Texas, Sam Houston Coliseum.
      Radio Show done live after the gig.
7   New York City, photo session in Central Park with Linda
      Eastman.
8   Demo session of my songs with a duff drummer.
9   Recorded two songs of mine with Robert Wyatt.
10   Chicago, Illinois, Auditorium Theatre – two shows with
      The Association.

11	Davenport, Iowa, Col Ballroom ($19,000).
13,14	New York, mixed two of my songs.
16	Baltimore, Maryland – TV show, interviews.
	Columbia, Maryland, MerriWeather Post Pavilion ($16,000).
17	Atlanta, Georgia, Municipal Auditorium with Vanilla Fudge and Eire Apparent – two shows.
18	Tampa, Florida, Curtis Hixon Hall.
20	Richmond, Virginia, The Mosque – two shows.
21	Virginia Beach, Virginia – two shows.
23	New York City, Flushing Meadow Singer Bowl – New York Rock Festival with Janis Joplin. 18,000 people came ($32,000).
24	Hartford, Connecticut, Bushnell Memorial.
25	Framingham, Massachusetts, Carousel Theatre – two shows.
26	Richmond, Virginia ($14,000).
27	Recording – two new tracks, one of them mine, *Little Miss Strange*.

Even with twenty years of hindsight and having taken in others' views of what was happening, it is still difficult not to see the story in the little details that seem inconsequential. Why did we always seem to leave for gigs in the middle of the night? Mitch was at his nuttiest on the road. In the early days, he and Chas sometimes shared a room and he'd nearly drive Chas crazy. Even if we were doing a one-night show, Mitch would unpack and put away the contents of all his three suitcases, paste his toothbrush, lock and chain his door, put his phone under a pillow under the bed, and take a sleeping pill. By which time it would be time to leave and Gerry would be hacking through the chain, waking, dressing, and packing Mitch up while Jimi and I waited grumbling and half dead in the car. Sometimes Jimi would disappear and I'd be put in charge of getting Mitch to the airport while Gerry'd look for Jimi.

We were travelling salesmen of music. At times, simply bored brainless with The Experience Show, we could hardly imagine going on a minute longer. The management insisted that our growing (younger) audience only wanted to hear the same cranked-out hits. If we tried to change we got static. Somehow we did some very good shows, jamming our way through our standards. We'd lost that driving energy though, and strangely, Jimi and I were both thinking ahead to softer, more melodic songs played on a variety of instruments. And I wanted to try my own material.

I made the mistake of overestimating my adaptability, expecting to play my new six-string Epiphone bass without coming to terms with the close string spacing. I never got a second try – it was stolen before the next gig. The more I wrote the more I felt like a guitarist again, so I got a Fender six-string bass. But my fingers were still too big for the string spacing.

In Texas, we asked for a drink and were told the gig was 'dry'. That was it. Forget it! We flat out refused to play without drink. Finally a police car pulled up outside the gig and we were taken out. We were getting a bit nervous. Texas had a terrifying reputation for locking you away for life for possession of a joint. The boot opened and inside was as close to a full bar as you could imagine.

In Connecticut, Chas wanted the lights down for our stage entrance. He was passed from person to person until he finally found someone who ordered, 'Beat it, fatso.' Whereupon Chas replied, 'If you don't turn down the lights, you'll have a riot. I'm their manager.' He was handcuffed and jailed in Bridgeport for threatening the local Police Commissioner. In Richmond he was arrested again – 'security error'.

Near Boston, we sampled our first grass pills – pure THC. Continuing the last century's trend, the chemists were busy making something chemical from something natural. Chemically synthesised and concentrated, the difference between, for example, psylocybin tablets ($15 a go) and peyote buttons (free) was more than the price. THC was unbelievably strong, the high wasn't cool, and the accompanying paranoia gave us the horrors about going on stage until the receptive crowd filling the circus tent made us feel welcome. We had to get back to New York, but the driver was way out of it. Only Jimi could keep it – loosely – together. The drive took well over five hours and he borrowed my glasses to see the road. Suddenly, I remembered other occasions when he'd borrowed them to check on something and realised he really could use a pair, but was too vain to wear them! Then I remembered all the other times he'd driven without them . . .

On days off we worked on *Electric Ladyland*, which was taking forever. And Jimi was trying to find time to produce other groups, too, doing rush jobs he wasn't always happy with. On 27 August, speeding and coked up, we worked from early evening until ten the next morning. We blew the next day as a result. The words day and night had no meaning. Day was whenever we happened to be awake. I'd pry my eyelids open with a snort of coke just in time to go all-night jamming with friends like Robert Wyatt and Larry Coryell. When I jammed with The Tremeloes, I realised how different our musical worlds were. They did wonderful arrangements but didn't jam. Since Jimi was determined to record jams for ideas, that means of relaxation disappeared into work and worry for him. I stopped making an effort to go jamming as that's all we seemed to do at gigs anyway.

New York was full of Londoners who were trying to establish English outposts in America. You'd run into the same people all the time, like Rik Gunnell who was there on behalf of Polydor. We rarely, perhaps never, gigged with groups not signed to Jeffery or one of his business associates unless it was a local group put in by the promoter. In late August we headed West with Vanilla Fudge and Eire Apparent.

September

  1   Denver, Colorado, Red Rocks Park ($13,000).
  3   San Diego, California, Balboa Stadium.
  4   Phoenix, Arizona.
  5   San Bernardino, California.
  6   Seattle, Washington, Center Coliseum ($18,000).
  7   Vancouver, B.C., Pacific Coliseum.
  8   Spokane, Washington.
  9   Press Interviews.
        Portland, Oregon.
 11   Photo session for *Life* and another magazine.
 12   Interviews.
        Two radio shows.
 13   Oakland, California, Coliseum.
 14   Autograph session at Hollywood record shop.
        Hollywood Bowl ($30,000).
 15   Sacramento, California.

Few places had anything to offer in after-gig entertainment. We spent more nights in our rooms listening to records and watching our new (gift of Warners) portable TVs – hotels didn't have them then. I kept in touch with 'real' life by watching and loving *The Three Stooges* and, I admit it, *I Dream of Jeannie* and *My Favorite Martian*, until we left our TVs in the office between gigs and they were nicked. For lack of anything else to do in Utah, we took acid and went up into the breathtaking mountains – a welcome relief from city hotels, city air, city noise. That evening we went out to be entertained by the Everly Brothers. This was a definite improvement on our usual after-dark arrival at the airport, car, hotel room, gig, car, gig, car, hotel room, car, airport. We visited cities that I'd never recognise unless you showed me the hotel or dressing room. We felt much better for our outing.

Denver was a huge, flashy gig featuring a police escort to and from the concert, but Jimi was having an off-night and Denver had little to offer in terms of post-gig entertainment. The lure of the big outdoors must have got to us because in San Diego we hired boats and saw the Pacific. We nearly missed Spokane because the operatives at Vancouver airport didn't like our looks and refused us seats. While negotiations took place we shared a joint with Spooky Tooth in a convenient phonebooth. I can't remember which airline condescended to fly us, but we couldn't complain about overcrowding: no one would sit near us. Back in the Bay Area, we made our own flying arrangements after meeting A.S. Owsley and his high-specification purple tabs.

Having flopped so dismally at the Hollywood Bowl first time around, we were particularly anxious about our return engagement. We fretted. We reflected. We even rehearsed. As we walked on stage, a bass string broke for the one and only time in my career. The snap scared the shit out of me. The show went better than anyone could have anticipated and our relief was audible in the music. Relief too that the water splashed by fans invading the stage-front pool didn't lead to mass electrocution. Jimi introduced Buddy Miles from the audience, but the police beat him up as he tried to get on stage. In Sacramento we ended up in a bar singing rugby songs with Eire Apparent.

Settling into Los Angeles for a couple of weeks of time off it was impossible to find refuge in a hotel. There were chicks phoning constantly and somehow managing to get into our rooms. Girls were anxious to try both American and English guys and some of Jimi's steadiest women visited me when Jimi was in a bad mood. Some ladies carefully bedded the whole group before heading on. We were anxious to sample every delicacy available. As white ladies were drawn to Jimi, black ladies were curious about Mitch and me. I knew lovely ladies of all shapes, sizes and shades. But to sleep, we were forced to book a room one place and crash elsewhere until we rented a house in Benedict Canyon for an astronomical fee – $1,000 per week, I think – where Cary Grant had once lived. It gave us a feeling of privacy and togetherness until it too degenerated into a round-the-clock, LA-style party. There was always an excuse for one – Buddy Miles Express opening at the Whisky, jamming with Graham Bond and Eric Burdon, anything.

We had weeks off, but my passport was away getting stamped or something. In desperation, I decided to chance it without documents, hopped on a plane with Mitch and actually got into England (and back into the States) with no trouble, not even a search. Neil showed up and *Mr Moonshine* was born to add to the growing Fat Mattress songlist. Mitch and I conferred about the most likely place in London to hustle some living money. We knew we had LPs on Track Records and we knew we'd never had royalties from them. Conclusion: they must owe us something. Over at Track's office, Chris Stamp handed us each £500. No questions asked. My first and last Track income.

Methed to the eyeballs, we got on a plane with Canned Heat, flew to LA, then on to Hawaii to continue the tour.

October

5	Rehearsal.
	Honolulu, Hawaii, Honolulu International Center.
6,7	Photo sessions.
10	Rehearsal.
10-12	San Francisco, California, Winterland with Dino Valente, Buddy Miles Express – two shows each night. Now an LP, ($20,000).
18	Recording.
	All Along the Watchtower released in England.
20	Free Clinic Benefit with Murray Roman.
	Recording (nothing done).
21	Recorded a new track. Had a jam with Buddy Miles and Lee Michaels.
22,23	Recording.
24	Photo session in the studio.
	Recording (nothing done).
25	Interviews.
	Recording (nothing done, again).
26	Bakersfield, California, Civic Center ($13,000).
28,29	Recording.
30	Film session.

Jeffery was to be found more often in Hawaii or at his country house in Woodstock. Incredible as it seems, Jeffery became a real groovy-hip-man-babe-far-out-flowerchild-acid-head. Now he rarely appeared in the office or at a gig, leaving the details to Gerry. We dosed ourselves frequently with acid – lots of acid. But as the quality of your trip depends a lot on your physical and mental condition (and the quality of the acid), and as I was invariably tired, drunk, and troubled as well, the trips remained weird. Initially, we liked LSD for the creative space it opened up, the different perspective it showed us, the fresh slant on a variety of thoughts and pleasures, not to mention the great swirling colours and the physical tingle which made it fun to fuck on. We fell into the habit of taking just a touch to cheer ourselves up and make the hotel room look prettier. After a while, I found sitting in the bathroom for hours contemplating suicide and/or my navel while watching my face melt in the mirror a bit distressing – educational, but emotionally draining. Sooner or later the surface pleasures are pierced by a multitude of hidden thoughts and feelings demanding attention. Then come the choices – open your mind or close it, play with the dark side of life or the bright side. These crossroads can present themselves at any time in your life – drugged or not. Though I feel drugs helped in some ways, they hindered me in others as I lost control of them and became rundown physically. Nor did I take time to assimilate the insights gathered or put the bits together. This is asking for it.

I've had some strange thoughts come out with acid and seen some weird things, but I've never known anyone to kill themselves while under it's influence. One heard stories about the person who supposedly tried to fly and failed. Who knows? People damage themselves every day in many ways. Just don't damage anyone else. I mean, if you are absolutely certain you have to jump out of a window, don't land on anybody.

The worst thing about taking any illegal drug is that little niggle at the back of your brain constantly reminding you that the police can take you away and throw away the key. Add to that fear the paranoia that the substance just swallowed might be of inferior quality and you get freaked. If that happens, you can end up getting pumped full of the frightening thorazine in a hospital, when a friend, a beautiful place, and some relaxing music could have pulled you round. Once tripping with one of our accountants, the Seattle police stopped us for some reason as we headed for the airport. I kept saying, 'You can't stop me, I've got a plane to catch,' but I took it very badly when they asked me to sit in the police car while they laid it on the accountant quite heavily. He was quivering afterwards. A month later tripping in Hawaii, he remembered that threat, fell apart with paranoia and freaked. He took some time off, which is what you should do. We didn't, never took the time to make compost out of the shit, to grow and gain from our losses.

Despite his overdeveloped flower-child tendencies, Jeffery didn't forget about business. He viciously attacked me on various issues. I was due to have my second song on the new album (*Electric Ladyland*) and was busy putting together more material. Jeffery wanted to know what I was writing for him, for he, as publisher, was on the lookout for one of his major sources of income. Writing goes something like this: a creation brings its creator something called 'copyright', the right to authorise usage. Permission granted by the owner of the rights (known as the publisher) results in income for the publisher and, in the best of worlds, the writer/composer. *She's So Fine*, for example, was assigned to SeaLark and Yameta (Jeffery's publishing wing) who then assigned it to Warner Brothers Publishing, who paid the writer and publisher two cents per record.

The writer need not assign his/her songs to a publisher, but may instead retain the copyright and publish the songs him/herself, or make an agreement with a publisher to administer the collection of money due. Usually, however, the writer signs up with a publisher who administers the rights to compositions and pays the writer a portion of the income, typically between fifty and eighty per cent. The third option, tragically common in the history of popular music, involves the writer's selling a song to a publisher for a flat fee (i.e. the writer gets no cut of future royalty income). The writer may still be credited, but will not be remunerated. (The late Tim Hardin sold many of his tunes for a flat fee and suffered accordingly.) A top vocalist, such as Presley, often does deals which are seemingly good for a writer in that they get him/her exposure, but at the cost of a portion of the publishing. Even disc jockeys have managed to claim publishing credits in exchange for playing records.

Publishing is one of the most lucrative aspects of the music business and can provide substantial incomes for years following the demise of the groups or individuals who first brought a song to prominence, and not surprisingly, following the Beatles, many record companies prefer to deal with groups which write their own material. The song often outlasts the singer. Publishers get paid quarterly and writers half-yearly, so publishers get to accrue income on unpaid royalties. Some huge-earning groups reportedly have publishing deals in which they get 100 per cent of the royalties – the publishers work just for the interest they earn between pay periods.

If you have your own publishing company, your manager will hate you and will probably try to take his management/agent percentage from your songwriting earnings too. From an unscrupulous manager's point of view, the ideal arrangement is to own the publishing, charge the writer through the publishing company for collection, earn interest on unpaid royalties because of the delayed payment period, and take the management percentage off the top of the amount finally paid the writer. Someone signed up in this way, and with a nominal 50/50 split with the publisher, may end up with something like thirty per cent while the publisher/manager collects twenty per cent.

I knew very little about this, but I did know that there was some advantage in having one's own publishing company. Jeffery was adamant: 'Look, you have no rights to anything you write. I own it all.' I was bummed out, but reacted with a vengeance one evening in Hawaii when we were all tripping. I dressed up in drag – dress, tits, make-up, the works – and Mitch was kitted out as a clown. We hid behind a bush and as Jeffery, also tripping, strolled past with one of his flower-child pulls I appeared at his shoulder. 'Hello, Mike, kissy kissy,' then Mitch popped up and Jeffery was gone. We gave him a satisfying and memorable case of the horrors, totally freaked him.

Innocent – but getting better – of publishing, I was also totally unaware of how lucrative merchandising could be. Jeffery and Jerry Goldstein and Steve Gold of FarOut Productions, Los Angeles, flew in photographer Ron Raffaeli to do a session with us. G&G were planning a series of full-colour booklets devoted to various rock bands, and Ron was contracted to their printing company, The Visual Thing. Ron came up with some great stuff, including the poster with the two half-nude blondes. Jimi gave G&G the rights despite Steve Weiss's warning. Ron spent hours with us on Maui, in the lava fields, astride horses. He did close-ups of Jimi while cruising along in a beach buggy (Jimi freaked and crashed it). The result was *Electric Church*, which was sold at concerts for $3, none of which, needless to say, found its way back to the group.

If the Hawaiian trip was meant to serve as rest and recuperation, it didn't work. Back in San Francisco we played a couple of shows at Winterland (recorded for release) and they were good examples of how the band was feeling: we were past the point of being able to leave our problems off stage while we played good music. I stood there fading in and out of a deep resentment. I was terminally bored with Jimi's style and his moodiness. Mitch pissed me off, making me feel inferior with references to his Ealing address and theatre training. I must admit that a couple of times I deliberately played badly in order to put Jimi off. I didn't particularly enjoy doing it, but it was wholly in keeping with The Experience vibe at that point. I couldn't stop seeing those weeds in our Garden of Eden.

Jack Casady, the bassist with Jefferson Airplane, jammed with us for the first night and somehow between the leapers and the THC we managed to play well. Our reward? Bill Graham gave us rings to complement the watches he'd passed around earlier. Jeffery, of course, got the tapes which, naturally, we knew nothing about at the time. I couldn't stop seeing those weeds in our Garden of Eden.

There was no time to hang out with Eric Clapton and George

Harrison, who had joined the California scene. For relief, Murray took me to the Los Angeles Free Clinic Benefit. Coming from England with it's free medical services, the cost of American medical treatment horrified me, so I was glad to help as long as I didn't have to say anything on stage, where I generally limited myself to a few 'thank yous', some 'Stonefrees' and a couple of 'Let me stand next to your fires'. I was suspicious of Murray and I was right. He introduced me straightaway with the accolade: 'You all know this man who's coming up. He's had the clap ten times!' Oh great! I got a cheer, but all I could mumble was, 'I've never done this before. Try not to get the clap.' At least you didn't die from sex in those days, unless it was a crime of passion.

We were returned to the studio under duress and struggled to get it together. A year had slipped by since our last LP and we were being kept alive by means of the October single, *All Along the Watchtower* b/w *Long Hot Summer Night* (UK) and b/w *Burning of the Midnight Lamp* (US). I'd stalked out of the *Watchtower* session and Dave Mason had sat in on bass. Jimi may have redone it as he was rarely content, even if it was perfect. The attitude towards sessions grew more and more nonchalant. Lee Michaels and Buddy Miles dropped in to party. We managed only the slightest amount of work in several days. Jimi was trying too hard to be experimental, but he was so out of it he changed his mind every other second, not even knowing when he had it right.

Some of the girls liked the star treatment a lot less than others and during the *Watchtower* period Mitch and I got a tip-off that some girls had put the police on to us. It wasn't too surprising. Jimi had tried to beat up a girl in my room and Eric Barrett and I had grabbed him and thrown him out. Jimi went outside and carried on beating up on her. Tipped off that the cops were on their way, Mitch and I cleaned the house and when Jimi failed to show up we went in to tackle his room. The state of it knocked us out. We found an amazing amount of an amazing number of substances in every pocket, every drawer, on the floor, under the bed, *in* the bed. I'd expected a sizeable stash, but this was preposterous. We gathered it all up and buried it in the garden. The squad arrived and we were clean. All The Experience needed was a drug bust on top of an assault complaint.

In October 1968, two years after the group's inception, we had our first accounting. The Are You Experienced Inc. c/o Jeffery and Chandler Inc. statement was not fulsome in its detail but:

In: Last tour/29 gigs grossing..$365,817
    Net income from Warner Brothers (this could be royalties,

    advances, or loans to Jimi and Jeffery)...........................$49,046
Out: Jeffery and Chandler Inc. (commissions) $82,972
    Advance to Leon Dicker (no explanation)....................$10,000
    Advance to Stickells (no explanation).............................$8,598
    Advance to Jimi for Electric Lady Studios...................$28,450
    Unpaid expenses from the spring tour (no
    accounting for this tour)..$9,928
    Legal costs/settlements (PPX and Sperber) $32,390
    Agents' fees (GAC)..$54,872
    Hotels and travel:
      Noel Redding $2,673
      Mitch Mitchell...$4,283
      Jimi Hendrix..$7,101

On a 50/25/25 basis, the group shared *ordinary* expenses of $45,478: publicity and photos, musical supplies, equipment maintenance and freight, wages/travel/hotels/food for the road crew (and all this time I thought they ran on uppers), limos and truck rental, house rent, accounting fees, recording and miscellaneous expenses. Legal costs of $32,390 were classed as *extra-ordinary* expenses, and this was the device whereby I was compelled to pay a portion of Jimi's legal costs despite my refusal to sign an agreement to that effect. The balance of the income was divided on a 50/25/25 basis and then *direct* (that is, individual) expenses and *personal advances* were deducted from individual shares (as well as withholding tax).

I was left with considerably less than ten per cent of the gross earnings (which I left in Hecht's account). This impressed me no end: an accounting whose outcome leaves me with money in the bank. A happy man, I headed out in a much better state and further buoyed up by the news that Jeffery had been talking with Warner Brothers about getting support for recording I wanted to undertake on my own.

We completed the finishing touches to *Electric Ladyland* and in early October, Chris Stamp showed up to collect the masters for an early November release. Having managed – somehow – to deliver the *Electric Ladyland* masters, we still had studio time booked, but no one had the heart to use it. We shifted to partying without recording. I didn't see how The Experience could even think about another album without at least a year off. It was best simply to let it rest for a while.

The move out of the studio, however, didn't signal a change in working commitments. The schedule, October through November 1968, was full of record-breaking audiences – so much so that Jeffery kept turning up to check on receipts!

November
1   Kansas City – broke the house attendance records.
2   Minneapolis.
       Interview with Tony Glover, filmed for the BBC.
3   St Louis.
7   New York City – photo session.
11-14 London
15   Cincinnati.
16   Boston, Boston Gardens – broke attendance record held by
       the Beatles.
17   New Haven, Yale University, Woolsey Hall.
22   Jacksonville, Florida, with Cat Mother.
23   Tampa, Florida – got shoes, a gun, and a Gibson guitar.
24   Miami.
27   Providence, Rhode Island ($10,000).
28   New York City, Philharmonic Hall – two shows.
       An Electric Thanksgiving.
30   Detroit.

December
1   Chicago, Coliseum.
3   London.

There was no shortage of standard cock-ups. In one venue the PA was
so dreadful that the crowd wouldn't stop shouting their complaints.
We agreed, but what's new about a duff PA? Jimi left the stage and
Mitch and I had no alternative but to follow him off. Stickells was left
to try to fix the gear and calm the audience, but the promoter panicked
and threatened to stop the show, a pretty feeble response given that it
had already stopped. The cops were eager to clear the hall and try out
their new 'flying wedge' riot technique which would have produced,
no prizes, a riot. Jimi was finally persuaded to come back on and we did
a real slow, calm version of *Red House*. A close call.

On 11 November, Jeffery and Hillman came up with another
agreement concerning The Experience. Suddenly we became 'both
individually and collectively known as the Jimi Hendrix Experience'. I
was a new legal entity, but then again I was an old legal entity. The
Nassau accounting circus was still under way and Chandler and Jeffery
were found to be still owing $26,000 to Yameta, so a deal was agreed
whereby Jeffery and Chandler would pay their debt in exchange for
Yameta's promise not to sue them in the future. Yameta relinquished
claims on commissions on money earned by and advanced to Jeffery

and Chandler and on royalties yet to be paid. Yameta would take fees from Jimi only on pre-31 December 1967 income and fees from everyone else up to 31 July 1968. Jeffery and Chandler were no longer Yameta employees.

And on and on and on. I was becoming an expert at looking at legal documents without taking in their significance. Jeffery would decide which Yameta artist contracts would be terminated and which would be assigned to him; if assigned to him, he would be responsible for the lawsuits. Yameta assigned Burdon to Jeffery. Jeffery got all Yameta income not yet paid out from its artists' contracts. Hillman could still be Burdon's lawyer unless Eric sued Yameta. Jeffery and Chandler took over Yameta's contract with SeaLark. Yameta would protect Jeffery and Chandler from any lawsuits based on Yameta's failures; they promised not to sue each other. And more, more, more.

In Miami, we arrived to find the hotel ablaze. We tried to base ourselves in New York but got thrown out of the expensively hip St Moritz for being too noisy. We were no longer welcome at the Waldorf-Astoria because one night, in order to get into the orgy in Jimi's room, one had to undress in the busy hallway. We all quickly found ourselves on the street. When the Hilton banned us, we discovered the PennGarden near Madison Square Gardens. It was fine and they left us alone. Handy for group therapy on Mandrax with several lovely ladies. It must have worked. The next night, we played a two-hour, good-sounding gig in Providence.

The plush velvet comfort of the Philharmonic Hall was a dream come true. The red, deep-pile carpeted dressing rooms, with a grand piano as polished as our personal uniformed waiter, was built to accommodate an orchestra. Why was I in a rock band? The acoustics were impeccable. The subtlest nuance carried distortion-free to the furthest corners. We'd been bashing it out in fields and barn-like sports halls to miles of people who couldn't hear us well enough to bother listening. It was sobering to follow the New York Brass Quintet and harpsichordist Fernando Valenti, and difficult to adjust to the thought that every vibration of every note would be heard!

I visited Hecht and listened while he explained what publishing was all about. He suggested that I contract Barbra Streisand's lawyer, Richard Roemer, and as he struck me as a nice guy, I hired him. Jeffery joined us at our second meeting and within ten days, something had been set up. Exactly what, I'll never know. Jeffery brought out a new set of papers (I never saw any of the old contracts I had signed) and I signed on the dotted line. I was then sent to see the accountants where I signed and probably – who knows? – gave them the right to sign and collect on my behalf. I thought I was the owner of a publishing company, but in actuality I owned only a name, a dba (doing-business-as) or aka (also-known-as), a thing called Joint Music, c/o Steingarten, Wedeen & Weiss, thereby nullifying the whole point of the exercise. Warner Brothers files show that *Little Miss Strange* was registered to Joint Music, c/o SWW, in September; transferred to Arch Music (Schroeder), then reregistered in October to SeaLark (Schroeder) and Yameta (Jeffery). Since then my catalogue has been acquired by Interworld Music, sold on to Ariola/Arista, then to Chappell Music, which became Warner/Chapell. Since it seems to have 'come home', I guess it'll stay there. Call me naïve, call me a rock musician, call me Experienced.

Jimi nearly missed the 30 November 1968 gig in Detroit. Trixie Sullivan, the office secretary, knew that each of us might refuse to play a gig for one reason or another, but Mitch and I could be persuaded to get back on board when it was pointed out that no play equals no pay. But a couple of times Jimi refused point blank to play. In all my time playing pre-Experience there had been only three occasions when a group member didn't show, but at least I had been the lead guitarist, so could scramble around and come up with something. We weren't particularly worried when Jimi missed the plane, but when people from the record company were waiting for us at the airport and took us to a hotel, we knew that something serious was going on. Jeffery was on the phone. Jimi had freaked and refused to play. No details. Jeffery and Jimi had a strange relationship. Jimi was always going on about getting rid of Jeffery, but he never got anywhere and Jeffery managed to retain control. In any case, Jeffery managed to change Jimi's mind and a Lear jet was hired to get him to the gig.

Jimi suffered badly from depressed panic attacks. I believe he felt threatened and hounded. Many interests, some heavy, were constantly hustling him. As Chalpin organised his first LP for release, PPX began trying it on in Europe against Jimi/Polydor/Track, saying the Warner's settlement applied only to the US. It seems the phrase 'for the world' had been left out of the settlement contract. Instantly, both Polydor and Track put a hold on all royalties due The Experience and filed a countersuit against Jimi and J&C. It was all on Jimi's head, now that he'd signed documents protecting Jeffery from all future suits that might turn up against him in Britain. This suit devastated Jimi. And there was little free love for him either. Judging by the amount of paternity suits, Jimi must have been the most potent man ever born, or else he just attracted chicks with their own future security in mind. Whatever it was, he slashed his wrists. This was kept *very* quiet, but we all felt horrified. I wanted Jimi to get things off this chest, 'Jimi. If you're depressed you *have* to talk about it. It's the only cure. You can't be pessimistic because we don't see things as they are.'

Fortunately, the tour was ending. If only every gig could have that 'last night feeling'. Knowing it's over, that there is no plane in the morning, that you don't have to pace yourself in anticipation of tomorrow, inspires one to exhaust that last little bit of energy and throw everything into the set. Ravers abounded. So we grabbed as many women as possible and all jumped into a very overcrowded bed. And then we fucked off into our own lives.

It was so good to see Mum, the usual haunts and faces. Suzanne, a Danish girl who had popped up a couple times in the past few months, appeared and boldly requested the fare to Denmark for a couple of months at home. Why not? I was flush and I suspected she was having immigration problems. What's one chick more or less with at least five steady ones on the go? I picked up my life as I'd left it. A few sessions with Jim Leverton and Eric Dillon (drums) were a total contrast and a relief from recent Experience sessions. In two days, we put down twelve tracks for the future Fat Mattress LP.

A guest appearance on *Top of the Pops*, an opening party at the Speakeasy Club, Eire Apparent's press reception, a jam with Jim Capaldi – but nothing could compare with arriving at the Tandoori Rooms on Fulham Road and spotting Spike Milligan dining there. In my very best Goon Show/Seller's voice I quivered: 'What are you doing under that car young man? I'm not doing anything under that car.' He gave me an acknowledging wink and two bottles of champagne promptly materialised, 'Compliments of Mr Milligan.' I'm a Goon Show addict (especially *Robin Hood and his Merry Men*, *Bridge Over the River Wye*, and *China Story*) and when I turned Jimi onto them, he really appreciated their humour. A session that started as a songwriting collaboration between Jimi and I ended up as an impromptu Goon Show when he pulled the studio crowd into a skit because it was getting crazy beyond words. This is now making the rounds under the title *Devil Jam* and features both of us on guitar. But like other demos, it was registered as a Jimi Hendrix song.

As I started mixing Mattress material, the studio began to take on the flavour of an Experience session. Mitch, photographers, Mickey Waller, Ron Wood, Mick Avery (Birdcage) and more appeared, bearing brain-changers. This time we were lucky and a song came out of our all-night party. But I knew how easy it was to let creative drive collapse into chaos. As these were my sessions and because I had to watch pennies, I tried hard to maintain control.

Happy Birthday? Another year was gone, I was twenty-three years old and depressingly homeless. Capricorns need a home. Being in England always reminded me that I had nowhere, no shared house, no grotty hotel room, no flat. My bits and pieces were in a box in Mum's attic. Hating London, I'd decided to settle in Kent. So when I went home to Mum for Christmas and saw a place nearby for sale, I promised myself I'd have it. Jeffery had hired us English accountants on Hillman's recommendation. They directed me to Michael Balin, Jeffery's personal English lawyer, who murmured encouraging things and made me feel good. After all, I was only begging for £11,000.

We had rowed about Mitch's and my desire to include England in our 1969 European tour. In the past year, we'd spent ten months in the US. A European tour would generate less than half the income of another American one and take longer, especially if we included England. To tour America at this stage, we'd only have to do a couple of weeks' worth of huge concerts in major cities spaced across the country. To get Jimi off the hook, Jeffery told the press that I wouldn't tour. In fact I was the only one saying that if we didn't tour we'd break up immediately for sure. My side project was a tonic I was happy to spend more time on. Mitch wanted time off to record with Graham Bond and others. And Jimi had Chalpin waiting for an album.

We waited around for the European tour to start. One night a crowd went nuts and started ripping off gear from the parked van. Lost were: Fender Strat, twelve-string Fender, half of the drumkit, two two-hundred-watt Marshall amps, one hundred-watt amp, and a Marshall column PA speaker. A notice offering '£75 reward if returned within seven days' bore no fruit. The Roundhouse hosted a huge pre-Dutch-tour (with Traffic) on the 27th, but we never made it. When the plane to Utrecht was still missing after a four-hour wait, the show was cancelled with the papers saying that Jimi had injured his leg and that Mitch and I would play with Traffic. This added fuel to the fire. After Cream and Traffic broke up (the first time), the press started on The Experience. If any external factor besides the lawsuits contributed to our break-up, it was the journalists who played us one against the other looking for headlines. Apparently, it was too much for them to think that we could have personal projects and still have time for The Experience.

Instead of becoming a new plateau for the The Experience, 1969 became the dregs. Once again we spent less of our free time together, not even attending business meetings together. Usually I went alone with Gerry, rarely Mitch and never with Jimi. When we got together for gigs, we were often short-tempered and peevish. We'd use girls to get back at each other. Jimi still hated it if I pulled a girl after or instead of him. He retaliated with nasty tricks like spiking her with acid.

Our lack of 'normal' life, whatever that was, destroyed us more than anything. Living in a void, the empty days between gigs drove me crazy with confusion and apprehension. We no longer had much in common with our friends, who had grown away from us, and we'd replaced them with fan-type acquaintances so we wouldn't feel so alone. Road life was filled with travel, light pre-gig entertainment followed by the show, followed by getting smashed and laid. The gigs were so huge that it had been ages since we could nip out of the hall between shows to relax or even leave our top-security dressing rooms/prisons. It was simply too physically dangerous. Only Stickells' careful planning saved us from being ripped to shreds several times. If the dressing room was a mile away, like it often was in sports stadium-type places, I learned how to wait a few minutes on stage after we finished before crawling on hands and knees through the crowd. My rule of survival became: As much as possible, stay away from people.

January 1969, and we were off.

1,2	Interviews.
3	Interviews.
	BBC TV, *Lulu Show*.
7	Canadian TV show.
	Interviews.
8	Gothenburg, Sweden, Lorensburg Cirkus – two shows.
9	Press reception with The Outsiders.
	Stockholm, Sweden, Konserthus – two shows.
10	Copenhagen, Denmark, Kalkoner Centeret – two shows.
11	Hamburg, Musikhalle – two shows.
12	Düsseldorf, Rheinhalle – two shows.
13	Cologne, Sporthalle.
	Jam at Storyville Club: Jimi on bass, me on guitar.
14	Münster, Halle Münsterland – two shows.
15	Interviews.
	Munich, Deutsches Museum – two shows.
16	Nuremberg, Meistersingerhalle – two shows.
17	Frankfurt, Jahrhunderthalle – two shows.
19	Stuttgart, Liederhalle – two shows.
21	Strasbourg.
22	Vienna, Konzerthaus – two shows.

23   Berlin, Sportpalast.
      Press reception.
29   Interviews (The German tour earned £23,000).

It was time for an image change. I was sick of people assuming that I'd
permed my hair to be like Jimi, so I had it straightened. We were
booked for the *Lulu Show*, which was so straight it was only natural
that we would try to combat that atmosphere by having a smoke in our
dressing room. In our haste, the lump of hash got away and slipped
down the sink drainpipe. Panic! We just couldn't do this show straight
– Lulu didn't approve of smoking! She was then married to Maurice
Gibb of the Bee Gees, whom I'd visited and shared a smoke with. I
could always tell Lulu was due home when Maurice started throwing
open all the windows. Anyway, I found a maintenance man and begged
tools from him with the story of a lost ring. He was too helpful, offering
to dismantle the drain for us. It took ages to dissuade him, but we
succeeded in our task and had a great smoke.

The idea was tossed about that Lulu might sing along on *Hey Joe*.
We cringed. Still, it had to be her who would finish up the show. But
midway through our two millionth rendition of the song, Jimi stopped.
Perhaps he was feeling sentimental about Cream's break-up or just
avoiding a duet, but he broke into *Sunshine Of Your Love* after a quick
dedication to Cream. This was fun for us, but producer Stanley
Dorfman didn't take it at all well as the minutes ticked by on his *live*
show. Short of running onto the set to stop us or pulling the plug, there
was nothing he could do. We played past the point where Lulu might
have joined us, played through the time for talking at the end, played
through Stanley tearing his hair, pointing to his watch and silently
screaming at us. We played out the show. Afterwards, Dorfman
refused to speak to us but the result is one of the most widely used bits
of film we ever did. Certainly, it's the most relaxed.

On the whole, I can't understand how anyone who saw us on this
tour could have liked us. There was a lot of filming for Swedish TV
and compared to similar films in 1967, we were a different group. Jimi
was sullen and removed and actually slagged off the audience during
the first set. He rarely bothered to sing. I paced grimly in my corner
and turned my back on him. The sparkle was gone, very gone, replaced
by exhaustion and boredom which showed in the sloppy repeats of the
hits as we stared at the crowd with dead eyes. We hated playing
Sweden. Always the same problem – no drugs. We were forced to
drink the killer Schnapps, and it brought on Jimi's mood for the first
set. In desperation I went out between shows and with much persis-

tence managed to score a leaper. We huddled anxiously over the dressing room table, crushed the pill into a powder, shared it out, and snorted it. The second show was much more together and enthusiastic. But no wonder Chas was leary when Jimi approached him about management during our Swedish tour. Besides, Jeffery owned Jimi. And even Jimi didn't want The Experience to break up. It was his only sure earner.

Suzanne showed up in Copenhagen. In Cologne, I tried recapturing my youth by visiting the Storyville Club. You can never go back. I needed to talk to someone. Jimi listened. It was one problem he understood well. Emotionally fragile, I wondered if this was what a nervous breakdown was? If so, it would have to wait. The tour 'progressed'. The beer in Vienna was terrible. Berlin was very strange. The flight path to the airport took you directly between two tall rows of apartment blocks and you could have sworn that the wings would clip a wall. The show featured a political riot between left and right. We never found out any more of what it was about but we were told it was going to happen. There were rows of police in front of the stage. I actually saw some guy in the audience look at his watch, turn, and hit the person next to him. That was it. Eric was knocking people off stage with a mike stand as they came up in waves, some just hoping to escape the violence below. We were forced to stop. I just couldn't believe the stupidity of it.

Back at the hotel, promoter Fritz Row had a very stiff and formal press party going. You could almost hear heels clicking. We decided to liven it up and minutes later all the servings of ice cream contained flakes of Mandrax. We sat back to watch the show as everyone got loose. It was much better fun that the reception where a cameraman punched an advertising executive in the nose for getting in his way. The ad guy jumped up on a chair screeching, 'If anyone saw me get hit, please step forward and give your name.' It had to be in America – no other place in those days was so litigation conscious.

February

2,4	Fat Mattress rehearsal.
6	Film interviews for the US and Canada. Fat Mattress recording.
8	Cut the LP at Pye for £31.
9	FM rehearsal.
14-16	Experience recording.
18	London, Royal Albert Hall, with Traffic. The concert sold out and was filmed.

21-23   FM rehearsal.
24   London, Royal Albert Hall, with Fat Mattress in support. Another sell-out, also filmed.
26   Experience recording.
27   Interviews.

Back in London, Jeffery phoned, catching me dead drunk, and went on about my obligations to Yameta – two-thirds of anything I wrote. This worried me because we had finished the Fat Mattress tape and I was playing it to anyone who happened by. I went to see Jimi because we had just finished a co-written song (disappeared) which had made us both feel good. Chas offered to take the Mattress on, and Dick Katz said that my name guaranteed easy booking. I'd spoken personally to Mo Ostin of Warners about a deal and knew if we went for a huge advance, we wouldn't even have to worry about being a flop.

On the other hand, Jeffery and Weiss were now planning The Experience's biggest grossing tour, an estimated $1,292,000 for only seventeen gigs. It was due to start in April, simultaneously with the release of Jimi's *First Wave of the New Rising Sun*, whatever that was supposed to be.

All this talk of recording action translated into nothing. We were booked into Olympic Studios and, as I nearly expected, first day there was nothing doing. On the second it was no show at all. I went to the pub for three hours, came back, and it was still ages before Jimi ambled in. Then we argued. There seemed to be no way to get working. Either there was no one there or I'd show up to find the studio so crowded I had trouble squeezing in. Next day, Mitch was late. I suppose it was partly because we didn't want to get it together. The pressure from the public to create something even more brilliant each time, while basically expecting us to stay the same, was crushing. On the last day, I just watched it happen for a while and then went back to my flat. Jeffery tried to cheer me with a gift of some grass.

Late in 1968, Jeffery and Weiss – as promoters – had booked the Royal Albert Hall. They had contracted on a 50/50 share basis for G&G to shoot, distribute, and licence a full-length film of the European tour and in particular this gig. I remember signing a release for this film. We took this gig very seriously, even to the point of rehearsing.

After spending the day with journalist Richard 'I never eat when I'm drinking' Green, including the mandatory Fat Mattress tape-listening session, I felt well up for the Tuesday show. We were driven to the gig in a Rolls before setting off with Traffic (now known as Mason,

Capaldi, Wood and Frog) for a twenty-minute trek through snow and ice to the nearest pub. I never realised how bereft of pubs that area of London is. We played Jeff Beck's *Truth* in the dressing room to get into the mood. Jimi was relaxed and happy. Instead of his usual non-stop jumping, he played in a variety of poses and we went down well with a minimum of effort. Over one and a half hours we did all the hits, a track from *Axis*, and closed with *Purple Haze*. At the close, Jimi tossed his guitar in the air. But the motion now oozed routine rather than inspiration. In a funny way, though good, the show was listless – polished but lacklustre. Mitch was subdued as well, and even a jam of *Voodoo Chile* failed to take off. Was it a reaction to the pre-show chaos? Or to the coke? Was Jimi trying to break his wildman mould on this film?

Next day even the filmed rehearsal had sounded good. Baffle shields hung from the ceiling to break the echo. Mum and Vicki came up. Before the show, I was knotted up with doubts waiting for Fat Mattress, with Manfred Mann's drummer Mike Hugg sitting in, to debut supporting The Experience . . . in the Albert Hall! Please don't let us be booed off. We weren't. I think we made a good contrast to The Experience. Mum's mothering had been needed in the dressing room that night. Everyone was nervous. Jimi poured sweat. He asked Mum to wipe his forehead and as she helped him cool down, he pleaded, 'Can you help me find my guitar?' Jimi said thanks by dedicating a song to Mum and the show settled down to feel fantastic. As we finished up, a small uprising (perhaps planned for the cameras) started in the huge crowd and thousands of people tried to climb on stage. Never underestimate a crowd. We ran to our cars, which were damaged by the crush.

Whatever was going on between Chas and Jeffery was going on between the group and Jeffery, too. After the Albert Hall, we called a meeting and the five of us met at Chas's. We talked for hours. The conclusion: to sack Jeffery. The Experience decided that we'd rather be with Chas if he and Jeffery were splitting up the partnership. None of us trusted Jeffery. He was hard to contact, and we all ran to Chas if we needed help and encouragement. Jeffery said nothing, and nothing changed. Many times we broke off with Mike and yet he was still there. Chas told us that when he'd quit the group in mid-'68, Jeffery had re-signed us. I tried to break the bonds by dealing directly with Mo Ostin about FM. Why did I need Jeffery? He was no help in the studio and I'd paid for the LP myself, so why should he claim a cut?

The renewed PPX quagmire slowly killed Jimi's creative drive, and therefore The Experience, by sucking him once again into endless hours of legal bickering, including one meeting attended by *thirty-two* lawyers. Warners had paid off PPX, right or wrong, just to hold on to Jimi. Now Track/Polydor were up against the wall. Jimi and Jeffery's solicitors, Goodman, Derrick and Company, suggested a plea that the action should be barred because of the American settlement, but they doubted that the argument would be sufficient to strike the claim.

Jeffery asked what financial gain would be available to himself, Jimi and the labels if they won, but was told that the reality of the situation was a potential loss of at least £10,000 in legal fees. The lawyers recommended immediately starting settlement proceedings. PPX were after Jimi for breakfast, lunch and dinner, too.

No wonder he couldn't concentrate. No wonder he was rude to an interviewer on the 27th, the day the arbitration with Yameta was cancelled. A meeting with Chas the next day lasted six hours, in spite of Mitch's non-appearance. The angry whirlpool of business was something I had never imagined, even in my worst nightmares. The meetings were so complex I never knew where I stood. On hearing my tape, Steppenwolf's manager said he'd like to manage me, but I was too tied up. Jimi went off to do whatever he had to do. And sometimes he didn't. He failed to turn up for a Dick Cavett Show booking and was told if he missed the next he would have a million-dollar suit on his hands. Nothing so dramatic for me. I only had a fashion spread for the *Daily Telegraph* and an interview for *Oz*.

I assumed Chas was my manager since the 'sacking', and so it was to him I took my test pressing. Meanwhile, I'd been kicked out of my furnished flat and lumbered with the aggravation and expense of damages and an assessor because the place had been wrecked while I toured. I was back in a hotel. I dropped my boxes of bits off at Mum's, but this time I also gave her a downpayment for the house I'd promised her. While visiting, I decided to have a go horseriding. Thrown immediately, I tried again. The horse had different ideas, waited till I had one foot in a stirrup, then bolted, throwing me over it's back with one foot trapped. It galloped down the main street with me hanging on for dear life, my head missing cars and the road by inches. Finally it stopped (tired, I suppose, since it had ignored my frantic rein-pulling and shouts), and I got a round of applause from friends and pedestrians alike, who thought I was doing a stunt. I don't ride anymore.

One dream come true was the second-hand Rolls Royce Silver Cloud Series II I purchased for £250 down and £2,250 to pay on hire purchase. It was beautiful! Smoked windows, pale grey leather upholstery, flash dash. Eric Barrett, who was hanging out while the band was on hold, drove me and insisted I ride in the back, 'What's the use of having a Rolls if you don't use it properly?' And I thought, what's the use of smoked windows if you don't use them properly. I made the whole cost worthwhile by rolling and smoking a joint while parked next to a police car. I fitted a speaker under the bonnet, so I could drive through town blasting out Mountain's music and talking to people. One 'Out of the way, please!' to a cyclist was enough to have him looking in the hedgerows and heavens for the voice. Denny Laine and I discovered that if you moo near cows every one in hearing distance will come running. Jeff Beck and I would cruise the countryside near Ashford, him in his hotrod, me Rolling away.

Chapter Six

Last Straw

Man is quite insane.
He wouldn't know how to create a maggot,
yet he creates Gods by the dozen.
MONTAIGNE

Not in the clamour of the crowded street,
Not in the shouts and plaudits of the throng,
but in ourselves, are triumph and defeat.
HENRY WADSWORTH LONGFELLOW

WE warmed up for this tour with photo sessions and recording sessions at New York's Record Plant, scheduled for midnight to eight in the morning. Compared to the low output of the *Electric Ladyland* sessions, even getting one track done in eight hours seemed a major advance. While Jimi was interviewed and photographed on his own, I was working on my Fat Mattress plans and hoping to get the album out before the Fat Mattress began touring with The Experience. We had cleared the first fence by going down well at the Albert Hall. I gave Michael Goldstein photos and clippings and he went off to organise a PR splash.

I was enthusiastic about the way things were shaping up. I had a group of friends recording my songs and touring with me. Mo Ostin liked our tapes and over dinner at a hamburger stand on Times Square, he said he was willing to go ahead with the LP – no problem. I didn't realise that Chas was still hustling Polydor on our behalf.

Track released *Crosstown Traffic/Gypsy Eyes*. We'd done *Traffic* in London and I didn't play on the B-side. We had a few recordings stockpiled they could pull from, but when *My Friend* appeared, my music had been credited to Jimi, when he only wrote the words.

April

11	Raleigh, N. Carolina, J.F. Daulton Arena – with FM.
12	Philadelphia, Spectrum – with FM.
14	Recording.
15,16	Recording and rehearsal with Experience.
17	FM photo session.
18	Memphis, Mid-South Coliseum – two shows with FM.
19	Houston, Sam Houston Coliseum – with FM.
20	Dallas, Dallas Memorial Arena – with FM.
26	Los Angeles, The Forum – recorded.
27	Oakland, Oakland Coliseum – with Jefferson Airplane and FM.
29	Photo session.
30	Recording.

Fat Mattress's upcoming American debut as occasional support band for The Experience had my stomach in knots. It would mean I'd play as many as four shows some nights. I wanted us to be different – no wild stage act, no heavy lead guitar, no endless jams, no stars. We worked to create concise, melodic listening music – although Neil loved to whoop and shout in every break, during every solo and after every ending. Someone came up with an idea for a photo session and we headed off to the Bowery with a mattress to try for some photos with the bums. It was horrible and depressing. We felt so bad we tried to leave the mattress for someone to sleep on, but the police quoted litter laws.

The Experience set off touring. Thank heavens because even our rehearsals were bad beyond belief. That horror drug PCP had come on the scene, once making me so badly smashed that I had to lie face down on the floor to keep in touch with the world. I never knowingly took it again. We were too spaced, too sensitive, too unsettled and too paranoid to maintain a simple relationship. Jimi was responsible for most of the time wasted; and after a particularly unproductive studio session complete with shouting match, he sent Mitch and I a note of apology for messing everyone around.

It was a strange, touching letter, which showed a side of Jimi's character it was easy to forget existed in the mayhem of touring and recording and drug-taking. In it, he wrote the kind of things we should have been able to say openly to each other once in a while, but didn't because when you're leading a life that's a succession of drug-induced highs followed by music-induced highs followed by more drug-induced highs, you forget to lend some time to things like friendship and sympathy. Though he often seemed aloof and spaced out, Jimi was, as the letter showed, acutely sensitive to what was going on around him, felt strong affection for me and Mitch as fellow musicians, and lived for the music we made. He was obsessed with the guitar – to the extent that he could sometimes be found strumming and picking away while seated on the lavatory, because he liked the acoustics produced by the tiled walls and floor. The Hendrix front was not just a defence for himself – it was also a way of distancing the band and the music from the media circus that now surrounded us at every turn. Perhaps this accounted for the wasted recording sessions and the moody gigs. Deep inside he may have felt that as our lives became more and more fraught, the music had to be that much better to compensate. The pressure from outside was enormous, but maybe Jimi felt his own internal pressure most – pressure to innovate, to produce more and more brilliant music every time we went into the studio, to perfect everything we did. That internal pressure must have conflicted painfully with the external pressure to plug away at the same old numbers on stage and innovate only in the sense of introducing new stage gimmicks. It's an old story: agents, managers, promotors always want to preserve a successful format, while the artist needs to move on, fearing always that their creativity – the source of everything – will dry up.

Jimi's gentle, rambling, apologetic letter somehow conveyed all this. He admitted things had changed for the worse between us, and blamed it on what he called the 'mumble jumble' that threatened to engulf us – the cynical, artificial environment of fame, a quagmire of superficiality, repetition and triviality. This was what was creating the emotional problems, despite the fact that we were basically a good, harmonious band – or should have been. 'I love you deeper than you could ever imagine,' he wrote. The Experience wasn't just a 'skeleton', 'it's three', a living entity that needed to be reborn. Outbursts and misunderstandings were inevitable under the circumstances, but shouldn't be allowed to get in the way of what we all wanted and had in common. We were on the same path, but needed to understand that in our own individual ways. Jimi apologised for the fiasco of the previous night, and admitted that he needed help and advice just like anyone else. He ended with a plea – 'please help me as I would love to help you' – which I guess amounted to a plea for us to respect each other more and accept that we needed to work things out together.

We were getting terribly self-destructive. Jimi – especially – bore the brunt of the attitudes of fans – they had paid for his good life and they expected him to put out, even to burn out, but at any rate to stay the same forever. I'm sure Jimi felt heartsick at the turn of things. His music wasn't a formula, it was meant to evolve. I consider his use of heroin a sign of his lost optimism and a desire to distance himself at all costs.

Overnight Los Angeles had flooded with music-related businesses, including Motown, as they split New York trailing London entrepreneurs. Marshall Brevitt opened a club called The Experience on Sunset Strip which tried to keep in a supply of English beer. We were encouraged to jam whenever we felt like it, with groups like Led Zeppelin and the McCoys, and to treat the club as a home away from home. The Factory was also a favourite haunt; and Barney's Beanery. A few things went east. Bill Graham opened his Fillmore East in the old Village Theatre off St Mark's Place as the New York scene moved from the Beatnik grooviness of the West Village to the hip poverty of the East Village.

Warners continued to treat us very well. We did our most fun photo session on their movie lot, where we watched Tony Curtis filming. We were pointed in the direction of wardrobe and given a free hand to reappear however we fancied – Hell's Angels, bandits, or cowboys, which is what we settled on for the poster.

Press parties, opening parties, closing parties, premieres, private parties, intimate parties. Take the parties out of LA and I'm not sure there'd be anything left! We even had a pre-gig party at the Forum and together we relaxed and worked our way through the mountain of Mexican grass, leapers and coke. The show was a very good one indeed – a whole hour and three-quarters for the bootleggers. Oakland was just as big.

May

2	Detroit, Cobo Arena.
3	Toronto, Maple Leaf Gardens.
4	Syracuse, New York, Memorial Auditorium – with Cat Mother.
7	Tuscaloosa, Alabama, University of Alabama – with FM.
9	Charlotte, N. Carolina, Coliseum.
10	Charleston, W. Virginia, Civic Center.
11	Indianapolis, Indiana, State Fair Coliseum – with Chicago Transit Authority.
16	Baltimore, Maryland, Civic Center – with Cat Mother.
17	Providence, Rhode Island, Arena – with Cat Mother.
18	New York, Madison Square Gardens – with Traffic ($105,000).

21	Interviews.
23	Seattle, Washington, Coliseum – with FM.
24	San Diego, California, Sports Arena – with FM.
25	San Jose, California, Pop Festival – with Eric Burdon and War.
31	Radio Interviews.
	Honolulu, Hawaii, Waikiki Shell – with FM.

June
1	Honolulu, Hawaii, Waikiki Shell – with FM.
5,10	Photo sessions.
11	Rehearsal.
16	Recording.
20	San Fernando, California.
	Newport Festival/Devonshire Downs ($100,000).
29	Denver, Colorado, Mile High Stadium.
	Denver Pop Festival.

Following a horrific flight, coming into Toronto Jimi was busted at customs for possession of heroin. The grapevine had warned us to make sure we were clean coming into Canada, but the Customs guy just unzipped Jimi's flight bag, fumbled about, and came up with a packet of hash and heroin. I couldn't believe it. Surely, Jimi wasn't so stupid as to think he would be exempt from a search, especially as we'd been warned. After the LA house clean-up, I knew he didn't keep track of his stash and accepted gifts all the time from fans, as we all did. Jimi swore that someone had handed him a packet and he had simply slipped it into his bag. But this was too much. You don't put a gift of drugs in your flight bag if you know you are going to be searched – it wasn't like we'd never be able to score again. Perhaps the stash was planted . . . It certainly couldn't have come at a worse time. Was the Toronto bust just a way for someone (from a long list of possibilities) to remind Jimi that he was very vulnerable and depended on others to get him out of tight situations? It put Jimi in breach of, at the very least, the original Jeffery/Chandler contract.

We tried to contact Jeffery, but he seemed to have disappeared off the face of the earth. Finally the New York office answered our increasingly frantic calls. They thought Jeffery might be in Maui, contemplating a multi-million-dollar investment in a vast holiday resort. The police held Jimi while I continued my efforts to contact someone. Finally, wheels turned and Jimi was released on $10,000 bail. After all, we had a show to do.

We fled, freaked, to the hotel and attempted to recover with legal drugs – we drank a lot. The gig went surprisingly well, but the bust knocked any positive feelings Jimi was holding onto out of him. Civil actions were one thing, but criminal law was scary. He spent nearly nine months in agonised suspense before being acquitted on 15 December with the help of friendly testimony arrange by the office.

The tour took us down the Southeast coast and it was *déjà vu* time: we were replaying the Monkees tour, same halls, same crowds, same horror. The two-stopover Charlotte-to-Charleston flight in an old prop plane was a lesson in fear. The audiences were creepy and there were no chicks afterwards. It went nowhere from then on. We did a show with Chicago Transit Authority in Indianapolis on a Sunday (a dry day in that state); we drove to Baltimore from New York for a terrible gig, and then had to drive five and a half hours to get back; only to set off to Providence for a mediocre show. Perhaps we were unconsciously holding back our energy for the forthcoming Madison Square Garden show, but we needn't have bothered. It's a barn, far too large and impersonal for the action on stage to get out to the audience, in addition to which the route from dressing room to stage is a mile-long, body-packed obstacle course. I used my crawling technique to good advantage, but this was supposed to be a gig, not a survival course. We played for an hour and a quarter which worked out at $1,400 per minute, but it was not a night to remember for its high points.

After the gig I escaped to the Scene with Keith Moon and John Entwistle, where we got up to the usual excesses. Moon was always a pleasure to be around. He was crazy and spontaneous and always kept the show going. His lifestyle is well documented, but I remember in particular one event which summed up the Moon style: drunk as usual, he fell down a set of stairs, broke a leg and ended up in a thigh-high cast. At home, he took a bath and discovered that the cast was dissolving. Attempting to get out of the tub to ring the doctor, he fell and broke the other leg. This slowed him up a bit, but just a bit.

With a couple of days off in New York, I called round to Roemer and chatted with both Chas and his preferred company, Polydor, who wanted to hear the Fat Mattress tapes. Chas had news for me. 'Reprise want to sue you and are getting very nasty.' Sue me! What for? It seems the $10,000 in studio fees hadn't been taken from my account as I'd asked, but had been covered by Warners. I had planned going with Warners, but with nothing owing, a clean slate. I wanted to avoid the mistake of starting off with a huge deficit. This bit of news was highly upsetting. I should have run to phone Warners before I lost my rapport with Mo, but I got drunk instead.

The San Diego gig represented a return to form, and we did a rare rendition of *Little Wing*. The concert was recorded and much later put out as *Hendrix in the West*.

It was good to see Eric Burdon going down well in San Jose. His new group War (formerly Nightshift) had been together for years in various permutations. G&G were tipped off by their bassist, Peter Rosen, who had been go-foring for them on the side. G&G brought Eric to the Rag Doll Club where Nightshift were backing LA star footballer Deacon Jones, then having a short go at a singing career. Eric got up with harmonica player Lee Oskar for a jam which clicked instantly. G&G signed them all up, except Deacon, and also promised Eric they'd get his money back. They soon had an LP entitled *Black Man's Burdon*, with a visual concept based on the reverse of The Experience look – a white guy backed by a black band.

By the time we got to Hawaii we were falling asleep on our feet. I woke at five a.m. and saw a centipede on my pillow. Oh well, live and let live. I brushed it off. Through my half-sleep I felt a tickle on my chest. I scratched but it felt funny. I pried my eyes open and looked. My body and bed were covered in centipedes, both whole and mashed: insect horror comics come true. I peeled myself off the ceiling and fled. There were also saucer-sized hairy spiders, which a local lady brushed off into her hand as I stood on a chair having a case of the shivering creeps.

Besides that, Hawaii was wonderful, and so was the pricey beach-front house we rented at the foot of Diamond Head. We swam, took Owsley acid and ate THC cookies in the sun. The standard Experience pace proved too much for Mattress bassist Jim Leverton, who ended up having to be nursed by yours truly through two tabs which had hit him hard. Luckily, the pressure of the upcoming gigs forced him to pull himself together.

The first concert started very well. Perhaps Fat Mattress's relaxed vibe suited the pace of Hawaii, for the crowd was very responsive and enthusiastic. After a short rest for me, The Experience went on for what should have been a marvellous performance. But Jimi simply stopped the show, refusing to play because of a small amp buzz – nothing more than an earth hum. I felt he was a right bastard for that one. I wanted to scream, 'Stop being a star and play the guitar!' I couldn't believe he would do it to such a huge, eager and pleasant audience. Or to Mitch and I – who were completely embarrassed at being forced to trail off after him yet again. I think the Mattress went back on to stretch out the show.

We tried to relax for a fresh feeling towards the next day's gig by going horseriding, but the stable owner came running out screaming, 'Fuck off you hairy load of cunts!' Our roadie retaliated with equally wonderful threats and everyone felt like shit. Thank heavens the PA hum was gone and all went well.

With three weeks off, I headed for London, only just avoiding being thrown off the flight, with Eric Dillon, for being drunk. Customs caught me trying to bring in a Gibson Stereo guitar, confiscated it, and fined me £120.

I caught up with business. In the Jeffery/Warner – Chas/Polydor struggle, Chas won partly because Warners were inextricably bound up with Jeffery who kept on telling me: 'I'm your manager and I'm entitled to twenty per cent no matter how you get a deal.' I'd reply, 'Well, if you're my manager how come I'm broke and you're doing OK? Why are you only around when there's a bunch of money coming in?' No reply.

Of course, the rest of FM had a say, too. They were excited about the prospects and eager to sign with Polydor for the very reason I was sceptical – a huge advance, the biggest ever given to a British band without even an LP to their name. I would have been satisfied with a no advance/better royalties deal, but I succumbed and went along with it. However, if you go with the flow, you must realise it isn't always going to flow where you want to go.

I met with the label president and Danny Kessel, the label rep, and on 6 June we were photographed signing the relevant papers. Why isn't anything dated properly? I have FM contracts dated while I was still in Hawaii. The set-up was something like this:

UK AND EIRE: Each artist formed a company to which he signed as a salaried employee for five years. Mine was Matula (ninety-nine shares to me and one to Chas) and the directors were myself, Chas and a representative of Stigwood's. The secretary (to whom correspondence is normally sent) was Chas's accountant. We agreed to work a minimum of 150 days per year doing recording and personal appearances. Each artist, through his company, then signed a five-year management agreement with Montgrove Investments Limited (which I thought was Chas's, but later found out was Stigwood's) who received 20 per cent. Our companies then signed with Polydor for recordings sold in the UK and Eire for three years and each provided a side letter guaranteeing the terms of the agreement with Polydor. The advance was $55,000, less 20 per cent management and seven and a half per cent legal fees.

OVERSEAS: We signed a five-year agreement with the flourishing

Constellation Overseas Limited (whose parent company was Stellar Growth Unit Trust, Isle of Man). Other 'new faces' recently signed were Led Zeppelin, Ginger Baker, Eric Clapton, and Jack Bruce. Constellation had also recently acquired companies owning the services of Frankie Vaughan, Diana Rigg, Susannah York, Ken Hughes, Judy Geeson, Alan Bennett, and many more, and advertised the fact with a big glossy brochure. This contract covered personal appearances and recording outside the UK and Eire with a salary of earnings less management expenses and Constellation's 5 per cent handling charge.

For recordings made outside the UK and Eire, the three-year contract was between Montgrove *pro* Constellation Overseas (the party who received income, did the administration, and got the tapes back when the contract expired) and Polydor, with a side letter from us to guarantee the terms. Advance: $120,000 minus percentages.

For management outside the UK, it was Montgrove signing with Constellation for recording and appearance at 20 per cent. Then there was a loan-out agreement between Constellation, Montgrove, and the artists, according to which Constellation loaned out artists' services to Montgrove. Finally there was mention of 'cross-collateralisation' – a concept about which I was woefully ignorant. (Basically it means that if the record company can't recoup it's advance through one kind of royalty – record sales, for example – they can claw it back through another, publishing income, for instance: a tails-we-win-heads-you-lose arrangement.)

Jeffery threatened to sue me, though he never dared wave the countless contracts I'd signed for him in my face. I wish I had called his bluff and told him I'd see him in court. Jeffery finally said he would allow me to sign with Chas if he could have my publishing. I don't know, but I imagine he did retain some at least. I just wanted to see the last of him. Mo asked Jeffery if he should reimburse Warners for my sessions by taking money from 'Noel's account'. That's the first and last time I heard anyone refer to my account at Warners.

I felt Chas was trying to do it right, but he only got headaches in the end. None of the band, including me, took our contractual commitment seriously enough. Contracts all signed, we had our bits of papers and we thought it was great. Of course, sheaves of papers in reality indicate little more than the fact that you've paid a lot of money to lawyers to write them.

I celebrated the Fat Mattress deal by getting involved with the Mothers of Invention gig at the Royal Albert Hall. At Zappa's instigation, their road manager and I danced an impromptu ballet during their set.

I moved, at last, into my house. It wasn't fancy, but it was comfortable, quiet (until I moved in), and was located near the home of Jeff Beck, so we had a good house-warming jam. I was all settled into suburban living until I visited my local pub, The Walnut Tree, and was asked to leave – not by the publican, but by the established toffs, who wanted me to regret moving into their area. When I returned with my Roller, I was welcomed . . .

Chandler got me in to do some backing vocals for one of his other groups, Eggs Over Easy, and while in the studio I heard a 'live' Experience album. This was a surprise, to say the least. It may have been the Albert Hall gig, which was meant to be released as the soundtrack to the film. It was released on the Ember label in France by Entertainments International which was owned by Bernie Solomon, Gold and Goldstein's former accountant. Later, at Chandler's flat, I was amazed to hear my song *She's So Fine* used as a backing track for a television club scene. The artist is always the last to know. And the last paid (if ever).

Still fuelled by optimism, I headed back to Los Angeles after giving Montgrove authorisation to sign papers on my behalf. Jimi had been settled into the penthouse suite of the Beverly Rodeo Hotel in a vain attempt to isolate him from distracting influences. I'd been after Jimi for years to cut down on the size of his crowd scenes, and management had finally twigged, but even with access restricted by a private elevator, his suite looked like Grand Central Station on a late Friday afternoon. His crowd not only lived with him at home, but followed him out in public. I sometimes refused to go out for a jam because I couldn't face the Jimi entourage. Jimi called me a stick-in-the-mud, but I couldn't stand being with him in those circumstances. You just had to look at his face to see what a pain it all was. He was just this side of screaming, but he didn't have the nerve to tell them all to fuck off. His hangers-on cluttered up his living space and ran up bills on his room account. Mitch and I would occasionally clear them out, but the hordes soon regrouped. In a way, Jimi's ego fed off the attention, but in the end he was forced to become 'Jimi Hendrix' round-the-clock host to parasites. They fed off his celebrity and he fed off the drugs they provided. He paid the bulk of the bills, though. Members of his inner circle would turn up at the office carrying scrappy notes signed by Jimi with the message: 'Give them $$$$.' I imagine that many of the requested autographs had demands for cash added later above the signature.

Jimi spent plenty of money on himself and he gave plenty away. He bought guitars all the time (in addition to being given many free) although he used only a few favourites. He gave money to his family. He paid out settlements and kept lawyers and managers in style. Once he gave two girls $3,000 to go shopping just to get rid of them. Costly studio time, however, did not result in sellable product, yet this was the one expense which might have been justified. If we had been able to produce anything in the studio we could have financed The Experience, but Jimi's insistence on taking charge of everything in the studio ensured that there was no output, just bills.

Jimi was obviously trapped. 'I still want to play with you guys and we'll do our own things, too,' was what he said, but in reality the only way things could get done was if Jimi was handling all the chores, and he wasn't up to it. When I said, 'We must get on with the music,' Jimi said, 'Don't worry, we'll get rid of Jeffery,' as though that single act would solve everything. If I did discuss Jeffery with Jimi, I would immediately receive a heavy call from Jeffery warning me off.

The Newport Festival at Devonshire Downs was billed as the biggest festival to date, a three-day venture staged in the suburbs of Los Angeles and featuring – among many others – Creedence Clearwater Revival, Booker T and the MGs, Eric Burdon and War, Steppenwolf and Three Dog Night. We were scheduled to appear on 20 June 1969.

Jeffery was geared up for this one in the same way he was geared up for the Monkees tour. This was good business, our biggest return for the least amount of effort. All he had to do was make sure we were standing on stage for one short set in front of miles and miles of audience. The backstage area was a circus, with rows of caravans for the sideshows and groups. A sea of colourful and happy people milled outside our wire mesh enclosure and watched us in our cage. A helicopter dropped us off backstage, the only possible way in. I scored some grass and headed for our caravan.

The interior of the caravan contained a world quite different from that outside, where a hippy/peace/love vibe prevailed. The caravan was packed with about eight black heavies who dwarfed Jimi. He looked petrified and I was chilled to the bone by his appearance. I don't know what they were on about, but Jimi looked so relieved to see me that it was pathetic. I told them to get the fuck out of our dressing room. I didn't know anything about politics or the black equation.

I really hated those people who were always trying to get at Jimi. Though 'Love Everyone' was a highly political thing to say in those high-intensity Cold War/Vietnam times, Jimi wasn't politically active and would only question things he read about if he was stuck on a plane and there was nothing else to do. Probably saved himself a lot of aggravation. You can pretty much do what you want until you start getting people to think, and perhaps vote, differently. The White House invited him to meet Nixon and play for a Youth Telethon. I suppose Nixon needed some credibility with the voters of the future. Thank God he didn't do it.

If the management didn't concern itself with Jimi's personal happiness, neither did those who hovered round him. They only worried that someone else was sucking his blood and they wouldn't get their cut. He was being pulled so many ways, it's a wonder he stayed together so long. Band of Gypsies was the closest Jimi got to submitting to the pressure to work exclusively with soul brothers, and it was short-lived. Buddy Miles was used to his own stardom; and there's one thing I know about Jimi – he liked being Top Cat.

Jimi had an open and loving mind, even if he was sometimes violent. In a personal discussion he'd ask questions and try to understand the other viewpoint before going over and beyond any walls. We swopped jokes all the time – including racial ones. He'd tell us the jokes black people told about whites (and some were pretty close to the bone), and we took it for what it was - humour. We shared a lot of laughter. Many comedians of the era based their humour on knocking everyone. Grooviness meant being able to laugh at the world. You are what you are. If you can't laugh at yourself, you can't laugh.

The Experience did not have a race relations problem – that was one of our strengths. Any aggro about social equality in the band stemmed from from a class difference between Mitch and I. Though I have a lot of time for Mitch, we were always playing one-upmanship games with each other.

With the caravan cleared, Jimi was a bit shaky and somewhat withdrawn and troubled. I settled him down and we relaxed with the grass. After a couple of drinks and a snort of coke, we were perfectly primed and ready to go at eight. Then we were rescheduled for ten-thirty. That was the worst thing about festivals. You never went on when you were scheduled, but you had to be there and be ready at the appointed time, having planned your high and your energy levels all day correspondingly. When we did get on, Jimi just couldn't pull himself together. I don't know whether the pressure was internal or external, but I suspect the latter. He played with his back to the audience for twenty minutes and walked off. Maybe it was just his way of saying to Jeffery, to the heavies, and maybe even to the fans: 'Look, I'm terrible. You don't want me. Leave me alone.' Whatever it was, I never did get used to having one-third of the group walk off the stage in mid-set. I was angry. I split to the hotel instantly without trying to see Jimi, and passed out.

Next day the pressure was on for us to make up for the short set, but I was sick of the whole thing. Jimi decided to go on with Buddy Miles on Sunday, when they did a good jam with Eric Burdon. The fans and promoters were happy, but it was a bit late, to my mind.

Waiting it out in LA for the Denver concert to come round, I ran into Jimi often in The Experience Club. We had pleasant, general talks about business and the future. He'd often say in public that we should be splitting the Experience income in thirds as we were all working equally hard. But he had no say. These talks were followed by typically heavy phone calls from Jeffery.

I hung about killing time. David 'Lord' Sutch pulled the two Lord Sutch and Heavy Friends LPs together by hiring Jimmy Page, John Bonham, Jeff Beck, Nick Hopkins and myself for some sessions. Crazy times, crazy people.

The final concert scheduled for this tour was the Denver Pop Festival, an outdoor, two-day affair staged in the middle of a field on the outskirts of town. The first day we were spectators, enjoying Joe Cocker and Creedence before crashing early. The next day, everything was going fine until somebody said to me, 'Are *you* still with the band? I heard Hendrix replaced you!' Seems some eager press person had reported that I had split because I hadn't been consulted about the 'expansion' of the band, whatever that was supposed to mean. This was the last straw. It did my head in. I was uneasy enough about our future, but this rumour just blew me away. From some reason, I jumped to the conclusion that Jimi had actually done an interview saying I'd been replaced, and it hurt. I suddenly just wanted to get away, to be alone, to recover. We'd already agreed to do a revival tour in 1970. That was OK, as it was months away.

As if the rumours weren't enough, the concert very nearly killed us anyway. These big shows were just too scary. We went down fantastically well – too well. The crowd went berserk. Thirty thousand fans wanted to be on stage with us. The police panicked, and I don't blame them, when the crowd started to move *en masse* towards us. We didn't feel too calm about it either, but kept playing, hoping it would ease up. The police had tear gas, so they used it but forgot to check the wind direction first. Of course it was blowing towards the stage. Tear gas is wicked. We started to choke and feel the burning tears, but there was no way off the stage, which was now completely encircled by a solid mass of surging bodies. If we had jumped or fallen into the crowd we would have been mauled. Gerry came through for us, and I believe he saved our lives. He backed a huge panel van right up to the stage and we stumbled blindly, choking, inside. He locked us in. The crowd immediately swarmed over the van, and the din inside was frightening as the roof began to buckle under the weight of countless bodies. We huddled in silence, each lost in private thoughts and prayers, fighting in our own personal ways to stay calm in the dark, windowless van, with the roof creaking closer to us and the door locked. How could this nightmare have emerged out of all the good feelings and music? As calmly as I could I concentrated on rolling a joint. Thank heavens I had my stash. I always said that grass made it easier to relax. Well hell, this was the test. I truly appreciated that smoke, which seemed set to be my last. Then the engine started. Gerry had somehow made it back to the driver's seat. He couldn't wait for the way to clear and just eased the van into motion and hoped for the best. It was a good mile back to the hotel. There were still fans hanging on to the top and sides of the van when we arrived. We had to run for our lives to get through the hotel door. To this day, I get a horrible feeling in the pit of my stomach when I think about it.

I fled for England the next day. It was the end of the world as I'd known it for three hectic years. For the first time in ten years I stopped keeping up my diary. That was the last show The Jimi Hendrix Experience ever played.

Chapter Seven

Win Some, Lose Some

I have lost friends, some by death . . .
others through sheer inability to cross the street.
VIRGINIA WOOLF

IT came as something of a surprise to discover how easily and effectively you can be destroyed by getting what you want. Adulation in particular sets you apart from reality and, more devastatingly, from the relaxed sincerity of close friendships. No one sympathises because you are envied, not liked, and come to despise yourself for daring to be distressed when your dreams come true, for not continuing to thrive and improve on your success. Some people find depression creative, but I just find it . . . depressing.

I sat, usually alone, getting drunk on pints of vodka and ginger beer day after blurred day, but the alcohol didn't even touch the residual leapers, though it blotted out the brain just fine. I'd lost the urge and/ or ability to think ahead, only being called back by the necessity of getting the Mattress together. I threw myself completely into interviews, photo sessions, and the 'many exciting possibilities for Noel's future' Chas raved about in his press release. I wanted it to be true. Polydor had coughed up the recording costs to repay Warners and with the LP delivered and the single finished, Neil suggested a quick holiday in Copenhagen, where I saw Suzanne. After seeing Jimi busted, I never again carried 'substances' through Customs. Neil and I searched ourselves thoroughly and chucked out everything we found. Only I arrived in Copenhagen with a lump of hash in my pocket I *know* hadn't been there before . . .

I did a two-and-a-half-hour jam to benefit a busted friend and was amazed that the audience was willing to just sit and listen for that long. When was the last time anyone had actually listened to The Experience when we played live?

August

9	London Jazz and Blues Pop Festival
11	Bath
18-20	Recording.
22	Lyceum, London. Midnight Court with Reflections, Kelly James, Village, Junco Partners and Andy Dunkley (£300).
24	Tofts, Folkestone (£121).
26	Marquee, London (£250).
30	Isle of Wight Festival (£300).

September

| 1 | Redcar (£175). |

Fat Mattress began gigging without the accompanying splendour (and guaranteed crowds) of The Experience. We even played Tofts, where The Lonely Ones once had a residency. I was relaxing in my room before the prestige Marquee show with a lovely girl, when there was angry banging on the door. It was Suzanne, 'Let me in! Let me in!' Did she think she owned me? 'I'm asleep. Piss off and leave me alone.'

It was time for the first Isle of Wight concert – a mad party from the moment we boarded the ferry. The weather was great and the gig was good. We went on at midnight and left at dawn to drive to our gig in Redcar, North Riding.

Murray Roman appeared in London. He'd been on an American TV show, *The Dating Game*, in which an up and coming star takes his/her pick of three unseen contestants by asking silly questions and judging the response. A girl called Michelle chose Murray, then scriptwriting for the Smothers Brothers, over Bill Bixby (pre-*Hulk*) and the prize was a trip around the world. Probably due to Murray's sense of humour, they became lovers in Bangkok and married when they returned to LA.

A bit more romantic than my wedding. Out of the blue, in late September, Suzanne got in touch with me. 'I'm pregnant and it's yours.' What happened to birth control? Considering myself a gentleman, I offered to marry her and had her mother flown over for the ceremony on 6 November 1969, at the Registry Office in Ashford, Kent. All I could think of was that this might be the beginning of something good – marriage to a girl with home-loving instincts who didn't mind a musician's life and who shared my dream of an idyllic country life. But I was wrong. The Mattress was off for a German tour with The Pretty Things and I thought my bride would settle in to make us a nest. But she refused, and refused to stay with Mum, returning to Copenhagen instead.

I was very worried about the Mattress. Would it make it? Was it even any good? I was now in Jimi's shoes. No one had any good or bad criticism to offer for fear of alienating me – the goose who'd laid a golden advance. I felt something wasn't quite 'right', but couldn't put my finger on it. Chas reassured me, 'Don't worry. You have thousands coming in every day from The Experience.' In fact, Track was forced to release *Fire/Burning of the Midnight Lamp* on 14 November due to the lack of anything else. 'So if this doesn't make it, it doesn't matter.' Chas insisted we had a good chance since the strength of my name would get us gigs and a listen. As if to back up Chas, I even got a sort of statement from Are You Experienced Inc., showing a healthy balance being held in Hecht's special account.

I was right to have forebodings about the Mattress advance. It was the worst thing that could have happened. The band went berserk, spending money like water instead of playing it out slowly until we caught on. Eric bought a Bentley and an Afghan hound, which got run over. Neil spent tons on a London flat, a house with a £9,000 mortgage, and a Jaguar. Too rich, too easy. Too poor, too soon.

We were treading a weird line between stardom and dues-paying, acting like stars when our gigs were only paying a couple of hundred a night. We got too smashed to play properly. In Kiel, as I went to sing, I missed a step and fell over into the drums. The amps went over, drinks flew, and I continued playing laid out safely on the floor. We staggered back to the hotel with some girls. When the staff wouldn't let us in, Neil tried to buy the hotel. Later, Jim went into the bar, where a pianist and drummer were quietly doing their bit, and shouted, 'Come on Ginge [Ginger Baker], give us a solo', successfully clearing the bar of customers, before they threw him out. We were very obnoxious.

I stopped off to rattle around in my empty home before our Stateside promotional tour starting on 3 December. Obviously we weren't going to take off like The Experience, if at all, but we were working and warming up. Four days into the tour, the Mattress came unstuffed. We argued and without saying a word Jim, Eric, and a roadie split to London. I believe the last straw was a dispute over a sax player who Jim and Eric had invited to jam at our New Jersey Action House gig. I hadn't heard him and they barely knew him. I did know the Mattress was skating on thin ice until we could get a record to break. Reluctantly, I agreed to his joining us for the encore after our set was over. When they brought him on early in the set anyway, I freaked, horrified that they could jeopardise everything so casually. 'If you ever do anything like that again, you can get out your bow-ties and go back to Humperdinck.' Even The Experience had jammed only very rarely, and then only on one or two numbers with Jack Casady and Traffic – people we already knew musically very well. In our dodgy circumstances, we couldn't afford to fuck up on stage. However, my attempts at control were obviously resented. No one insisted the guys return for the rest of the tour. It was simply cancelled, and I took the blame via a press release which said I'd had a nervous breakdown. Probably very close to the truth.

The empty house was very lonely when I returned five days before Christmas and my twenty-fourth birthday. My sister Vicki took pity on me and we drove to Denmark to collect Suzanne. I could hardly wait for the comfort of her arrival. Everything was going drastically wrong – no group (the group kicked me out), contractual obligations, tax problems, no musical future, and agents and venues threatening lawsuits. But when Suzanne arrived, she made it quite plain that she wasn't interested in me or the house and complained constantly, especially if musicians visited for a jam, or even if I moved my wedding ring to another finger while playing because I couldn't play wearing jewellery. I felt confused. This relationship was her idea. On Christmas Eve, arriving home in a bad mood from a party with Mum and some old friends, she announced: 'I'm leaving and it's not your baby anyway.' I was dumbfounded to say the least. I had a small birthday party planned, but Suzanne split early and returned late, 'I don't want to talk, I'm leaving.' In no condition to argue, I accepted her imminent departure. She stayed a week longer, speaking to me only through third parties.

At six in the morning on New Year's Eve, my home-manager Bill Black and I travelled to London to collect a friend. Suzanne asked Bill if she could be dropped off in London. While we drove in uncomfortable silence to town, I asked her questions – to no avail. On Kensington High Street, she asked Bill to stop, took her case and went off without a word. Later that day Chas phoned. Suzanne had walked into his home early that morning saying I had thrown her out. He advised me to get a lawyer. He had recommended his own lawyers to her and proceedings for a judicial separation had been started. I couldn't believe it. They immediately obtained an injunction allowing Suzanne something she already had – free access to the house – and they froze my assets, such as they were. It also prevented me from 'molesting' her (when we hadn't even shared a bed since her announcement). The Happy New Year started with Suzanne and her friend, Lynn Collins (who soon married Mitch, briefly), beginning a series of visits. They'd arrive without warning and ignore me – except for Lynn asking for money, 'You'll be better off if you give it to her.' Well, she was confirming the Beatles' observation to me anyway. Money can't buy you love.

The only thing remaining was Jeffery's big plan for an Experience 'reunion' tour. It was a nightmare, but I couldn't wake up. Truly the end of an era.

The hippie revolution had taken place, and with it a new freedom and disregard for the established machinery was supposed to have arrived. But groups like us, the symbols of freedom, were tied to large corporations with an interest only in profit. Many managers and record companies rarely saw their groups after the initial signing. They'd simply terminate a contract with a letter when the initial flood of income slowed or stopped, usually taking with them the production company that was the sole authorised receiver of income and the owner of any tapes made. Not to mention the poor groups that were signed by recording companies specifically to be shelved because the company needed tax losses.

Real people had spent the last few years getting their heads together and coming to terms with their future lives. But the groups never had the time or the social contact necessary to do this. I must have signed my contracts in blood, for I felt I'd lost my soul, that I was just a cog in the money-making wheel. Jimi was a big earner, but sales had fallen off, and how much longer could he go on living off his past image? Pretty smashed most of the time, not writing much, and deeply troubled, he too was at the turning point. Should he fade away, expand the existing set-up to generate new interest, or chance a complete change of direction? It might be weeks, months, years, or never before he could get reorganised and the audience learned to enjoy the new material.

Jimi had met Alan Douglas, producer of Duke Ellington, Billy Holliday, Charles Mingus and John Coltrane, and of film, record, book and TV packages of Lenny Bruce and Malcolm X. All dead. He offered Jimi help with his idea of filming four shows a year to maintain exposure while he recovered. In fact, Jeffery was already working on two film projects – *Berkeley* and *Rainbow Bridge*. Douglas organised some jazz jams, taped them and wanted to release them. But Jimi thought they weren't up to scratch, since he was playing in an unfamiliar field; and Jeffery didn't want to change Jimi's image. Nor did he like Douglas moving in on his property. Douglas contemplated a book on Jimi; others thought it premature.

On New Year's Eve and Day, the Band of Gypsies played concerts at the Fillmore East. The group featured Billy Cox (an old army buddy) on bass and Buddy Miles on drums. Jimi, like me, had opted to play with old friends. He admitted in interviews that he was going through changes and was very, very tired. The band never got off the ground, but Chalpin got his album.

Periodically, Jimi tried to break his love-hate relationship with Jeffery. During one of these periods, Jimi was kidnapped, put in a sack, and driven off. A couple of days later, he was rescued. By Jeffery I think. Was it staged to frighten Jimi? Or Jeffery? To let one or both of them know what could happen . . .

First Jimi said he'd do Jeffery's grand reunion tour, then he said he wouldn't. Jeffery sent me a plane ticket and by the end of January we'd met, talked it out, been interviewed by *Rolling Stone*, and signed a document authorising Jeffery to contract three major tours: a US tour to gross between $750,000 and $1,000,000; one major tour of western Europe and the UK; and a tour of Japan. Net profits were to be split 50/25/25.

In 1969 Jimi and Jeffery had leased a building on New York's 8th Street. The initial plan was to open a nightclub, probably inspired by Jeffery's successes in Spain. But the New York club scene was rather more ruthless. And surely Jimi was sick of clubs? We'd been in hundreds of strange clubs with thousands of strange people, and left many of them feeling totally fed up with the whole scene. Considering how much time Jimi spent recording, Jeffery's idea to build a studio was better by far. Jimi went into a 50/50 partnership with Jeffery in Electric Lady Inc. But the building chosen was plagued by subway noise and damp – $369,126 disappeared and hardly anything had been done. On 11 February 1970, Jimi and Warners made a deal (with Jeffery as administrator). Jimi got $300,000 against future Experience and other royalties to complete the building of Electric Lady Studios. They figured they'd recoup the loan with the proceeds of an idea called *Wave*, which probably ended up as *Rainbow Bridge*, produced by Jeffery as Antah Kar Ana, Inc., later Karana Productions. Jimi guaranteed the loan by promising to write enough original material of Experience quality to cover it.

This was risky. Whenever anyone asked Jimi to do a film, he'd say, 'Yeah, man.' If you asked six months later how it was going, he'd say, 'Well, I have these two tracks that might suit . . . ' and he'd offer some old material that had been laying around. *Rainbow Bridge*, released in 1971, included four tracks recorded prior to the latest agreement. I played on one of them, *Look Over Yonder*, which was recorded in 1968!

The other songs spanned the period 1968 to mid-1970. The reunion tour would certainly raise needed funds and take the pressure to write off Jimi at a time when he was finding it very difficult to be creative.

The contract also contained a 'certain guarantee' reference. Jimi consented to Warner Brothers deducting 20 per cent of royalties due him from all Warner sources, 'for the purposes set out in the Jeffery guarantee'. Was Jeffery making sure his percentage was paid off the top before the loan repayment of six semi-annual payments of $50,000 plus interest was deducted, even though he and Jimi were partners in the venture? The studio opened for business late in the summer of 1970, and did good business on the strength of Jimi's name.

Roemer billed me for $2,000 worth of services rendered plus his $600 monthly retainer and expenses. In England, the taxman arbitrarily billed me for £112,000 and forced me to travel back to speak with them, and to hire Ivor Casson and Bernard Winters, who proved to be worth their weight in gold. Once it was all laid out I discovered I only owed £5,000. After expenses, taxes, and fees, they discovered I'd cleared only slightly more than £1,000 per year from 1965 to 1969.

I got in a lot of trouble by ignoring the simple piece of advice Chas and Jeffery gave me: don't talk to the press about your earnings. But I liked to brag, perhaps for reassurance. Suzanne based her suit on my wedding day boast to the press that I was worth £250,000. The realisation that I could only afford and actually preferred a 'poor' lifestyle must have been a disappointment. My idea of the good life is not travelling at all and quiet evenings in front of the fire sharing a chat and a pint with friends. I never could get into all that 'Meet you next week in France' stuff. Suzanne charged me with 'cruelty' for having thrown her out of the home and demanded half of everything I'd worked so hard for, plus £25 a week for a London flat and additional spending money. Pretty good for ten days together. The visitations for cash continued. Still insisting the baby wasn't mine, she said she planned an abortion. I wished she'd go back to not talking to me. How was I expected to keep coming up with cash when my bank account was frozen and nothing was coming in? A subpoena ordered me to pay maintenance. I sat in at the Roundhouse with the Mattress for some cash.

Rehearsals for the reunion tour were scheduled for late March in New York. I went over and was met by Bob Levine from the office. He kept repeating, 'I know this drummer. Have a play with him.' So I jammed with this fifteen-year-old drummer next day to fill the time while waiting for rehearsals. Days went by. I phoned Jimi regularly but his lady friend, Devon Wilson, always answered and said he wasn't in. Finally, I phoned Mitch's hotel. His chick answered, 'They're rehearsing. Didn't you know?' Nobody had had the decency to tell me they were rehearsing with Billy Cox. Then it clicked why Bob had been pushing this drummer. Now he started to say, 'Don't let it bother you. Why don't you nip into the studio and do a quick LP, try out some of your new songs? I know a place where I can get cheap time and then Mike and I will get you a deal with Polydor.'

I thought, 'Fuck it!' and went for a whirlwind LP at the Sound Center with Michael (Skip) Juried as engineer, Roger Chapman of Family on vocals, Paul Caruso on harmonica, a guy named Jerry on organ and the young drummer, Steve Angel. I meant to enjoy it and I did. We recorded at a good but leisurely pace and though I was covering all the expenses myself, I paid Joe Oldrich for orchestral arrangements. Then I hired Marc Rolands to design the cover. Bob reassured me that the office would get a deal for it instantly, so I used it as an experimental opportunity. I found working with an orchestra difficult, especially when I tried to get the string section to ad lib! The rough tracks came quick enough: *Walking Through a Garden* (I hadn't liked the Mattress version); Eddie Cochran's *Nervous Breakdown* (one of my favourites); a quick country bit; *Highway*, with Neil showing up for vocals; *Gas Class* (my *Classical Gas*); *Wearing Yellow*, with Lee Michaels on piano; *Blues in 3/4*; *Friends*, with Jimi on guitar; and *Rough* (vocals and lyrics by Roger). The Churl's Bob O'Neill helped out on vocals, and the doorman from the PennGarden Hotel played bagpipes on a few tracks. Jimi stopped by one night, sort of to say he was sorry, and had the grace to look embarrassed. He offered to play guitar and gave me a snort of coke which was heavily laced with smack and made me violently ill. I called the whole thing *Nervous Breakdown*. It went through a lot of hands and is now sitting in Electric Lady Studio pending payment of thousands in storage fees.

The initial recording buzz wore off and NY became depressing, knowing Jimi and Mitch were rehearsing. I escaped to LA on one of the first Jumbo flights. It took nine hours – two hours late taking off, then a passenger had a heart attack and forced us into Phoenix where no Jumbo had ever landed before. In case the runway wasn't long enough, out came all the emergency gear – which then waited until we took off again because, obviously enough, a Jumbo had never done that there either.

Mitch and Jimi arrived in LA not long after me for the 25 April start of their tour at the Forum. I consoled myself during the gig by spending a lovely evening with Mama Cass. I couldn't avoid Mitch in

LA and we'd sit and speculate about The Experience, Yameta and our past income. I was having cash problems. The LP, hotels and travel expences had eaten up my reserves incredibly fast. I was also getting bills from the FM tour, paying thousands in US taxes, and so on. Even worry-free Mitch, second biggest spender on the road, was feeling the pinch. Murray Roman listened. 'What kind of royalties are you guys getting?' 'None,' I'd say, trying to explain the situation as it had been explained to me. One day he said, 'Something's wrong and you guys need a good lawyer.' But that was the trouble already: too many lawyers. He took us to one. Our position was dodgy since all agreements had either been carefully kept verbal or we had no copies of anything signed. The first thing he did was to draw up a document stating the essence of our share agreement and Mitch was put in charge of delivering it to Jimi for his signature. Whatever he did, the document disappeared.

I tried to forget that Jimi and Mitch were touring without me. Murray threw a huge party with Eric Burdon, War, and John Hartford (banjo), and we recorded a background for Murray's new LP, *Busted*. I felt time slipping away as I headed back east to mix *Breakdown*, between parties with Manfred Mann and the Jefferson Airplane, sessions with Johnny Winter and trips to the Village Gate or Vanguard to see Mose Allison. Neil rang from London to say he had recorded *Highway* for the second Mattress LP after hearing me doing it. He added a few words and claimed 50 per cent of the writing royalties. Neil hadn't been able to remember all the chords, but hadn't dared ask me for the correct ones. Then he had the nerve to ask me to rejoin. I declined. They were falling apart. Instead of hustling gigs they were sitting waiting for someone to do it for them. And no one was interested.

Jeffery could still talk me into things. In May, he presented a document in which I acknowledged that I was still under contract to Jeffery per the contract of 11 October 1966. The gist of the rest was 'I (Jeffery) will give you half of your publishing as I already own it all. Therefore, sign this paper saying you'll give me half.' It also gave him the authority to take funds from Hecht's Joint Music account. I signed it because he said that if I didn't all my Experience income would be held up.

New York was still abounding in acid. Someone stopped by to ask if I wanted some pure crystal acid. 'Oh, yeah', says I, wetting my little finger, sticking it in and licking it clean. 'Uhhh, you should have only licked like maybe a pin clean.' Bill Black did the same and we dashed off for some serious business discussion at a lawyer's office. An hour went by. Suddenly, a tingle. I looked at Bill and knew he'd felt it too. I stood up. 'We have to go now, bye!' By the time we'd reached the street, we were tripping madly, the air and concrete thick with swirling colours. I clutched Bill's arm, repeating, 'We *have* to get to the hotel.' Somehow we got there, I swallowed a Mandrax, sank into a chair, put on the TV to keep me in touch with reality, and held on to the arms of the chair for dear life. Hours passed. People drifted in and out. I had to slide along the walls to get to the loo and had a hard time getting out. So much for my gluttony.

As we got more run down and neurotic, the 'bummers' became more frequent. Jimi got caught out badly when the Band of Gypsies played at a peace rally at Madison Square in January. Mitch and I were there, having been asked to come on stage later in the set for a couple of numbers. I was hovering in the wings behind the PA speakers, and before Jimi went on I saw Jeffery give him a tab. Perhaps he thought it would pep him up and liven up the act. But Jimi freaked instead, saying to a girl in the audience, 'Are you having your period? I can see it through your yellow knickers.' I suppose the shock of having said that brought him around. He added, 'We're not getting it together,' and walked off stage in the middle of a song.

Poor Jimi was obviously having serious problems. He gave very strange interviews at the time, saying things like, 'I figure that Madison Square Garden is like the end of a fairy tale, and that's great – the best ending I could possibly come up with.' More often he was inclined towards the temporary escape of heroin. Headwise, that was a huge barrier between us.

I finished my LP on 21 May, complete with artwork and photos by Ira Cohen. (Ira had done a really spectacular session with The Experience in our declining days. It had been awkward as we weren't speaking that day. He'd photographed us one by one while Jeffery had dispensed coke downstairs to those waiting. The results were incredible multi-faceted, mirror-image, full-colour psychedelic extravaganzas.) The LP had cost most of what my rapidly dwindling account contained. Polydor turned it down and the master tapes disappeared. From my first accounted tour earnings I'd bought two houses (one for Mum) and a car. With the second accounted tour, I'd paid for an LP, lawyers, accountants, and lived in New York and LA. With my FM advance I'd paid English taxes, accountants, and living expenses including alimony granted at £2,000 per year. Jeffery kept insisting our back Experience earnings were just around the corner. I'd left my brother in charge of the house and arrived home to find fifteen people living there and wearing my clothes, and the TV nicked. Jeff Beck, with whom I'd been discussing a joint effort, informed me he'd put together another band. Then the gearbox went on the Rolls.

Then Suzanne arrived to collect her things. Something she could have done anytime while I was away. To her, everything I did was wrong. She threatened to have me arrested for drug possession. Why had she married me? I knew she still had plenty of other boyfriends because someone was always making it their business to let me know who she was seeing. What did she want? To be divorced and independently wealthy? To stay in England? I knew she loved the publicity generated by the wedding and divorce, with her picture, and stories about how much money I was earning on the world tour (!), all over the papers. I began to receive hate letters, 'We agree with your wife and hope you get thrown in prison.'

The taxman had a new claim: £50,000 this time. I had to employ a barrister to talk to the judge. You tell your solicitor, he tells the barrister, and the barrister tells the judge, after translating what you've said into legalese so you're not even sure he's telling the same story, let alone the right version. It's like the children's game, Chinese whispers, in which a message is passed round in whispers until it emerges completely and hilariously distorted. In court you rarely feel like laughing about their translation of your problem, and you can't even stand up and say, 'Wait! What's wrong!' I feel that whether you are defending your actions or complaining about somebody else's you should be able to talk directly to the judge in everyday English. It might increase the chance of justice being done. However, in the interest of job preservation, I doubt anyone in the legal profession would support this. Presently it seems you hire a barrister so you can have someone in court on the same 'social level' as the judge. Proceedings can then be livened up with 'in' jokes about who is playing golf with whom.

After a meeting with the divorce lawyers I'd been forced to hire, upset and tired, I stopped on the way home for a drink. Nearly home, I got stopped by the Ashford police for doing fifty in a thirty mph zone. It was all over. Just under twice the legal limit, I received a £100 fine and a twelve-month driving ban.

With everything collapsed in England, I fled to New York where I saw Jimi at the official opening party of Electric Lady Studios. He now had what every songwriter/musician dreams of. He could record there and present half the cost to Warners – up to $10,000 – to be recouped from future royalties, if any. We didn't speak much in the hubbub of what was essentially a press party. 'How are ya! We're going to Europe, I'll probably see you there.' Friendly but preoccupied. I didn't stay long.

Jimi should have been conserving his energy for the Isle of Wight gig. When he arrived in England on 30 August he had been up all night and had to wait until two a.m. to go on. I didn't attend, but Mum was there. She was utterly shocked at how tired and rundown Jimi looked. She had a soft spot for him, and he for her. He made sure she was taken care of and took her up on stage for the show. For most of the concert Jimi had his back to the audience and pumped his guitar, trying to drive the bass and generate excitement. Billy had become deeply paranoid and it was said that he refused to eat because he feared his food had been poisoned. Maybe he had picked up on the bad vibes surrounding Jimi. After the show Stickells telephoned me and asked if I would be willing to step in and replace Billy. Of course I would. I had wanted to be on the tour from the outset.

It must have been terrible for Jimi, plodding away like this. The European tour was a nightmare. You have to see the film made in Stockholm to believe it. I'd never seen Jimi looking so drunk on stage before. Next was a festival on Fehmarn, a German island. I think Jimi was too tired to care. The set was horrific. A riot started. The rest of the tour was abandoned and Jimi went for a breather in London.

He saw Chas and once again asked him to help sort out his music, as he'd lost touch with what he wanted to do. Jimi had been complaining to Buddy Miles about his situation. He knew money had been 'lost' that he would never know about. In self defence, he tried to stop trusting people. About Jeffery he probably thought, better the devil you know . . . Even though Jeffery had been fired several times, he still did interviews saying, 'Jimi never wanted to change management, even though there were times I just couldn't devote energy to helping him. People outside the circle mistook this for discontent. If he wanted to split, he would have split.' Jimi phoned Steingarten saying once again that he wanted to leave Jeffery even if he had to stop working until the contract ran out. Steingarten said he wanted evidence against Jeffery. There were also meetings about PPX. I didn't give him the nickname 'Henpecked' for nothing. He stood them up.

Jimi looked up old friends, he hung out, he jammed at Ronnie Scott's with War – staying in the background but enjoying a relaxed play which was well received and pleased him no end – he thought he was finished in Europe.

He had lots of girlfriends, some steadier than others. But this time he was seeing one of his less frequent companions, Monika Danneman. Why her, I don't know, but Jimi hated to be alone. When he was, he'd often do his 'bat' routine, sitting in his room with the curtains drawn and the lights down, feeling weird.

Interviews with Monika tell this story: On the night of 17 September, Jimi asked Monika to drive him to 'some people's apartment' near Marble Arch. She can't remember where. He told her not to come in because they weren't his friends and he didn't like them. She picked him up an hour later.

Back in her hotel room, Jimi relaxed and wrote a poem, later entitled The Story of Life. They ate, they drank, they took sleeping pills, and went to bed. Monika woke a few hours later and noticed Jimi had been a bit sick. She felt something was wrong and soon afterwards decided to call an ambulance. Not much later, on 18 September 1970, Jimi Hendrix was dead.

As I lay struggling through the aftermath of a heavy night on the town, the phone in my New York hotel room insisted on waking me.

'Hello. A friend of yours is dead.'

'Oh, yeah, who's that?'

'Hendrix.'

I hung up, numbed. A thousand thoughts and feelings flooded my head. Was this a joke? If so, it wasn't funny. He couldn't be dead. People don't die when they're only twenty-seven.

Jimi was the first person I was close to, my first intimate friend, to die. Suddenly, I felt mortal and very alone. The next few hours were unreal. The phone rang unceasingly. Girls pounded on my door, crying and hoping to commit suicide from my hotel room window. I was forced to leave for privacy and sanity's sake and was drawn, unexpectedly for me, into a church. More expectedly, I then gathered up the ladies, took them to a bar and began to get drunk. I ran into Paul Jones, who kindly kept me company in my misery and soon . . . oblivion. If your high reflects how together you feel, I had reached a new low.

There are lots of questions surrounding Jimi's death. Jimi had taken several sleepers – the German brand Monika took called Vesperax (which has two barbiturates in it, slow and fast acting, plus an antihistamine which may be there to counteract a tendency for the drugs to congest mucous membranes) with a normal dose of half a tablet – and he had been drinking wine. A very dodgy mixture. Plus he'd taken something at the flat he'd visited.

On 21 September, the pathologist at St George's Hospital, Westminster, checking Jimi's blood, urine and liver, found evidence of

Durophet and amphetamine – the main ingredients of a Black Bomber, which normally contains some downers too. This may have been the source of two of the barbiturates found – Seconal and Allobarbital. He found evidence of the three ingredients of Vesperax – Brallobarbitone, Quinalbarbitone and a unidentifiable substance which he guessed might be a possible metabolite of hydroxyethyl hydroxyzine – the antihistamine. The only base detected was nicotine. Alcohol in the urine was 46mg/100 ml, so blood alcohol was probably 100mg at the time he took the Vesperax.

The ambulance crew strapped Jimi into a sitting position for the trip to the hospital, though the usual position for a person being sick is lying on his side. He vomited and choked. There was no attempt to use resuscitation equipment. The post mortem showed 400ml of free fluid in the left chest with the left lung partially collapsed. Both lungs were congested and swollen with vomit even in the smaller bronchi. Contrary to some reports, Jimi was still alive when he reached the hospital. There is much speculation over the twenty-to-forty-minute period after he reached the hospital. To my knowledge, no files have been found, and neither the ambulance crew, hospital personnel nor the pathologist have been available for questioning, though many fans have tried to trace them.

My theories include accident, suicide, and murder. Each treads on toes.

A more frequent girlfriend of Jimi's, Devon, was in London and was very likely one of the people Jimi had gone to see when Monika dropped him off near Marble Arch. Devon, who later died under mysterious circumstances (falling out of a New York hotel window), was a junkie and *may* have supplied Jimi with drugs that night. Upon Jimi's return, he and Monika stayed up talking until the sleeping pills took effect – not surprising given the amount of speed in his system. At about six a.m., she says he complained that there was something wrong and wondered whether someone had slipped him an OD. If only he'd seen a doctor then.

Suicide didn't seem to be on Jimi's list of things to do, but you never know. Monika says Jimi had urged *her* not to commit suicide. Had they been discussing it? The poem Jimi wrote earlier in the evening has been called a suicide note, most widely by Eric Burdon. But Jimi had been talking of new beginnings, of rediscovering his own amazing creativity, of waiting the business mess out, of taking a year off to study music, to try jazz, to write and perhaps expand into films. If he did take nine downers, it's extremely difficult to believe he could have swallowed that many without knowing, though Monika insists that Jimi never took any drugs at all and has tried to persuade me to say the same. How could I say that? Jimi *had* taken drugs, though he'd also started to look at his drug use more objectively, and did an interview saying, 'You know the drug scene has come to a head. It opened minds, but it let in other things that people couldn't handle. Music can do that without drugs.' Another argument against suicide is Monika's presence. If you really want to kill yourself, you don't have people around who might save you. I know lots of people who have 'tried' suicide. I mean, you haven't lived until you've felt like bumping yourself off – darkness before the dawn and all that. But they tried it in circumstances where they'd be found and helped.

Jimi had also spoken recently to his father, telling him he'd put some money away and would tell him about it as soon as he returned from Europe. He seemed too full of hope and plans for suicide. But then again, his career was entering the crunch stage, there was no guarantee that any of his future plans would prove successful artistically or commercially; and anyway, Chalpin was still hanging over everything he'd done or planned to do. He died on a day when he was due to attend heavy legal meetings over PPX. The pressure on him was unimaginable.

You could argue that it wasn't the pills which did Jimi in, but the way he was 'rescued' – that he died from sheer stupidity, his own and everybody else's. He could have radically misjudged just how many drugs he could take. Or if he truly felt he had been slipped on OD, he might, in his depression, have gone along with it. There weren't that many drugs in his system for a person with a large tolerance, but Jimi was always covered in spots and blemishes, symptomatic of a rundown condition. The cumulative effects of bad health and complete fatigue could have precipitated an accidental death. Bodies do give up. And Jimi did take heroin, which due to the control of the market by unscrupulous profiteers is often cut with dangerous contaminants. But at that period of time in London, more deaths were caused by some unusually strong heroin being made available as the Chinese made a play for the market. I'm sometimes amazed that I made it through alive when so many of my friends didn't. But anyway, Jimi died from choking on his vomit, and that should have been a preventable cause of death.

An interviewer once asked Weiss if he had any reason to suspect that Jimi died from other than natural causes. Weiss looked stunned, 'Do you mean poison?' The interviewer was stunned, 'No. Suicide.'

The really paranoid theory is that someone was paid to kill Jimi. Or scare him. I think murder is a distinct possibility. Jimi may have been under surveillance. Were the ambulance men really ambulance men? Was it a plot, like the kidnapping in the sack? Recently, while working in Italy, I was told that a French hitman had definitely been hired to kill Jimi, and did it by getting him to take something at the house he visited. There is no question that Jimi was a mess and was involved with some pretty creepy people. Billy Cox wasn't the only one to feel threatening vibes. In an interview, jazz musician Sam Rivers once discussed the possibility that Jimi was murdered by organised crime because of his determination to set up a union to arrange concerts and produce and distribute records. I can't see Jimi being able to do this, but his participation would have attracted many to the effort. Or might there have been a personal vendetta – a pregnant woman, a rejected lover or business associate? I doubt that anyone will ever know for sure – unless there is a murderer out there.

The coroner gave an open verdict, which was kept very quiet. Both Warner Brothers and Jeffery and Chandler Inc. had Jimi insured for a million dollars. Generally, insurance companies don't pay if it's suicide, though I believe some do if the policy has been held for more than two years. No one bothered to look for clues or call for a police investigation, preferring him to go down as just another musician who couldn't handle his additives.

Alan Douglas flew to London and with Stickells brought the body back. Someone suggested a Madison Square Garden extravaganza with the body on display. During our touring days, there were times when we'd discussed our deaths and how we wanted them to be. Jimi had always said he wanted to be buried in England, where he'd been given a chance and had 'made it'. Jimi's family brought his body home to Seattle, but they had control over very little else. I'd only met Jimi's father a few times and found him to be a gentle and sincere person – too nice to be confronted with this freak scene. It was bad enough to lose your son, without having the tragedy commemorated with a circus. Jimi had been away for such a long time. Suddenly he was a star, and suddenly he was dead and all these vultures were hanging around trying to be photographed with the family. As next of kin, Jimi's dad became surrogate 'star'. How could he hope to cope?

The funeral was a complete nightmare for me. The coffin was open. I think it's a ghastly custom. Everyone was expected to parade by and look, but I just couldn't. Mitch and I cried and held hands for strength. I looked around and was horrified. Everyone was vying for attention. Everyone had been Jimi's 'best friend'. Some who hadn't cared a jot for him alive came because it was *the* place to be seen. There were about twenty-five limos. The preacher went on and on when he should have just said, 'We loved him. He played great guitar and gave so much and now he's dead.' His white Fender guitar should have been buried with him, but instead it disappeared.

Jimi always said he wanted a party when he died. We rented a hall, gathered up a few instruments and gave him a good sendoff: Buddy Miles, Johnny Winter, Mitch and myself were the nucleus of a jam session that lasted hours. Jimi would have enjoyed it. Photographs have recently surfaced, but I don't think I want to see them.

Once the formalities were over, it was business as usual. In fact, it was better than usual business. There were, of course, many, many financial considerations. To a record company, a star is better dead than fading. During a star's 'natural' career decline, an unsuccessful album release can do serious damage to the back catalogue. Death, however, tends to bolster sales, unloads all those albums languishing in warehouses. The public panic-buys: 'That's all there is; better get it.' The marketing of Jimi Hendrix was well developed while he was alive, but with his death it was raised to a new level, and far more Hendrix product has come out since his death than came out while he was alive.

From my point of view – and Mitch's as well – Jimi was the only honest link with the rats' nest that was The Experience (and Experience Inc.) and his death severed our last connection with the earnings generated by the three years of work. It also made it impossible to answer many questions central to our legal concerns. Our ongoing negotiations with Jimi, with management, with the troops of lawyers and accountants were suddenly swamped by claims over the right to administer Jimi's estate. Jimi had died without a will, so there was a lot to be sorted out. Because they had become Jimi's personal lawyers,

Steingarten, Wedeen and Weiss took the driving seat and were soon in charge of *all* income from *all* sources. All claims to Experience income – including mine and Mitch's – were put on hold because of the set-up whereby much Experience income was collected in Jimi's name before being redistributed. The European royalties, of course, were still tied up by the PPX suit.

Mitch was so overcome by paranoia concerning the outcome of negotiations over the estate that he begged me not to do any interviews for fear that I'd tell stories about on-the-road escapades which might spoil our claims. Hendrix had died, but somehow Mitch and I – though tired – had survived. I met people who deeply resented this fact.

Al Hendrix, Jimi's father, travelled to New York to collect what was left of Jimi's effects. Most items of value had already been taken from his apartment by various scavengers. Only a very few of Jimi's possessions – the least valuable and least important – ever reached Jimi's family, and stolen items (film, tapes, clothing, guitars) continue to show up on sale.

The rest of the Experience's gear did a quick disappearing act, too. There had been about thirty guitars and a number of small amps at the studio – all gone. The tons of gear from the European tour were taken to Mitch's house and there I saw a huge room full of speaker cabs, amps, three drum kits, an Altech PA complete with monitors, etc. A Sussex dealer told me that Mitch slowly sold off the gear. At least he had some right to do so.

There was plenty of activity taking place on the fringes. With Steingarten's knowledge, some people in Hollywood (Michael Moriarty and Kathy Brody of Our House Productions) planned a 'memorial concert' and contacted me by telegram on 6 October. I ignored them. Then there was the Jimi Hendrix Foundation, set up by a Seattle group which included the owner of a porno-house chain and a carnival booker (reported by Jerry Hopkins in the 2 December 1976 issue of *Rolling Stone*). Hopkins's story includes a photograph of Mr Hendrix at home with some 'friends', including Jeffery's and Bob Levine's girlfriends. Exploiting the innocent Mr Hendrix, the 'foundation' took advantage of everyone they came in contact with, including groups who played (usually for nothing) at the 'benefits', and the kids who bought memberships and merchandise thinking they were helping to build a concert hall and museum. Finally, they fought amongst themselves over the money and disappeared overnight, leaving nothing but the bills. Two of the people involved tried to sign Mr Hendrix up for another foundation. Thank heavens he said no.

Steingarten officially became administrator of the Estate on 25 September 1970. Income I had been getting as a member of The Experience stopped for ever at this point. In Account No. 2, an escrow account controlled by Steingarten, Wedeen and Weiss, Jimi and Are You Experienced Inc., Mr Hendrix found only $12,367.81. After Jeffery warned him not to expect too much of a legacy, only a further $21,000 could be dug up, a ludicrous sum. Where, just for starters, was the money from the recently completed tour? Jeffery's attempts to convince Mr Hendrix that The Experience cupboard was bare led Al to worry out loud to an acquaintance, Herbert Price, who suggested that he tell his story to showbiz lawyer Leo Branton.

Branton had a lot of experience – with Nat 'King' Cole, promoter Norman Granz, and Dorothy Dandridge, to name but a few – and he had connections with a useful Panamanian company, Presentaciones Musicales, SA, founded in the early 1950s, through which taxes could be avoided. In Panama there was no tax on foreign source income, no tax on bank interest, complete confidentiality with regard to bank details, and the assurance of anonymity for account holders. Branton had retired to Mexico City, and a planned move to Sweden in 1968 was forestalled when thirteen members of the Black Panther Party were arrested in Los Angeles. He offered to defend them for free, got a name as a heavy lawyer, and later defended Angela Davis. It looked like Mr Hendrix was on the right track.

At the end of September, Branton met with Mr Hendrix and other interested parties in New York to review the situation. There were a lot of claims coming in: from the landlord for the cancellation of the studio lease, storage fees for Jimi's gear, funeral expenses, and of course taxes. Meanwhile, Steingarten rounded up tapes sitting in Wally Heider's studio in Los Angeles (they had $2,859.61 owing on them), met with Warner Brothers, and shortly after that met with Chas and others to talk about the tapes.

By mid-January 1971, Branton was taking over. The next meeting Steingarten had with Warners included Branton sitting in for the Hendrix family. Back in New York, Jeffery received $20,000 in management commissions due as per the contract of October 1966. Jeffery's fees were the only things being paid at that point, aside from Jimi's personal-expence debts. Branton saw how much money was being contested and he took a strong line. SWW were easily disposed of. The threat of a simple conflict-of-interests suit was adequate to shake them out of place. Branton had up-and-coming New York lawyers Kenny Hagood and Ed Howard appointed attorneys of record.

Obviously neither Al Hendrix's musical background sympathies nor

Branton's righteous indignation extended to Jimi's fellow (white) musicians who had helped bring in the cash, and Mitch's and my interests took a back seat at this point. There was no one in our corner, and that was that.

On 11 February 1971, Steingarten gave up control and presented to the court his educational final accounting as administrator: my, Mitch's and Jeffery's rights were laid out, but only Jeffery received payments in advance of settlement. As Jimi had feared, his tax payments had been neglected. The taxman nabbed $210,695 and wanted $13,000 more. Then the State of New York took another $40,567 and New York City took $5,673.

When Jimi died, Jeffery was still in place as his manager, and only he could renegotiate the three-year foreign contracts that were on the verge of expiry. Jimi had died just at the right time as far as Jeffery's interests were concerned. Branton recognised that he needed Jeffery and probably recognised as well that he was dealing with a sharp operator. Jeffery had taken a trip to Nassau (paid for by the Estate) to cash his latest $25,000 payment from Warner Brothers. He used his new company, Karana Productions (registered in New York on 28 July 1970) to renegotiate the Deutsche Grammophon (Sweden and Germany) and Polydor (Eire, Holland, Britain) contracts. Pye in Spain and CBS in Italy went over to Polydor, who were in the process of merging with DPG (Polygram). These moves consolidated his control over much of The Experience's worldwide income. Jeffery signed the DPG contract on the same day that Hagood and Howard became the official administrators of the Estate, 19 February 1971. The DPG contract was for an advance of $150,000 and a royalty of six per cent on the three Experience albums plus another $150,000 for *Hendrix in the West* and *Isle of Wight*. Warner Brothers retained the US and Canada. The Barclay contract (France) had yet to expire, but negotiations had begun for an advance of $150,000 and a royalty of twelve per cent.

Steingarten's fee for administering the Estate for four months was $27,000. He also claimed against Jeffery, on Jimi's behalf, $33,000 in foreign-source royalties already paid to Jeffery.

Ignorant at the time of all this heavy wheeling and dealing, I had expected that Steingarten would sort things out for me. He had always assured me that everything was OK, that we should have no trouble. Why should Jimi's death affect my income? Suddenly, nothing was happening.

I fled to England and got lost in a drunken blur. Chandler was having a go at restuffing the Mattress – our advance had left us with heavy recording obligations. Without a tour, the first album had flopped. According to him, if we worked hard enough, we might be able to recover the momentum on a second album. A Berlin television programme we did went well enough, but my heart wasn't in it. I just didn't feel close enough to the other band members.

I picked up a few bob doing small-time gigs. In January 1971, I was arrested on a drugs-possession charge. I guess the neighbours didn't like my pink tortoise. Or perhaps Suzanne had carried out her threats. Anyway, a carload of police walked in to my house. Expecting a huge haul, they'd followed my supplier from London. I was upset, of course, but let them work away. Grass smokers are generally peaceable, law-abiding people who are not inclined to hit policemen or anyone else. You don't see fights at a pot party. A terribly disappointing search revealed 2.52 grams of hash and one LSD tab. To quote my lawyer, 'There were more pills in twenty-five-year-old Mr Redding's bed-room than in a chemist's shop – and they are all on prescription.' Lucky for me. If I had been forced into stopping my well-established sleeping pill habit suddenly . . . I hate to think about it. I received the maximum fine of £100 for the hash and £50 for the LSD, with two months to pay because of my financial ill-health.

In New York, Roemer refereed the battles between Stigwood and Schroeders for the right to collect for Fat Mattress. My previous contract said I'd bring anyone I wrote with to Schroeders. The squabble cost me. Of course, I also involved Roemer in my divorce. I could have personally got the accounts from Hecht, but I let Roemer do it for £250 plus expences. Then came another bill for $75 from ASCAP for 'processing' cheques and accounts. I could have opened the envelopes and banked any money myself, but I didn't. When I later wrote asking about any ASCAP royalties, the reply was that there were 'only blank statements and miscellaneous correspondence which I threw away'. Expensive waste-basket . . .

My friends treated me like a multi-millionaire, but my lawyers knew the truth. I was too broke to want as a client but too troublesome to ignore. It seemed my every move required lawyers who required fees. As my cash dwindled, so did their interest – just when I needed them most. Lawyers can be as fickle as lovers. And here was innocent me hiring lawyers to 'get' other lawyers just because I was 'right'. It doesn't work. It's nothing to do with right or wrong, and everything to do with money. An old print shows two farmers fighting over a cow. One pulls the head, the other the tail. The lawyer happily milks away in the middle. The games people play are nothing to the games lawyers play. Try bucking a large corporation and you soon realise why they keep whole departments of lawyers on permanent payroll. Some change their ethics more often than their underwear. I once made chocolate cookies with ground-up grass stems and then had a legal visitor. I warned him, but he insisted on eating them anyway. When he got spaced and didn't like it, he reported me to the police.

Mitch and I were getting steamrollered. Accounts showed $560, 434 due from Warners alone for the last two quarters of 1970. After Jimi's death, fourth-quarter (October-December) sales soared 450 per cent over those of the third quarter. But we had to *prove* our entitlement to Experience income! It wasn't enough just to have played in the band. To make things more difficult, Branton had cornered the market in Experience files – and Hagood had fired Hecht and taken his files and books.

Meantime, Mitch was in the thick of it because Jeffery had asked him to mix an LP from the tapes of the last tour. Mitch felt Jeffery called him because he had no choice – Mitch had actually been on the tour and in the studio with Jimi. Mitch ploughed through a jumble of hundreds of boxes of tapes. Then he'd phoned Mo Ostin: 'I hear you have Albert Hall. Would you consider releasing them, as they are far superior to those we have here?' The reply was a definite 'No.' Eventually, with Eddie Kramer's help, *Cry of Love* came out in March 1971. Jeffery was busy 'executive producing' *Isle of Wight*. When the Estate decided to sell Jimi's share of Electric Lady Studios, Jeffery was able to fork out $240,000 and take on the balance of the Warner Brothers loan.

I felt lucky enough to be out of it. Literally. Trying to make some semblance of order out of the chaos, I fell into a regular routine – get up, go to the pub, get smashed, feel ill. Relaxing was more work than work. I took more acid, disturbed my neighbours with my looks (I wore slippers and a dressing gown to the pub in case I fell asleep, and walked barefoot down the streets of Folkestone!) and my friends and my regular bash jam sessions with Jeff Beck. But Jeff had an ulterior motive for dropping in. We'd flail away for a while, me on guitar and Jeff on bass, and then Jeff would sneak off to the kitchen for big juicy bacon sandwiches he could only dream about at home due to his lady's vegetarianism.

I kept going, but couldn't have organised myself out of a brown paper bag. Being a pop star was the end of the rainbow. And maybe the end of my life. Is there life after *Life* magazine? For rockers tired of rolling with the punches? My brain swam. Living meant little. Had Jimi reached this spot and lacked the strength to get past it?

Sometimes out of the blue, you meet someone who becomes a treasured friend. A local agent/manager, Bob Steptoe, and I had become friendly after he'd asked Mitch and me to judge a local band competition. One night after a game of pool in Birchington, he suggested a visit to a local dancehall. The band, Wild Colour (aka Tristram Shandy), featured Les Sampson on drums and Andy Keeley on guitar. Always attracted to a good drummer, Les really impressed me. He was so nervous when Bob brought him round next day. He was a plumber by trade, engaged to be married, and only nineteen. When Jeff dropped in for a play Les was speechless. Well, he knocked me out, so I proceeded to rearrange his life. (I think he's finally forgiven me.) I told him to get un-engaged and go pro. He took my advice and we started jamming together regularly, sometimes with Jeff or Norman Hale (piano). For Les it was a lot better than practising in the hallway of his family's semi-detached house. His neighbours must have been wonderful people. Or deaf. Les was fresh and enthusiastic and loud – a lifesaver to me.

My wonderful cat, Kat, lost his eye to the hounds when a hunt decided to make a shortcut of my garden. Bill, who'd stuck with me, saved Kat and pulled the Head Bastard right off his horse. This turned us into animal rights militants and we joined up with Jeff's lady, Celia Hammond (who is still working for the benefit of animals with her London-based CHAT Charity), and an anti-cruel-sports group to picket hunts and drive past the pack shouting, 'Whooo, whooo', which puts the dogs off their track. Kat got his picture in the paper.

I had to get away. I stripped my bank account and took Mum (who had been having a very rough time with her private life) on a Caribbean cruise. I partied like there was no tomorrow, played with the band, and won a tie in the talent competition.

Looking for something to smoke, I tried mime. After five stops for cigarettes the taxi driver sussed that it was grass I wanted. He took my $20 (I took his licence) and he returned with an armload wrapped in newspaper. Getting back on board ship was no problem, and as the word got round I was surrounded by curious straight people who were dying to 'see what it was like'. We'd smoke like chimneys and eat the beautiful food on the Italian boat until we couldn't move. I'd hardly eaten in four years and weighed seven and a half stone. Even with twenty-four-hour smoking by willing and determined volunteers, we couldn't finish that stash. I knew there was no chance of getting it into England and I was right – I got searched immediately upon landing at Heathrow. Somehow you never really get used to being searched. Mitch would be sarcastic and start undressing as soon as he got off the plane. I didn't like FBI guys flashing badges, calling me by name, taking my shoes off and tapping the heels. It was spooky. I duly reported my return to the police.

The film *Monterey Pop* came to Folkestone and Les dragged me to the Opening. It was warming when the audience cheered my screen appearance. And I was certainly glad of their support when the police search party stopped me as I left – they regularly hassled the 'hometown boy made good'. We were immediately surrounded by two hundred fans (mine). Aware of the odds, the police backed off. But one of them messed me around a lot before he split to Australia with funds he had accumulated on the side while on the force.

Leas Cliff Hall still had Saturday dances. Status Quo (an up and coming group) asked me to jam. The place was packed. Lights flashed at midnight, but the band played on. The crowd went nuts and the hall manager called the police and threatened to pull our plugs. I threatened to smash my guitar over his head. Status Quo never allowed jammers after that and they certainly aren't likely to ask me again.

Chandler and Jeffery were not exactly leaping forward with offers of help in sorting out the Experience mess. Finally, Jeffery rang with the words I wanted to hear: 'There's $100,000 waiting for you here. Come over and pick it up.' Music to my ears. But after catching a flight to New York and showing up at Steingarten's office, I got the bum's rush. The money wasn't exactly 'available'. It was being held up by a lawsuit. And Jeffery had already moved on.

Mitch and I asked SWW officially to represent us, and Barry Reiss, a newcomer to the firm, was put on the case. Again, I was paying lawyers to talk to lawyers, making sure that as few members of the legal profession as possible were without work. Reiss started by writing to Dicker, Roemer and Hecht for documentation proving the relationship between Mitch and me, Jimi and Yameta. Dicker said that Hillman had the relevant documents, and Reiss's second request brought the information that Hillman had now received the first letter and would send us the requested copies if he actually had the documentation. Nothing, in short, changed. Everyone was making hay. Goldstein and Gold had the Albert Hall film and a contract for it with Jimi, and Jeffery and Warner Brothers had a plan for release, but nothing could be done while Mitch and I still had claims to be met. (Remember, if you still have your ticket stub, you were promised free entry to the film!)

In New York, Jeffery's Karana Productions was run from an office staffed Joyce Roben, Stickells, Tappy Wright (ex-Animals roadie who recently sold two Hendrix guitars I didn't recognise at a Sotheby's auction), Bob Levine, and office accountant Nigel Morgan. Jeffery himself spent most of his time in London, with French excursions which regularly coincided with royalty cheque times – our LP's went gold in France. Whether or not Jeffery shared the Barclay royalties with the Estate, I can only guess, I guess no.

Reiss's efforts were fruitless. First Clinton's replied that, ' . . . all files and documents have been handed over to Goodman, Derrick and Company [working for Jeffery and the Estate on the PPX suit] and if there are any documents you require we feel sure they will have them.' Well, they might have them, but they replied to our request with 'We act for the Estate of Jimi Hendrix and so we are not in a position to supply you with any documents which may be used in litigation against the Estate.' Checkmate.

Reiss begged Hecht for an accounting and an affidavit regarding the 50/25/25 split and finally got a skeleton accounting of my expenditures deducted from an unverified earning total up to 17 September 1970. A full year gone by, and my account is empty . . .

With no alternative, I sold my house to finance Les's and my participation in a new venture – to be called Road. It was a move back towards the three-piece, loud bash sound. A jam in England had resulted in an Australian tour offer, so we felt positive. We went to Detroit – a strange place with THC and heavies in abundance – and rented a house for living and rehearsing. Atlantic and Motown sent scouts. Atlantic passed. I was glad when we decided the best thing would be a move to LA, where the whole music scene had reassembled. I sent for Bill Black to help manage us, because I expected we'd be touring soon. And then, because he couldn't keep his mouth shut and got stroppy with an immigration man, I had to post a $2,000 immigration bond for him. We tried Warners, but Mo passed, saying the group needed stronger vocals. Tom Wilson (producer of early Dylan, Simon and Garfunkel, Frank Zappa, and many, many others), then with Motown's new 'white' label, Natural Resources, liked our sound. Tom and I had been friends for a while. I thought he was a really nice guy, and he liked me because he said I sang like Dylan! By autumn, Natural Resources was ready to sign us. What a relief!

Murray was wonderful and concerned. He and Michelle took us into their own home until we got settled. He went to meetings with us when Motown started negotiations and introduced me to his lawyer, who agreed to work for 7½ per cent of anything we signed plus fees, a percentage of any other income and $50 – 100 per hour for any other business. He put us on to business managers Sterling, Salyers and Altman, who also handled Three Dog Night and Black Oak Arkansas. I asked Murray to manage us and he invited Warren Duffy to co-manage.

In New York things had ground to a complete halt. Chess again – moves and countermoves. The Estate completely stopped talking to us. Reiss filed an official claim and a 'Bill of Particulars' which outlined our demands: a split on a 50/25/25 basis of an unknown amount accrued by The Experience since the October 1966 contract, which Jeffery had cited to collect his 20 per cent. Reiss then advised the Estate lawyer, Hagood, that Mitch and I were each entitled to a third of the gross income. It must have been like putting a red flag in front of a bull! Although Jimi had often said that we should be getting equal shares, it was never agreed – not even between us. And although Mitch and I were entitled to shares of the things we'd worked on, we were not entitled to a share of *everything* Jimi had done. Upon receipt, Hagood freaked. He filed a formal rejection of my claim – 'It's not a valid debt of the Estate' – and the delays really started to stretch out.

Reiss retaliated by objecting to any payments for Mr Hendrix, who had declared himself the sole proper recipient of all funds. I didn't mind Mr Hendrix getting something to live on, but Reiss said he should wait until all the creditors were satisfied, including the taxman. The paternity attorney felt the same. Eventually Mr Hendrix was forced to borrow when the court shoved his application in with SWW's unpaid fees.

As Hillman stalled by again asking for the same authorisation we'd posted to him three months earlier, my visitor's visa ran out. I had to grovel hard to get another three months. Reiss served Are You Experienced Inc. and the Estate with a summons to court. Hagood filed notification that he was the defence lawyer. This took a month. Now Mitch and I had to cough up a large fee before the court would proceed because we weren't New York residents. Mitch had trouble with this expence, too.

By the end of 1971, Jimi's debts had been whittled down to a few basic claimants: one determined paternity suit; me and Mitch; PPX; the New York City taxman; and the 1968 Pop Music Festival. A hearing was set for 22 December, but out in LA I heard nothing and figured nothing was happening. So Road's agent introduced me to *another* lawyer, who wrote to Jeffery c/o Electric Lady and Chas c/o Stigwoods. And got ignored.

Road rented a house in the Valley to rehearse and live in – a real American house with a fireplace of glittery quartz and a sofa covered in plastic. Immigration weren't about to renew Bill's visa (it took a year to get the bond refunded), so Rod hired a Detroit friend, Victor Guy, to replace him. Everything was going great. We rehearsed, we composed and were scheduled to record. One night Les and I visited

Frank Zappa to gawp at his new space-age synthesizer. Frank's pretty straight so it was a very sober evening. We left early and started down the long flight of concrete steps. I guess I wasn't used to being sober. I missed a step and ended up at the bottom of a fifteen-foot wall. I panicked! Did I break the bottle of Vodka? It was OK. I felt nauseous and gradually my arm began to throb. Les drove. I tied my arm to my body and took a Mandrax. Next morning it didn't look or feel like just a bruise any more. Citizens Emergency Hospital were incredulous. 'How are you still conscious?' It was a very neat break, just below my left shoulder. A couple of weeks later I read in a newspaper that I was suing Frank for some enormous fee due to a cancelled tour . . . Frank called. 'What's going on?' I hadn't a clue! What tour? Seems the lawyer with the white Roller recommended by our agent had started proceedings. First he'd kindly referred me to a doctor in Santa Monica. I'd gone a few times to have my shoulder rubbed softly and heated with a lamp, and come away with a load of painkillers and downers which I distributed to Rod and Les. If I'd taken them as prescribed I'd have been comatose.

In order to play I had to hold the guitar nearly behind me so my left fingers, now strapped to my right shoulder, could reach the fingerboard. I had plenty of time to sit and get wrecked and babble to anyone, interested or not, about my troubles. Coke and heroin were readily available now, Valium was holding it's own, and Quaaludes were the latest trendy pill. But I already had a Mandrax habit. At least the arm earned me a three-month visa extension. I settled into LA, feeling like an old-timer in that transient town. When I felt optimistic, I reckoned I could wade through the whole muddle. But when I felt down, everything swamped me. I counteracted this by stopping thinking whenever possible – for days at a time, then weeks, eventually even months.

My twenty-fifth birthday found me mending my arm and hoping. Others were trying to piece themselves together again, too. The last few years had ripped up a lot of musicians. Faces drummer Mick Waller, who had been messed around over payment, went back to college, studied law, sued, and won! Mitch had played with Terry Reid and Jack Bruce and now joined forces with guitarist April Lawton in Ramatam. He worried to me that his playing was getting a bit rusty (a musician has got to keep playing) and admitted that he hesitated to get back into the tour scene. He'd rather play in a relaxed way than be Number One. Mitch was still depressed from his months in the studio being pressurised to think like Jeffery: 400 boxes equals 400 LPs. He hadn't been allowed to scrap the bad tracks, and new recording techniques made it possible to layer one track on top of another and make even rubbish vaguely listenable. Mitch was determined not to put out any shit – it was his reputation, too. Billy Cox, recovered from the horrors, moved to England for an LP called *Nitro Function* with Robert Tarrant and Char Vinnedge.

January 1972 – Happy New Year. With *Rainbow Bridge* and *Hendrix in the West* out, the Warners accounts showed $323,622 due even after paying another $14,391 to Electric Lady in session costs. Track Records started a 'Backtrack Series' featuring The Experience. Phillips in Holland and Barclay brought out LPs. By February I was worried, 'Why hasn't Jeffery come forward with an affidavit to help us? Why this runaround?' Busy? But not too busy to nip to Nassau to cash another $25,000 cheque. And he'd changed accountants again – to Schecter and Epstein this time.

I faithfully did my 'walk up and down the wall with the fingertips' exercises to help my arm heal. Road, as Plate Productions, signed with Motown on Saint Valentine's Day. It seemed a fair contract. I only objected to Motown's absolute insistence on owning our publishing; but not wanting to rock the boat, I signed, in spite of my affiliation with Schroeders. Shit! Contracts were getting long. This one had twenty pages. One look and my mind just blanked out, boggled by the sheer bulk of the legalese. Am I alone in my horror at the sight of a sheaf of scarcely punctuated small print? How can I understand that? I've got to hire someone to tell me what it says. Then what happens if, after being billed for many hours spent in discussion with the 'other side', you still get a bad contract? Fairly recently a very well-known group were presented with a contract. Both sides put their 'teams' of lawyers on it and for a few days they attempted to thrash out the meaning. The legal bills totalled £25,000, and they never agreed over the contract's meaning. If you don't understand it, don't sign it. Beware of clauses like: 'In lieu of making payment directly, make payment to the manager/production company c/o somebody else's address . . . and all payments so made shall be deemed made to you . . . ' That means somebody else gets your income. Salyers, my business manager, was thorough and intelligent, but it still took over a month to OK. We got our $15,000 advance, but after expences, percentages, taxes and all, I pocketed about $1,000.

At long last we got into the studio. Les and I only had until 10 April to get out of the country. The minute we walked into the studio, the LA Musician's Union got heavy – pay out to join up or get out. We joined. In LA the MU is capable of pressurising associated unions. They can close a club by keeping the truck-driver's union from delivering booze. They can stop engineers, soundmen, and lighting guys from dealing with you, thus preventing you working. I've heard redeeming stories about the LA Union coming through for members, but most branches don't do much more than collect dues. Anyway, it meant more time wasted. The three of us got together with Warren and split an ounce of excellent pharmaceutical coke. It cost $1,000 but we finished the LP in four days. Rod finished his coke in a weekend, Les in a week and mine lasted two months. *Road* is definitely a coke LP. Even Tom Wilson was well into it. I have to feel like raving to listen to it now.

Les and I even found time before the coke ran out to record with ex-Spirit guitarist Randy California. Randy was like Pigpen in *Peanuts* – he only had to enter a room and a mess formed around him: flakes of tobacco, ash, cigarette burns, bits of skins, lumps of half-eaten food. During a non-stop-crazed fourteen hours in a Valley studio, working as Clit MacTorius (me) and Henry Manchovitz (Les), we put down tracks and put up lines as fast as we could go. Three spaced tracks ended up on Randy's *Kapt. Kopter and the Fabulous Twirly Birds*.

April: time up. On my way out of the country I stopped off in Miami to see Mitch, his wife Lynn (Suzanne's friend) and their baby. Aisha, a lovely but very precocious little toddler who gobbled your drink if you happened to set it down. Ramatam had filled out with Mike Pinera (ex-Iron Butterfly), Russ Smith, and Tommy Sullivan. Miami was the same as LA: all madness, no sleep, coconuts and coke at dawn by the water's edge, and liquid meals. Neither Ramatam nor the marriage lasted long.

In comparison, Mum's cottage in the small, unspoiled seaside village of Dymchurch, Kent, seemed trapped in a timewarp. Spring in an unheated house in damp England was refreshing after LA, and the countryside was rejuvenating. I went for long walks along the pebble beaches, bought winkles from the stalls on the pier, made the rounds of the old pubs hidden in the twisty lanes of Romney Marsh. It had been nearly a year since I'd been home, and I hadn't realised how homesick I was. The two months' stay did me good.

Back in the thick of it, Salyers extracted our lawyer from our affairs because we didn't really need him. The US tax people pounced because, like Jimi, I'd mistakenly thought Hecht had filed my 1969 return. Salyers grovelled for me, making my dependence on accountants the excuse. He wondered where my songwriting income was going and found out that Schroeders had paid my 1971 income to

Joint. I don't know where this income ended up.

A new champion then arrived on the scene. Publicist Sharon Lawrence had been a friend of Jimi's since 1968. She had got The Experience some interviews, testified on Jimi's behalf at the Toronto trial, and generally managed to help out. Her hope was to make things right for Jimi now that he wasn't around to do it for himself. She knew basically what had gone down and saw in me an ally, although she disapproved of my spaced-out approach just as she had disapproved of Jimi's. Her immediate concern was to stop Warners from cleaning up on the Jimi Hendrix films being assembled. Her idea was that the profits should go to a charity. The powers-that-be, however, were eager to strike while the commercial iron was hot. They intended to go ahead despite the fact that Mitch and I had a claim on the earnings from such a project. There was a lot of footage of us and, of course, we had played the music. Sharon had a meeting with Branton and the producer to check things out.

In a long letter, Sharon told me that Branton knew that Mitch and I had filed a suit in New York, and encouraged me to fight hard for the rights of the band. The longer I delayed, it seemed, the more difficult it would be for me to win. Her letter was full of advice, but despite the pep talk the years had taken their toll on me. I felt I was 'organised' if I could get from one end of the day to the other. I didn't even realise how scattered I was getting, how the days were flying past. What was all this about hurrying up before it was too late? Surely if things were urgent, Reiss would be aware of it?

Soon after I received Sharon's letter, Hagood answered our complaint by simply denying all of our claims and asking for a dismissal and award of costs to them. We denied Hagood's denial, so he demanded to see documents and his nit-picking queries ate up time and patience. He asked, for example: What is your name? What group were you in? Unless answers are furnished within the specified time, we will move to stop you from ever showing any evidence.

We asked Hecht for our accounts, but he had turned them over to the Estate and ' . . . therefore I cannot supply you with anything'. Dicker could no longer supply Reiss with the Yameta accounts. Eighteen months after Jimi's death and we had got absolutely nowhere.

I was adapting badly to being back in LA. I dreaded waking up. Each day brought new worries. I put them off, but they got bigger and closed in. Everyone expected me to understand so much. Where are my pills? What's all this about more lawyers? What about SWW? Let's have a drink. How can there be a problem when I'm right. I earned the money, how can anyone take it? Though I knew that everything Sharon said was true, admitting it, even to myself, was too much. For the first time it began to dawn on me how precarious my position was. Oh, God, just led Road play and make some music to drown all this shit out, I thought. But our agent never got past the Motown secretaries, who treated him like a bill collector. Les and I rented a flat where Tim Rose lived, after Murray pointed out that the house rent was whizzing through my capital. It was better. Our manageress, Barbara, was cheerfully helpful; and her boyfriend, Tom, made the best-ever morning-after Bloody Marys. We started rehearsing at Dress Revue Studios.

While I was standing around with nowhere to go, Jeffery was quietly and efficiently taking care of business, getting a credit as executive producer on all the Hendrix product coming out, and setting up a new company, this time in the Netherlands Antilles, to take collection of the Barclay royalties upon contract expiration in October 1973. With Schecter, Jeffery set up Suns and Rainbows (Company No. 6019), c/o Maduro and Criels Bank, c/o Curacao International Trust Co. N.V., Handelskade 28, Curacao, Netherland Antilles – a trust company managed by a Dutchman and with directors from Curacao and Surinam. Suns and Rainbows is managed by one of its subsidiaries, Curacao Corporation Company, first established in 1958 to represent, manage and promote the interests of third parties (this information is largely the result of the work of Caesar Glebbeek of the Jimi Hendrix Information Centre in Amsterdam).

Jeffery must have figured that I would try to cause trouble – that is, make my case – by trying to bring in my own set of West Coast lawyers to look into matters and fight my corner. I knew, after all, a fair amount about the way Yameta worked and was certain that the bulk of tour earnings had been processed through Yameta. Stickells was always wiring gig money to Nassau. The last thing Steingarten, Wedeen and Weiss wanted was for Yameta to be dragged into a lawsuit.

Reiss left Steingarten, Wedeen and Weiss to become director of business affairs at CBS and my case was thrown on to the desk of newcomer Theodore Rosenblatt. He started from scratch, writing the same old letters requesting documents and trying to figure out what the fuck had happened.

In July, Hagood applied to have his commission paid before tax payments were made. In the nine months leading up to this, $1,000,445 had come into the Estate and with $802,769 paid out thus far, he wanted his cut of the balance.

The legal clock ticked by and I was in danger of being barred by the

Statute of Limitations. I had only three months left or my claim would be struck off. I opted out of seeing Klein partly because he was in New York – which was crazy because the suit would have to be brought there – and partly because of the bad press he'd had after hustling for The Beatles and the Rolling Stones, the general gist being that although he had recovered funds for both groups, he had also come out, in the view of many, a bit too OK himself. In my paranoid state, I suspected him of working for Warners. I was considering Billy Gaff when Sharon came up with Michael Shapiro.

Young and eager, he agreed to take on the case.

Chapter Eight

Redding vs the World

It is quite a three-pipe problem.
SIR ARTHUR CONAN DOYLE

Never take anything for granted.
BENJAMIN DISRAELI

AND THAT was how I found myself sitting in yet another lawyer's office, cool and detached from the sweltering LA July day. Wall-to-wall carpeting muffled the office noises, and down below Beverly Hills rushed by. I relaxed for a moment. And then, yet again, I tried to explain the situation to a person who only vaguely knew the music scene and, though he'd heard of the group, didn't even know the names of our albums.

Even though I couldn't fully appreciate Sharon's advice and help then, her outsider's perspective, drive and willingness to come to meetings with me were invaluable. I doubt I could have summoned the optimism to have organised another lawyer without her. My (fading) dream was for Jeffery or Chas to suddenly pop up saying, 'Finally settled the mess with Nassau and PPX! Here's everything you're owed, and there'll be no problem about the 25 per cent in future.'

A very major problem was that I could not afford to litigate this to the end. I couldn't even stay in the country long enough to complete it. To do this case properly – even twenty years ago – I'd have needed at least $100,000 for fees and expenses. The decisive factor was that Mickey offered to do it for 25 per cent of the gross receipts under $500,000 and 20 per cent of any sum over that amount. I'd pay the costs too, but he promised not to spend any more than $25 without my approval. I signed a retainer letter.

Mickey summarised my case: I recalled signing an agreement with

Jeffery and Chandler in 1966, giving them 20 per cent and the right to negotiate for me. I had never seen any further contracts or had accountings, except for the last tour when I'd been charged for expences – including Jimi's legal fees – on a percentage basis.

Mickey realised right away that there was much more – I'd hardly even considered foreign royalties, or TV and film appearance income, appearance rights, or merchandising (posters, programmes, T-shirts). He also saw implications in the fact that SWW had represented Jimi, Mitch, me, Jeffery, Chas, and the various publishing entities. Michael Hecht, too, seemed to have represented everyone and everything. Mickey's idea was to jump in with 'a real motherfucker' of a complaint and threaten to file it with the court unless the 'bad guys' started to co-operate. Warner Brothers were obviously going to take the position that they had paid X, so I should look to X if I wanted to complain. Still, they wanted my consent for the Hendrix film and so would have to deal directly with me on some level. Mickey promptly threatened producer Joe Boyd with a lawsuit if they used my voice, image, music or any reference to me without my consent. Mickey felt strongly about the profiteering going on from Hendrix's relics, and felt the situation cried out for a moral resolution. He felt getting my royalties might be the closest anyone could get to changing the injustices going down.

Firstly, Mickey tried to help Les and I with Road. We'd returned from England with new visa stamps and found Rod sitting in his new Malibu beach house with his head in the clouds. The expected (and prayed for) tour was non-existent because he wanted only major venues at \$25-50,000 per night. I kept saying, 'We're not stars, Rod. No one knows us.' Motown wouldn't even put us on tour with Marvin Gaye. Rod eluded our demands for rehearsals. He played golf instead. Finally he came by to say that he had thought of the name Road and therefore owned the name and the group. But he hadn't registered it. So in case Les and I organised some work, Mickey put an ad in the paper saying that Les and I were doing business as Road.

Road managed one dreadful gig at Kindel's Back Door in Santa Ana. If we could only half-fill a small club, how could we fill a hall? It was such an embarrassing night. I hadn't made the transition to frontman at all, and Rod gradually disappeared behind his bank of guitar gadgets, spending most of the set with his back to the audience fiddling with his knobs. I knew it was over. Murray tore up the management agreement. At a loose end, Les and I kept rehearsing until we couldn't afford the fees.

Mickey suggested enlisting the help of an associate who practiced in Washington DC. Mark Sandground came to LA and the retainer letter we'd signed became defunct. Sandground insisted on a cash deposit of $10,000, to be credited to their account pending the outcome of the case. The retainer was 90 per cent of everything I had left. Mark listed a few costs I'd be expected to cover – extensive depositions, accounting fees, professional witnesses, travel and transportation, phone calls, telegrams, printing of briefs and regular court costs. The permission to spend level went up to $100. I signed it.

Back at SWW, probably assuming my case was on the verge of settlement, nobody had bothered to deal with Hagood's incessant demands for documents, which put me in a dodgy position legally. They had so rarely contacted me that I never thought of them as my lawyers. Only when I got their bill for $3,500 did Mickey discover that I was 'signed' to another lawyer.

Experience records sold like hot cakes. Two were now among Reprise's all time best sellers. In Europe, Jeff Kruger's Ember Records was doing well with *Experience* (Albert Hall) – Jimi Hendrix, Noel Redding and Mitch Mitchell, produced by Steve Gold and Michael Jeffery for Pomegranate Productions and Polydor Productions through Entertainments International and distributed by Polydor. With their film stopped, G&G began suing Warners for using some of their Albert Hall tapes to fill out *Hendrix in the West* (our San Diego show). Warners passed the buck, 'We got the tapes from Jeffery – sue him.'

Like Jimi, I was very easily intimidated in any confrontation. Business types with their high-pressure presence and gruff, slightly aggressive manner put me right off. At all costs, I'd avoid an awkward scene. Mickey forced me to phone Weiss. After I'd used up all the usual pleasantries, Weiss himself finally had to say: 'I understand you want to fire me?' I quickly said yes and changed the subject to the weather. I wanted to pick up the case files, but he said he'd be out of town. I asked for them to be left for collection, but he declined, saying he'd have to talk to his partner first because of his involvement with Jeffery. It was difficult because I knew he could be an important witness. He said goodbye with, 'Call me. You owe me money and I want to be paid.'

Prior to this call, he'd told Sandground that SWW was legally my attorney and representative in the suit. He also said he was Jeffery's attorney. Weiss warned Mark that there was very little in writing to prove my claim. He explained that he'd never filed suit against Warners because I had no agreement with Warners. Everything came to Jimi first (on paper if not in practice) before distribution.

Shapiro flew to New York and saw some of the files but was not permitted to make copies. Among other things he saw a letter to Weiss in which Jeffery had written, 'I want to help Noel and Mitch and I want to testify on behalf of the 50/25/25.' Weiss demanded his fees to date ($3,500) and Shapiro agreed to pay him from the settlement. While Hecht claimed that not all the foreign royalties were being paid to the Estate, Weiss insisted that they were and that 100 per cent of the stock of Are You Experienced, Inc. was owned by Jimi.

Shapiro had a plan of attack and ran around like crazy, gathering information, doing more in two months than Steingarten, Wedeen and Weiss had done in two years, and trying to make the 1 September deadline. There were four main earnings sources to be explored: publishing (via Schroeders which administered Joint Music); domestic royalties; foreign royalties; concerts.

Mark's job was to socialise on the East Coast. He started with the Estate. He met Howard and noted the firm's attitude, 'They distrust all whites.' Adopting the position that 'Redding and Mitchell were side men for Jimi Hendrix', Howard's proof was that we were all paid scale for the recording sessions and 'generously' for all personal appearances. (We were never paid session fees.) Howard likened the recording sessions to Mitchell and Redding being 'like members of the Tommy Dorsey Orchestra'. He indicated that 'these sorts of persons' would not receive special royalty shares so long as they got scale for sessions. It's nice to know that the whole Tommy Dorsey Orchestra chipped in a pro rata share of the recording costs and all other expences, and composed material and wrote all the charts and so on in return for scale. Must have made Tommy very happy. Mark noticed that we sometimes recorded 'off the clock' without filing union contracts (we never filed contracts) and in those cases no one was paid scale.

Howard insisted that the 50/25/25 agreement between the 'Jimi Hendrix people' had never been put on paper except for the 1970 tour proposal and that Jimi was the sole owner of Are You Experienced Inc., though no stock had ever been issued. He delivered the message that Branton would not settle without documentary proof of our 50/25/25 deal and that the Estate would go ahead with the film because I'd either signed releases for past events through individual promoters or I'd given Jeffery the right to sign for me. Alternatively, they'd just use the Tommy Dorsey angle. Regarding Yameta, the Estate reckoned they had a claim, but wouldn't pursue it due to the amount of work involved. They weren't planning a claim against SWW, but they weren't going to pay the administration fees either. Mark suggested that we try to cooperate, for everyone's benefit.

Now it was Hagood's turn, and he explained that the Estate's current deal with Jeffery for foreign royalties was 50/50 because Jeffery had 'some special European arrangement'. About $170,000 in royalties were being held up by the London PPX mess, where PPX was pushing for much more than in the US settlement.

Mark met Weiss and the first thing he did was try to make Mark nervous by suggesting that I would find myself in tax trouble. Weiss insisted that I had re-signed to Jeffery after Jimi's death – and I could well have – but offered no contract. Weiss felt that by promoting our tours, he'd saved The Experience at least 5 per cent. But as far as I was concerned, the missing words 'the world' in the first PPX release had tied up my share of the funds in English litigation.

Mark met and liked Reiss, finding him earnest and helpful. He admitted being present at several meetings agreeing to the split, and said that my English accountant had also referred to the 50/25/25 deal. Could we play this to the hilt? Reiss thought the Estate would suggest a settlement even though they were insisting I was a 'sideman'.

Jeffery was relaxing at his country home in Woodstock, well out of the line of fire, but agreed to meet Mark on his own turf – Electric Lady Studios. Mark's appraisal was 'a cool, cool character about forty, dressed Mod with long hair. Probably a very intelligent man.' According to Mike, Yameta was the villain. He claimed they owed us about $90,000. He claimed he wanted to help me with the Estate, but suggested that I might not remember things correctly because I was a musician. Then he proceeded with the story that I'd left the group in 1968, pointing to my absence from some LPs – *Band of Gypsies* and the posthumous *Cry of Love* and *Rainbow Bridge* (I'm on one track). Jeffery said Jimi had been emotionally upset and had this feeling that he had to do an all-black thing. Since I was white, I had found myself replaced by Barry (*sic*) Cox. Jeffery said that Hillman had been hired after Eric Burdon's lawyer had discovered him while looking for an offshore tax deal. He agreed that the first Warner Brothers contract was with Yameta for the services of the (whole) Jimi Hendrix Experience. He suggested seeing Leon Dicker, because although Price Waterhouse hadn't found any Yameta assets, Jeffery swore there must be some and Hillman should know where.

Jeffery admitted to co-operating with Howard and the Estate. And, yes, there was a 'special deal' on the foreign records both before and after Jimi's death. Steingarten, during his spell as administrator of the Estate, had authorised Jeffery to re-negotiate the foreign deals. Steingarten had also agreed, on behalf of the Estate, to pay Mitch and me. Jeffery said the Estate had confirmed this in writing – a 50/50 split between Jeffery and The Experience. On a $100,000 advance this should have brought me only $12,500. Just what were those 'special arrangements' that got Jeffery such a huge percentage? Jeffery then complained that Howard had got tough and forced him to cut his fee to 40 per cent. After cutting Mitch and me out, it would be 60 per cent for the Estate and 40 per cent for Jeffery. End of meeting.

A lot to consider, even if we did get a thirty-day extension.

I was asked to give a deposition (testimony), a stalling tactic as far as I was concerned. One thing had become quite clear: I had signed a general agreement granting Jeffery the right to sign for all deals and Jeffery had gone ahead and made deals which were obviously more beneficial to him than to The Experience. The current Warner Brothers situation revealed it baldly: Jeffery had granted the rights to make the film, but I hadn't. Even if Jeffery had my rights to grants, they couldn't be given without some payment.

My view, unencumbered by legalese, was that as no stock was issued in Are You Experienced Inc., dollars sunk into Electric Lady Studio were dollars in which I had a 25 per cent interest. If half the money used to buy Electric Lady Studios came from Are You Experienced Inc. via Jimi, then I should be entitled to a 12 per cent share in the studio. If no stock had been issued, then Mitch and I had just as much right to the company as the Estate did. My case would have been stronger if Mitch had come in with me, but he was sticking with Steingarten, Wedeen and Weiss. Grey areas abounded.

I was dividing my time between two thankless jobs: employer of lawyers and member of a no longer existing pop group. In Los Angeles I would open my door to be met with, 'May I speak with Noel Redding?' My response: 'Hold on and I'll see if he's busy.' On one occasion, summoned to Warner Brothers, I asked Les to fill in. No one even noticed. While I couldn't be recognised beyond the Experience image, dead Jimi had several living impersonators. Maybe this is what they mean by the 'legend who never dies'.

The entire summer had wasted away. Oh, sure, I'd been to a million press receptions, thanks to Sharon. Susan Pile had supplied access to film premieres. Mickey's lovely wife, Bonnie, had ins to the posh charity parties. Though LA abounds in lovely ladies, getting fucked became a rather smaller portion of my life than getting fucked around and fucked up. But worst of all, musically nothing had happened since our stillborn Motown LP. Les and I needed to play, it was our life, our sanity – besides the nightlife at the Whisky, that is. We tried finding another guitarist and rehearsed with Warren Klein from the Fraternity of Man (*Don't Bogart That Joint*). But we couldn't afford regular wages.

It was worse for Les watching his dreams crumble for the first time. He got into coke to buck him up when he was feeling bad. Not a good sign.

I spent much of the summer withdrawing from Mandrax after years of regular usage. In July, I stopped cold, just felt I had to. For three long months I woke several times every single night covered in sweat and stuck inside of terrible nightmares. When awake, every fibre of my body was at top tension. I chewed my nails up to my elbows. Relaxing was impossible with the endless muscle spasms that convinced me I had appendicitis. For the first time I was forced to consider the cost of being sick in America with no medical insurance, no bank account, no job. I felt terrible. If it got worse, I'd have to fly home to be hospitalised. I wondered if life was worth living without pills. The waves of anxiety drove me up the wall. I huddled in the flat and tried to counteract the nebulous fears and anxieties with more alcohol – moving from vodka to brandy, and most particularly Hiram Walkers flavoured brandies – apricot, peach, blackberry . . . At least one large bottle per day, plus beers. Luckily, in spite of the coke continually being offered, between the building's sauna bath which Les and I repaired and the excellent grass in LA, my muscles eased up and my appetite started to come back. I craved shepherds pie, smoked haddock, bitter beer. I started to learn how to survive and cope without tranquillisers and sleepers.

By September, I was pleading on my knees with Mickey to get me out of the Motown contract. 'Once that's done, I'm out of the profession,' I told him. I was tired of sitting in hotels and rented flats waiting for something to happen. I couldn't afford to go on, either, with the lawsuit to support. The kernel of panic I'd kept hidden grew. This was the feeling that I had been avoiding by getting smashed. And I felt responsible for getting Les into this mess. He'd given up everything stable he had to join this venture which had trashed his life and left him unhappy and confused. And I had visa troubles again. And my overdue retainer fee needed paying. Luckily, I had paid my US taxes, and Salyers even got me a $2,000 rebate, just in time to get me home. Sharon said she had business in London so came with me to Mum's.

First, Mickey and Mark accompanied me on a trip to my London bank where it took forever to withdraw the $10,000 retainer fee. I'd never had this much cash in my hands before. It freaked me. As I passed it over, I knew this was it. The last chance. I hadn't a thing left to sell, including myself. I also knew the case looked like a million dead ends, and I battled not to lose hope.

Next we visited Hillman in search of the elusive Yameta assets which would justify a suit. Hillman wasn't very helpful. He talked about boats in the Bahamas and half-heartedly said he'd look for helpful documents. But he did agree to make an appointment for Mickey with Sir Guy to see the cheque ledger and find out what funds had been channelled to Jeffery.

Harold Davidson of MAM Agency was next. Davidson hadn't done anything wrong, but simply didn't want to be involved because his company traded publicly. He suggested that the crook was Jeffery and that the good guys were Chas and Weiss (also his lawyer). Davidson said he'd always warned that the Yameta tax plan was dangerous, but his advice had fallen on deaf ears. He'd never understood why the group had come begging while regularly earning huge sums. To help, Davidson gave us eleven pages of early statements showing a lot of activity with Yameta and Jeffery and Chandler. At least it showed one thing – Hillman had been mistaken when he'd said no money from public appearances had ever gone to Yameta.

Mickey called it 'wearing more than one hat'. Rather than merely taking a commission, Jeffery had also scored as producer, taking separate percentages directly from the record sales.

Even though we were making some progress, and despite an extension of the deadline, it was heavy going. We had to work our way through the tedious and trivial questions in Hagood and Howard's bill of particulars, a task Steingarten, Wedeen and Weiss had managed to ignore. Shapiro quoted Hecht's records showing my share in expences and my right to an accounting from Are You Experienced Inc., as well as evidence that the settlement to PPX had been shared out. Now we were in a position to ask some serious questions of the Estate: how much have you got from all the record companies involved? How much tax is being demanded? Are you aware that Steingarten, Wedeen and Weiss and the Estate signed a contract with Jeffery dealing with collection and payment of foreign royalties? Have you executed any contracts regarding the film and did they relate to Redding? Do you have any documents relating to Are You Experienced Inc.? Because we had to file all this in New York, I had to hire a New York lawyer. At that point I was supporting three lawyers in three states as well as one in London for my divorce.

There were more delays imposed by Steingarten, Wedeen and Weiss and Mitch, and then a strange letter arrived, c/o a forwarding address that was three years out of date. It was from (what else) a lawyer, Rosenblatt, at Steingarten, Wedeen and Weiss. In it I was duly informed that Jeffery was exercising his option for my services under the 11 October 1966 agreement – as 'reaffirmed on 20 May 1970' – and wanted to extend the agreement for a further two years. On top of that, he claimed a five-year extension on the publishing agreement between me and Chas (11 October 1966, that landmark date again) which had subsequently been assigned to Jeffery. I was equally flabbergasted and furious by the news, but Mickey thought it really put the icing on the cake for a conflict-of-interest case.

Mickey hoped that the Estate would soften its isolationist stance as he was very keen to find out who they thought were the good guys and the bad guys in the story. He maintained that it was mad for the guys who'd made all the money to be fighting each other while those who had unfairly profited sat back and had a good laugh, and he was sure that he could convince the Estate of my entitlements.

It was a good attitude, but Hagood and Howard responded by getting crankier. They weren't into Shapiro's sincere 'let us all help each other' approach. They were happy to accept whatever documents we offered, but offered none in return. They wouldn't give an inch. Our gesture's only value was in buying time to complete answers to the interrogatories.

Hagood basically demanded that we prove our case, knowing that we didn't have access to the material we needed. The Estate's plan to depose me (legal grilling) on 10 October depressed Mark. Settlement hopes faded as the court date approached.

The Motown situation wouldn't disappear. When we'd signed with Natural Resources, Motown had agreed to handle our immigration problems and work papers, to cover recording and rehearsal costs, and to spend up to $100,000 promoting product. It didn't happen. I saw Tom Wilson many times. Tom would say, 'Great,' and nothing would happen. Our relationship with Motown steadily deteriorated. It was October before they met us and admitted that their delay had put their rights in jeopardy; but they refused to make a decision about letting us out of our contract. In a half-hearted effort to save face, Motown booked a session in November. We were advised not to do it, as we were on our way out. In the end (about January 1973) I had to give up all my rights to all royalties before they'd let me out.

Mickey took over my management. The growing thing of the early seventies was the 'Supergroup' – stray names put together and signed for huge advances. He introduced me to Elektra Records's Russ Miller, who gave me session time for four tracks with Les, using John Hobbs on (excellent) piano. The only trouble was the same as usual – lack of strong vocals. In fact very little vocal at all. They passed.

This is why I always tell aspiring musicians that it's important to learn to sing early and become relaxed at it. Not only will it give you more insight into accompanying a song instead of playing on top of it (and under, around and through it), but if things get tough, you can work on your own. You may be the greatest guitarist in the world, but most listeners relate to a voice first. Many who couldn't relate to Jimi's guitar work could relate to his vocal tone and his relaxed style of singing.

Another splodge of LPs came out. These releases were thrown together pretty thoughtlessly. The quality was nearly as bad as on bootlegs. Stickells, now managing Electric Lady Studios, said, 'There won't be much more after this. We have taken the best stuff. But if someone wants to release an album of jams there is nothing we can do about it. Our LP is *War Heroes*'. I assume by 'our' he meant Jeffery, who was still getting his producer's percentage. Working with John Jansen, Eddie Kramer produced both *Hendrix in the West* and *War Heroes*. I'm on both. At that point Eddie quit because his producer's agreement had been an oral one. Only one more LP would come out of the studio – *Loose Ends* was mixed and produced by Alex Trevor during 1973 for a February 1974 release.

Mickey felt optimistic at our 'progress', though I didn't think the snail-like pace really merited the description. The planned complaint against Warners should have been simple, but I couldn't afford to post the bond necessary or pay the expences involved in getting a temporary restraining order to keep Warners from paying the Estate – which was exactly what needed to be done.

If we deposed Jeffery immediately we could start proceedings. If he denied he had the right to receive various Experience funds, then he would be convicted by his own words. If he claimed the right to receive them, then we could point out that he must owe money to his clients. The relationships seemed incestuous. Steingarten represented Jimi, Mitch and I. Weiss represented Jeffery and worked with him on promotions. Jeffery represented Jimi, Mitch and I. The firm had represented me in a suit against the Estate, and a company set up for the band by the firm. In a position like this, who do you complain to if you feel something's wrong? And something must have been, for the legal fees were paid, the management was paid, but the group was not.

The whole mess seemed ready to blow up. Mickey needed to cash in on any lawsuit as soon as possible to get some payment in. I was broke. Hagood cancelled the October depositions and was elusive about when he could make it. He now positively refused to go in with us against Yameta because of 'conflicting interests'. Perhaps, and understandably, he was waiting to see what Shapiro could unearth in Nassau, a trip delayed for a month. Arriving in Nassau, Shapiro was given only twenty-four hours' stay. He found Sir Guy to be a classic British colonial type, but his residual sense of fair play allowed Shapiro to have a quick look at selected files, in particular ones dealing with the Warner Brothers settlement payments. Shapiro also managed to get copies of cheques and statements from accounts used occasionally by Jeffery. The basic problem, however, was trying to sue Yameta when – according to Sir Guy – there were no records of income, only certain expenditures. The accounting and banking laws of the Bahamas made finding anything else virtually impossible. In sum, the opposition had the documents and the income; we had a few papers and the prospect of a long, expensive court case with no funds to sustain it. We feared that our inquiries had tipped Jeffery to our course of action, but there wasn't much we could do to change that. Mark laid out our thoughts to Hagood in yet another attempt to get Mitch, me and the Estate together for an accounting action. We offered the Estate access to the files we had accumulated. All we wanted was my percentage, nothing more. In response, Hagood and Howard point blank denied our requests to see accounts of my earnings on the grounds that I hadn't yet proved any entitlement to an accounting.

Mickey tackled Mo Ostin at Warner Brothers and asked for statements which would give us some indication of what to ask for in a settlement, while reminding him that the only other way to approach the matter would be to try to block all royalty payments from Warner Brothers. Mickey hoped that Warner Brothers would wish to avoid getting dragged into a public mess which would result in little more than what could be accomplished through co-operation. Warner Brothers finally obliged by giving us copies of 1970-1 statements, but nothing more.

At the end of October, and not a whole lot further along in the progress stakes, Mickey hustled me some cash by re-signing me to Schroeders. The new contract included a 5 per cent royalty to him on any new material. After paying off expenses to date, I had only $1,500, barely enough to get out of the country.

Mickey sent Weiss a draft release document which Weiss rejected as inadequate as a 'general release'. In his letter, Weiss said that he had represented The Experience as a group, but not me individually, except in my claim against the Estate. He went on to boast that he had saved The Experience 'substantial sums' by negotiating favourable concert terms and agents' fees. He described how he had met Jeffery in 1967 and me at 'some concert', but stated that he had nothing to do with the October 1966 agreement. He then complained that he had been incredibly patient in waiting for me to sign the release for the film, and had co-operated with Mark in the case against the Estate – in effect he was asking what all the fuss was about. His letter ended typically enough with a claim for $282.92 in disbursements.

This letter pissed Mickey off no end, and he fired one back saying that new information had been found relating to Yameta accountings for July 1968, which showed that funds had been sent to Weiss. Needless to say nothing was sent on to me. Did Weiss represent me at this time? Or Jeffery or Chandler? Mickey also asked whether during this period and on 20 May 1970, 'certain contract modifications' were agreed at Weiss's offices. Then Mickey dangled the cherry of me signing the release if he got satisfactory answers.

A month later an imperious and indignant reply came from Weiss. He repeated that he had never represented me individually, and said that the reason I hadn't received any money from the July 1968 transaction was that I wasn't a party to this deal. He refused to answer the question about the May 1970 negotiations because the group 'was disbanded in 1969'. He said he was too busy to engage in a lengthy exchange of letters, but agreed to meet Mickey in New York. And he repeated his demand that I sign the release without further ado.

Mickey was enraged. Mark cooled him off. We badly needed support from the firm, since their testimony was bound to be crucial in any court case. And they still represented Mitch, whose claim was basically the same as mine.

Hagood and Howard were waiting for the court's reaction to our requests for documents and accounts. In New York, you have to establish your right to an accounting with an interlocutory judgement before you can see the accounts. The court sided with Hagood and Howard, and this meant that we couldn't get the information we required from anyone until after a trial to establish our rights.

Our New York attorney felt the judge was wrong because we had so many other causes of action pending on those documents, but any appeal would take too long and require too much money. If we could prove our rights, perhaps with oral testimony, we could get access to the accounts before any trial, and we could add 'unjust enrichment' to the original complaint.

No recompense for money from my account spent by Jimi, no recompense for legal fees I'd paid for Jimi, or paid for this suit, no recompense for money advanced to Jimi which should have been divided between the three of us, no recompense for gig earnings belonging to all of us which he may have spent. How Mitch fared is his story.

End of November and as Booker T had long ago reminded everyone, Time is Tight. Shapiro ran around with the Elektra tapes, trying for a deal. Atlantic passed, not too surprising given the vast fortune they hadn't made with Fat Mattress. I only had a couple of

weeks remaining on my visa. England had been nothing but hassle
since I'd 'made good'. Non-English-speaking countries were out of
the question. I liked the idea of Ireland – a mild climate and a relaxed
attitude to time – and I managed to arrange to rent a cottage in
Rosscarbery, County Cork, and started packing for the 14 December
deadline. Meanwhile, I bumped into Neville Chesters – now reco-
vered from meth madness and working for Emerson, Lake and
Palmer's Manticore Records which had signed American guitarist
Snuffy Walden and bassist Al Roberts. I suggested Les to them and
Stray Dog was born. After a two-album career, Les was stuck in the
States starving and getting experienced until 1975. On my way out of
the States, Hagood and Howard agreed to take my deposition on 14
December, but true to form they cancelled at the last minute. Goodbye
America, Land of Litigation.

Twenty-four hours later I was standing with swans and gulls gazing at
the Atlantic from the West Cork point of view. The effect of the Gulf
Stream was not readily apparent. It was easily fifty degrees colder than
California as Carol, who had come with me from LA, and I stood
shrouded in the heavy mist of a 'soft' day. Other differences included
no central heating, no films or concerts to attend, one radio and one
TV station with limited broadcasting hours . . . Suffering from media
withdrawal, culture shock, and from having barely two coins to rub
together, we just had to wait, huddled together in Joan and Ray's
Carbery Arms, drinking and staring at the few hours of black and white
TV – and some test colour tranmissions – every evening. Luckily
drinking is an accepted pastime in Ireland – and in the aftermath of LA
we were well able to compete. Irish brandy now, and real Guinness (18
pence a pint), which bears no comparison to the stuff exported in
bottles or brewed abroad. I did my best to fight an increasing tendency
to feel down, as bad moods only made me feel like drinking, and that
was easy enough already.

Life in Ireland was different in other ways, too: the misty, fairy-tale
beauty of the countryside, the lack of traffic, rush and pressure, and the
quiet warmth of the people we met. In America I often found people
went to bars to be alone, to escape. Here you go out to small, simple
public houses to savour the company of other people and practice the
art of conversation for communication's sake. A pub is judged by the
quality of the cosy rapport it creates between its customers. Because
fun doesn't equal fast here, a simple 'Hello' to a stranger can develop
into a leisurely philosophical discussion. I felt at home with this easy-

going, humane pace of life. The fresh, perfumed breezes were a revelation after the yellow exhaust fumes that passed for air in LA. I must have burned up a large lump of bad karma to earn the luck which brought me here.

One of my biggest surprises was discovering that the drug companies had beaten me to Ireland. You couldn't find the smallest bit of something smokeable, but it seemed everyone had prescriptions for tranquilisers and sleepers. In LA I had known people who prepared themselves for the day by waking up and swallowing a Mandrax or Valium. Even during my worst period of Valium addiction I had broken five milligram tablets in half before taking them, and never in the morning. I could understand it in LA, with the high-tension scrabble of the place driving your nervous system. But here? These were the most relaxed people I had ever met, yet prescriptions were being doled out for every conceivable symptom. Thinking of Jimi, I gave drug educations to people passing out on their feet as they struggled to take their ten-milligram lunchtime dose (four per day) and wash it down with a large whiskey. 'What are you taking?' 'Some pills the doctor gave me.' 'Did he mention drinking?' 'No.' 'Right then. Listen to me . . .'

On the Christmas Eve of my 27th birthday, Carol and I found ourselves drinking very late/early with a new acquaintance, Finbar O'Keefe. I was feeling so bad myself that I was surprised to hear him say how depressed he was to be 'sitting here on Christmas Eve drinking with two Brits and a Yank'. But drink we did – even the local moonshine called poteen, which winds its way down from mountain stills before winding its burning way down your throat. A home was the only Christmas present I wanted, and the local vet, Phil Crabbe, mentioned a place nearby. We saw it on Christmas day and it felt perfect. It was big enough for Mum, too. I couldn't raise the necessary deposit, so I talked Mum into taking a loan on her house, while I prayed for Experience earings.

The case in New York was on hold. We couldn't get the information we needed unless we went straight into the suit. Once into proceedings, we didn't have a lot going for us. New York has a 'dead man's statute' which prevented our testifying about our personal transactions with Jimi. Only 'non-interested' parties' testimony about our oral agreements was permissible. Who might they be? Hagood and Howard set my deposition for 6 February 1973, and they sent me a list of documents they wanted me to come up with – which looked to me like a list of documents they already had. I suppose they were double-checking that I had no copies. Their position was that any money I had received from the band had been a loan (advance) and was repayable. I had to prove them wrong. I returned to the States.

Arriving at Hagood and Howard's offices, I was struck dumb by the wealthy atmosphere – far more elegant than any offices I had ever been in. I went to a conference room where my deposition was taken. Mark had given me a crash course in avoiding being tripped up. Yet I felt all I needed to do was to stick to the truth. I was still naive enough to believe that was all I needed to do.

The deposition was a strange experience. The people facing me seemed to get all the breaks. As defendants they got to go first on all procedures, and I had to sit and respond to their battle plan. I felt very bitter watching their smug faces, their curled lips. They were screwing me and I could do nothing about it. They could use their money (and my money) to beat me. Why should I be answering questions designed with only one goal in mind: to make me look bad? They'd never known anyone in The Experience. They'd never played with the band, toured or composed or created anything or suffered anything, and there they were, asking me: 'What makes you think you're entitled to anything?'

It was bull. I had to tell the story of the group. They tried to say that Fat Mattress was tied to the Experience. They brought up my marital situation. They had chats with my lawyers – 'off the record' – out of my hearing.

The only royalties mentioned were those received posthumously. Any mention of foreign royalties brought an instantaneous denial that they were getting any at all. They said they had a few royalties from a short spate of sales after Jimi's death, but not much. There were no more tapes, and as far as they were concerned there would be no more albums.

I got through the session, but I felt like I'd been run over by a bulldozer. I had no real choice if I wanted to pursue the suit. In refusing to give a deposition I could only have threatened to hound them for ever and tell the world what had happened. They offered me $50,000. I felt that $500,000 plus my 25 per cent was more like it.

Going home I felt as if I'd ended up in one of Jimi's nightmares, homeless and on the streets. Mickey's energy was understandably declining as the case became more fiddly and prolonged. Instead of the millions we had once discussed, we were talking mere thousands.

I mentioned to Mark Sandground that Hagood's and Howard's snide comments during the deposition indicated to me that Jeffery was still on top of things and out to screw me. His suggestion that I write a book was not reassuring. I suppose what he really wanted to say was, 'Look, forget you ever played with The Experience and chalk it up to experience.'

We made preparations for a trial, something I seriously wanted to avoid. I was desperately craving an end to this madness. In the financial sea I felt like a drowning man considering a lifeline tossed by a cannibal.

Shapiro had made me promise not to talk to the press, but when Warner Brothers ignored our requests for more documentation, he gave a press release to *Billboard* magazine. Then he tried for a complaint for Breach of Contract by a Third Party Beneficiary and asked for an accounting and $350,000 or reasonable value for my services. All this was just to try to figure out what money had come in so we'd have some idea of what settlement to shoot for. Mickey no longer referred to my 25 per cent, but for me this was the prime issue. I would rather have had my percentage for the future than worry about chasing up the past. Mickey's goal was to settle fast and join forces with the Estate against Yameta, Jeffery, et al. He was working hard, but the ball was still in the Estate's court. Then things started to move very fast . . . and very strange. The catalyst was the ongoing PPX suit in which the Estate stood to lose more than anyone. Jeffery had Jimi's signature on a document which protected Jeffery from all future suits regarding the PPX settlement. Chalpin, however, got caught out. Besides claiming all sort of breaches of contract – as in the first, successful, American suit – he also tried to claim damages on the grounds that the *Band of Gypsies* album wasn't as good as he'd been promised, despite the fact that it was a huge seller. The English courts were not impressed by this claim and concluded that Chalpin's credibility was suspect.

Branton came over for the conclusion of the trial. PPX unconditionally withdrew its claims and, as per the English custom so loved by the tabloids, were ordered to pay the plaintiff's costs ($150,000). Chalpin could afford it. His income from his percentages on the Experience albums plus the *Band of Gypsies* album is estimated at $20,000,000. The plaintiffs confirmed Chalpin's rights to the thirty-three titles for which he had masters, and the Estate would receive artists' royalties from any use of those tracks. All of them would eventually be released. From my point of view, the major outcome of the trial was that the held-up European royalties were now free for distribution. It was a flood of (potential) income and a tax deduction would be handy. Quick. Settle with Redding. He's just this side of despair so he's ripe enough to fall for it.

On 2 March I received a telegram in which I was offered a flat fee of $100,000 for my claims on past royalties, the movie rights, and any claims I had on future royalties. No way. We scheduled depositions for Jeffery, Hecht and Reiss. I couldn't wait to hear Jeffery answer – at long last – the questions we had prepared for him.

The night of 4 March was very strange. For the first time since Jimi's death I dreamt of him. We met. I freaked slightly. 'What are you doing here, you're supposed to be dead?' Jimi answered, 'It's OK. I'm only here to take care of some business.' End of dream. I awoke spooked.

The next day, during a strike of French air-traffic controllers, an Iberian Airlines DC-9 en route from Majorca to London with sixty-eight passengers aboard exploded after a mid-air collision and crashed over Nantes. No remains were found and all aboard were presumed dead. Jeffery had been booked on the flight.

I have doubts. Contracts renegotiated, cash in hand, deposition looming . . . And Jeffery had a thing about flying. He would regularly book a flight, then miss it and travel on the next. He could have done the same on this Majorca flight and figured it was just the exit he needed. He was a quick thinker, and it would be completely in character for him to seize the opportunity and by virtue of his normal practice (lots of irons in lots of fires) manage to turn the situation to his advantage. He had already arranged for the Barclay royalties to be paid into his Curacao account; he had his 40 per cent from the new worldwide Polydor contract; he had numerous investments, especially in Hawaii and Spain. No one knew how much he had stashed away. It would have been as good a time as any to go away. So far he'd managed to avoid G&G's demand for a deposition regarding their suit over his use of their tracks on *Hendrix in the West*. Bob Levine (ex-Jeffery and Chandler Inc. and Karana) was suing him for $80,000 (10 per cent of the Hendrix royalties). Nothing was happening with any of his groups. My deposition on him was imminent. He no longer had access to the Experience's money to pay for legal fees.

A member of Slade, Chas's new band, later told me that – incredibly – Chas had laughed when he heard of Jeffery's death. Was it relief, or disbelief, or amazement at Jeffery's audacity? Jeffery sightings have been made in New York and London by people who used to work for him. Everything considered, I don't entirely believe he is dead.

Jeffery's death was not widely reported, and when I telephoned Mickey he freaked at the size of the spanner now thrown into the works. Our prime witness and *bête noire* was no more. The Dead Man's Statute was working overtime. The only hope was that we might get a copy of Jeffery's PPX deposition regarding the division of royalties in the band. Barring that, only Weiss's testimony could help us, but unless he would supply documents, his testimony would run afoul of the Dead Man's Statute. To quote Mickey, 'It's getting a bit sticky.'

Mickey was being threatened.

A long way from the action, I didn't have enough knowledge to assess the situation – besides which, I was drinking full time. I couldn't play. I couldn't complete the house purchase without cash, or even save Mum's house. To top it off, my dear Gran died on St Patrick's Day, 17 March.

I hustled the promise of another loan and managed to relieve some of the financial pressure. I notified Mark Sandground that a settlement of $150,000 plus future film and record royalties would make me happy. Mickey had by now indicated to Hagood and Howard that I would accept $100,000 not including film rights and with no mention of percentages. I contacted Mark before his California meeting with Shapiro and Branton and repeated what I had said in my letter: 'If you feel you can get more, feel free to wait it out.'

Branton pushed hard and gave Mickey what was purported to be an accounting of the Warner royalties from early 1971 to mid-1972 based on Experience recordings in which I had participated. Shapiro reckoned that $100,000 was the minimum due to me and that we stood a good chance of receiving a bigger offer. He asked me to authorise a settlement should we receive an offer within the next week of a gross figure in excess of $100,000 – no mention of film or future rights. Branton had admitted that the film definitely included the sound of Noel Redding on the soundtrack, but said that my image – now mostly on the cutting-room floor – wasn't recognisable. So how did he know it was me? Mickey replied to Branton saying that we estimated – conservatively – that I was owed a further $50,000 to bring my foreign royalties up to date. He pointed out that since my original claim for $250,000 included this, and a claim for future royalties from all sources, and a sum for the use of my appearance in the film, it was certainly modest and reasonable. Since I had now reduced my claim to $175,000, surely it could be settled quickly in exchange for a signed release for the film? Otherwise our side would proceed with the depositions. If fair settlement could be reached, Mickey offered to co-operate in all other claims.

Mark pushed to have the depositions postponed. I wanted to go straight ahead as we'd need the depositions in the case against the Jeffery Estate anyway. In a letter written on 3 April, I laid out my desires once again,

> . . . $175,000 plus all my *future* royalties domestic and foreign and 25 per cent of the film (and you know they will release an LP with it). I will not budge one ant's prick length on the film problem. Branton

contradicts himself regarding the film, and also why has Joe Boyd called me regarding a release for the film and to invite me to a screening if I'm not in it? How can I think about giving up future royalties? I didn't make those albums for a hobby. The Estate really pisses me off! There are now at least eight albums that I'm on. If you had a screening of the film and invited various critics, writers, etc and then asked them who was in it, I'm sure my name would be mentioned. Les saw a rough cut in LA last year and the only part I'm not in is the Isle of Wight.

6 April came and went. All was silent until the 13th when I received a cable from Mickey: 'New information re settlement. Please call me at Claridges in London on the 17th.'

I telephoned him and was shattered. The settlement bore no resemblance to what I had envisaged. I took Mickey to task on this, but he assured me that the settlement was in my best interests. I couldn't see it. The offer was for a flat $100,000 for everything, for giving up every right I had, past, present and future. Branton and Mickey had assured me repeatedly that there would be no more albums released, that there would be no more money coming in after the excitement of Jimi's death had receded from public consciousness, that the Estate was receiving no foreign royalties.

Our New York man was notified that, 'Through our negotiations in California, we have settled the litigation in NY. We feel that our settlement, although not a large one, is best for Noel's interests. We preserved in the settlement any right of action against Yameta.' Attached to the release was a note from Branton to the effect that the Estate looked forward to co-operating with Shapiro on those matters in which there was a mutual interest.

I flew to London utterly defeated, and when I laid eyes on the release I was horrified, aghast, and all those other words of dismay. The document released not only the Estate, but also Are You Experienced Inc. (now totally owned by the Estate), Warner Brothers Records – and all other record companies regarding past and future contracts – from any liabilities to me regarding royalties or compensation. I released them to do the film and assigned them the right to use my likeness and sound in connection with the Are You Experienced Group (*sic*). (It is a measure of their ignorance that they didn't even know the name of the band.) The release applied to worldwide rights to any recordings already released or mastered and released in the future. What happened to all those assurances that there wouldn't be any more albums? I promised not to sue or help anyone else sue, nor were my heirs, executors or administrators to do so.

The cheque from Hagood and Howard – written on Jimi's Bella Godiva Music Inc. account at Morgan Guaranty Trust Company – was deposited in Mickey's trust account and he posted on my share to me. His services had cost me $35,000 for nine months of negotiation. All the work and effort, the pain and the music, my creations, my mind and my face now belonged to complete strangers in exchange for a sum of money equivalent to what I spent on four years of legal advice. A real legal triumph.

Chapter Nine

Yameta Or Bust

*If a little knowledge is dangerous,
where is the man who has so much as to be out of danger?*
T.H. HUXLEY

WHEN I signed the release, I agreed to retain Mickey and Mark against Yameta, Jeffery, agents, lawyers and accountants. I'd never imagined that THE case would blossom into several. The original retainer agreement was re-applied to this case as discussion started about how to proceed.

The added-in 'you can sue Yameta' clause was little more than a pacifier, because in real life we hadn't the chance of a snowball in hell of suing them successfully. Even Branton, with his superior financial position, considered it pointless. Millions may have passed through Nassau and much certainly by-passed Nassau, but the documentation was pretty much non-existent, the accessible accounts were empty, the assets elusive. Even if I could throw buckets of money into a four-way battle between Yameta in Nassau, Hillman in London, Dicker in New York and Mickey in LA, the only result would be an empty bucket. Not only that, Yameta hadn't done anything against Nassau law, and Sir Guy was understandably upset about question marks hanging over transactions arranged by Jeffery in and out of the Yameta account of which he had had no knowledge.

On top of this, the Bahamian political situation had changed radically. Property investors now found they could only sell to Bahamians, many of whom could not afford to buy. Mickey had already sworn he'd never, ever set foot in Nassau again. He felt that those in charge would consider our case a 'white man's problem', especially now that Jimi, who had never been a black folk hero anyway, was dead.

We had the slimmest chance of getting jurisdiction over Hillman, whose tax consultancy role was perfectly legal, and Dicker could be forgotten completely. He was just a paymaster for US expences and his affluence indicated that he had plenty of friends in the right places. When Jerry Hopkins interviewed Dicker for his excellent 1974 *Rolling Stone* article, Dicker first examined Jerry's driving license, 'So I'll know I'm not talking to the FBI or CIA.' (Or IRS?) And he was as tight-lipped with Hopkins as he had been when Mickey went document-hunting.

Mickey was probably too young and too new to the music business to take on the dragon-slaying task he'd been set. His new partner, Andy Stern, who researched our legal position, was of the view that anything we did would merely help the Hendrix Estate, who would probably be only too glad to ride along on our coat-tails for free. At best, I'd end up with scraps of paper showing how funds got through to Yameta, who would then turn around and say, 'We were instructed. They got the money. Sue them.' I'd love to, if I could find them.

Stern observed that we might start finding out what went in and out of Yameta by starting proceedings in New York, where we might have some control, although statutes of limitation might restrict us to a short time-scale.

The obvious target was Jeffery, who had been involved at every step. Immediately upon his death, chaos had broken loose over the issue of his will. His wife, Gillian, from whom he had been separated but not divorced, stepped in, claiming the right to administer the Estate. Posed against her was Jeffery's ageing father backed by Michael Balin, Jeffery's attorney. In mid-April, Gillian's attorney applied in New York for Maxwell T. Cohen to be appointed New York administrator of the will. The lawyers apparently had a terrible time locating assets – for reasons I understood well – but fairly soon the value of the Jeffery Estate had reached $2,000,000. But Gillian, apparently, couldn't keep control of the Estate, and it went into probate (the judicial determination of the validity of a will). I don't know how Gillian fared, but as far as I know the Estate is still unsettled and Jeffery's father can't touch the $1,000,000 insurance pay-off from Jimi's death.

It was mid-May before Mickey seriously started to wonder who controlled the Estate. I know he doubted my determination to continue the suits after I'd used the settlement for a home for me and Mum instead of ploughing it all back into the next case, but I needed a home. The house I bought had lain empty for years, and was a 300-year-old, stone-built, wooden-pegged, slate-roofed miracle – a miracle in the sense that it was still standing. After moving we discovered we had a renovator's dream – rising damp, falling damp, horizontal damp, wet rot, dry rot, woodworm, furniture beetle, antique electricals, bizarre plumbing, and no heating. This could have been a wonderful challenge. But not on top of everything else.

It was with great relief that I answered a call from Mickey as manager: 'What about a Super Session with Wayne Perkins, Michele Rubini, and Jim Gordon?' Talk about mismatching, we were polar opposites, and again weak on vocals. We met in New York at RCA's expense, and I felt weird from the start. Rubini started bringing out sheets of highly intricate jazz in 92/26½ time, which of course he played brilliantly. But I don't read music, and the style didn't thrill my rock'n'roll heart. We did a three-track demo which has since disappeared. Perkins sang a Creedence song. I did an original, and I can't even remember the last one. No jazz at all. And needless to say, no group.

At least the house began to prove therapeutic. Labourers were out of the budget, so Carol and I spent an eternity hammering at the walls (pretending they were the latest aggravator's head: 'Take that, you miserable bastard!'), dragging out buckets and barrows of crumbling ancient lime and horsehair plaster. A childhood friend, Martin Emery, a magic plasterer, moved in to help. He lived with his wife Lil, and soon their child, in the habitable area. Carol and I camped out with a mattress in one hand and an electric frying pan in the other, keeping one room ahead of the demolition. Sometimes we coincided with it, as when one ceiling decided to take itself down in the middle of the night. When we got too tired to move, we headed for the comfort of the pub. Soon we were starting in the pub, as each day it became harder to maintain a positive outlook. Every morning became a study in hangovers. Life had little, if any, meaning and no charm as I searched for reasons to get up and stopped looking for reasons to stay sober – switching to gin and tonics (Cork Dry Gin, of course) chased by pints of stout mixed half and half with cider. At least I was avoiding pills completely.

With a £20,000 English tax demand for a year in which I'd earned nothing hounding me, Mickey took me to an accountant – £250 in advance please. Letter followed letter, and the accountant's advance soon ran out. I would have been better off paying the advance to the taxman, and writing letters myself.

I also needed a new divorce lawyer, since immediately after my settlement Suzanne had filed a supplemental petition, adding adultery to my list of marital crimes. She named an old friend of mine who, ages ago, had offered to give me a blow job in a closet before a gig, and had recently offered Mum a Danish newsclipping which said Suzanne was pleased to be pregnant with her second child, as was her husband (me!) currently touring the States! Feeling (wo)manipulated, I got Mickey to introduce me to Tony Russell of Bernard Sheridan and Company – £250 in advance, please.

English divorce laws were eras behind the States. We discussed nullity based on pregnancy by another man at the time of the marriage. All I'd have to show was: that I didn't know she was pregnant by another man at the time of marriage; that the petition was presented within a year of the marriage; that there had been no marital intercourse since discovery. No problems there. Her lawyers said they might take £2,000. I checked my finances and offered £500. It would be a year before she contacted her lawyers again. Russell worked away until he left the firm and passed me on to the next person, until he too left. Finally Bernard Sheridan himself started in. By that time they wanted another advance . . .

The action against the Jeffery Estate was filed in New York state court although Shapiro had wanted a federal suit. Seems we couldn't bring action in a federal court against an alien defendant. Mickey pleaded with Branton to join us, but he declined. I begged Mitch to leave Weiss and join us. He mumbled that he'd 'found something out' about Mickey, and said Weiss 'had some figures' and that Stickells had said everything was a mess. He said he'd spoken to the Estate, but wouldn't say which one. He said he'd meet me in London the next day. He didn't show. I guess he felt as confused as I did. At least I played my first public gig in a year, with Les and Stray Dog at the Marquee.

Carol and I started a sincere effort to pull me together. With her office experience and the acquisition of a portable typewriter and some pink stationery, the whole aspect of doing business changed for me. Copies of every letter sent and received were filed in a box according to subject matter and not just dumped in a pile. Carol knew next to nothing of the music business and had lots of questions. I realised that the simplest things were unknown to me. For example, my writing statements had a code showing where the various payments came from. I'd only ever seen copies of statements, and the code key was on the back of the originals.

We notified everyone of my new address and for the first time I got a writing check sent directly to me! This was a revelation. At last I could deal directly with business associates without a middle-mouth. I was very timid, barely able to communicate with friends, so strangers often threw me into a panic. Phone conversations were nearly impossible, but at least now I could write letters of the most vague and cautious variety. I knew I had a lot of questions to ask, but I didn't have enough knowledge to know what they were.

The ink was barely dry on my release when the film premiered. Out of the blue, an upset Sharon wrote to say she was horrified that I had reached a settlement, and complaining that she had lost a good deal of money trying to help out in our affairs. I understood how Sharon felt, but this whole situation had drained me. By now, none of us mattered anyway. Polydor did a block re-release of all the LPs. Both the Jimi Hendrix film and *Rainbow Bridge* opened in London. The former features interviews with people whose 'lives touched Jimi's', but not a word from the lives who made the music . . .

I plodded on but I admit that at this point I simply lost hope, not to mention my self-confidence, patience, positivity, and faith in my own ability to pull myself together. My health I'd lost years before. The abrupt end to my previous popularity (and income) left me in a state of limbo. Local people, hearing I was 'someone', asked, 'Who?'. Terribly embarrassed I'd mumble about The Experience, but inwardly I was asking myself the same question. I couldn't come to terms with what had gone down, rarely touching a guitar or even listening to music for two years.

Perhaps I should have stayed hustling in a city, but it would have been pretty grim for a broke(n), out-of-fashion rock star who'd already lost his identity and was consigned to the slot of 'Hendrix's bassist'. Isolated from the music scene, I took the opportunity to crawl into a hole while I gnawed away at myself over the horrific conclusion to the Estate suit, the knowledge that more suits would probably take endless years, Jeffery's death, the lingering post-pill depression that no amount of drink could touch, and a dreadful lethargy as the drink destroyed any drive I could muster and increased the confusion which my brain hated instead of helping me to forget. I was powerless to change events, to hit back, to get even. Jimi's death haunted me. The depth of my unhappiness became noticeable even to me when I found myself contemplating suicide. Even if I could find the road back, it would be damned long. The prospect did not encourage me.

Back at the 'ballgame', Mickey tried to formulate a heavy case by taking the few known facts and extending them with suspicions into a conclusion which would become The Complaint. Known: Jeffery and Chandler (through Jeffery and Chandler Inc.) had been managers of The Experience; Dicker and Hillman had been attorneys and agents for Yameta; Steingarten, Wedeen and Weiss had been attorneys for The Experience and Jeffery and Chandler Inc. – Steingarten for Jimi,

Weiss for Jeffery and Chandler Inc., and Steingarten, Wedeen and Weiss for the group. The facts went barely any further than that. The rest was supposition which would have to be aired in court. Somewhere in the shambles lay the truth about a great deal of money, but would we ever find it? We were asking for $3,000,000 plus interest at 7 per cent per year, but not a lot happened. I was so hard up for cash that I insisted on itemised bills from Mickey, who interpreted this as a sign of mistrust. I felt embarrassed – I was only trying to learn.

The trial was planned for the spring of 1974, nine months hence. The birth of a monster. In an opening skirmish, we filed against the Jeffery Estate to get Steingarten, Wedeen and Weiss listed officially as Jeffery's attorneys. Everyone wanted them out of the way and a suit would help force the difficult Weiss totally out of the battle for control of the Jeffery Estate. The Hendrix people said they would help us unofficially, but – as was their pattern – what they wanted was something for nothing. Mickey invariably believed them. He had no option.

The Jeffery Estate was in shit. Every time in his career when the tide had changed, Jeffery had changed accountants, partners and (less often) lawyers (although he'd gone through eight of them), and his past was littered with embittered former allies either claiming recompense or holding crucial sets of books. When – during that period – I had occasion to mention to Polydor that I had never received an accounting much less royalties from them (who at that time had fifteen albums on release) they said that their contract had been with Mammouth, Track and Yameta, not with me.

In London, I saw Chas at Eric Burdon's Marquee gig. Looking dashing in his new Rolls Royce, Chas politely made no mention of any litigation, though I wonder why Mickey didn't immediately grab Chas for our side since Chas always swore he never got his producer's royalties. Later he took me to a members-only private club on Jermyn Street, where his wife told me that all Jeffery's Spanish nightclubs were now in the hands of his parents. Did that include the apartments and boutiques?

The vibes deteriorated. Anxiety is not my favourite emotion. Like Jimi, I'd spent too much time worrying since 1967. Even in the era of love and peace, our world had put us in constant contact with 'love, piece or break your arm' types, who made you forget that you started playing music for the love and liberation of it.

By now various musical papers were realising that all was not 'love and peace and would you like another Rolls Royce' in the music business. Some ran articles and made some good points about how and why rip-offs happen. In *NME*: 'Most musicians are too broke, or too nervous to involve themselves in High Court actions, to confront the Mobile Cigars. Scared of reprisals. Dave Dee says, "When you're young you fall into traps. When you've got nothing and somebody comes along and makes an offer, you take it. Anything's better than what you've got. It's not until success arrives that you begin to be aware of the vultures hovering about. It's so easy to sign your life away." '

Or end up with no life at all.

I drove myself crazy with the thoughts that were breaking through as the years of pills cleared my system – the after-effect is long and hard. Contemplating the mountains of valium, librium and similar brain-blocking substances prescribed every year, I feel much of the world must be zombified. The changes my brain went through when no longer tranquillised and sedated were amazing and horrifying. I began waking Carol in the middle of the night to drag her (protesting all the way) to the typewriter. My mind paced the floor. Mickey took the brunt of this angst and called it my 'blue period.'

By mid-September, Max Cohen was confirmed as Special Administrator and negotiations began. He offered to talk settlements, but the meeting was a dead loss. Cohen was so 'straight' he didn't know Jimi Hendrix from Winston Churchill. Even to evaluate the case he needed a complete history of modern music, let alone of The Experience.

With that mess to deal with, perhaps the Jeffery Estate would settle quickly with us just to get rid of yet another headache. If we leaned heavily – pushing our annoyance value – we figured we might be able to avoid a full, costly offensive. Our main fear was that too many assets might be disposed of before a full suit could bring recompense.

Every time I opened a music paper I saw ads for Experience albums, many of them blatant bootlegs. From a group which made only three albums in its career there was (and is) an astonishing amount of product available: hundreds of titles now, and very few of them legitimate. Mickey wrote to me to try and put some things straight. He pointed out that I had now settled with Warner Brothers for all royalties from all sources; that I would not get publishing royalties; and that my permission was not needed to put out records based on masters – all they had to do was pay me any writing royalties. He wanted me to turn my interest towards the Yameta and Jeffery suits. 'I hope this helps you to cool out,' he ended up.

What I couldn't – and still can't – figure out was how Warner Brothers got involved with the settlement from Jimi's Estate? How did I settle with Warner Brothers when I'd been after the Hendrix Estate? Shapiro humorously referred to my case as Redding *vs* the World. It would have been better for me if I could have laughed, but it was just too hard. I was working on my creeping bitterness act and getting quite good at it. The irony of the case was that almost any participant could have joined with another and found common cause over something, but it was an irony I didn't much enjoy thinking about.

The value of the Estate grew as the inventory of assets – which included the film *Rainbow Bridge* – was put together, but as its dimensions increased so did the number of people crawling out of the woodwork with claims against Jeffery. Even from the grave (?) he was not short of ways to cause me grief. Cohen watched in horror as the value of the claims started approaching the value of the Estate. Would there be enough for his fees? He never knew Jeffery, but he must have been forming a picture of a man of unique talents. Even the fabulous Electric Lady Studio – state of the art – was such a labyrinthine financial construction that Cohen had to spend hours trying to pull it out of trouble. His dislike for 'rock and rollers' burgeoned and however much he seemed to recognise my claims to be real, he could do little but lie low and wait.

Time ticked by on the Statute of Limitations clock. Mickey had been on the case for fifteen months, and he tried to speed things up by giving a lead to *Billboard*: 'Redding sues Jeffery Estate: the action alleges that Jeffery converted to his own use money which should have gone to the trio. A similar suit against Warner Brothers won Redding a five-figure settlement according to Michael Shapiro.' Hold on minute. Against Warner Brothers? I thought I won it against the Hendrix Estate? I was clearly not on a purely legal wavelength, and small signals started to float through. I thought, for example, that I had a share in Electric Lady Studio because Jimi had used group funds to build it. Mickey told me that this kind of reasoning was mere 'theory'.

Mickey spoke to *Rolling Stone* magazine: 'While Jeffery managed the group, millions of dollars came under his control; he had an obligation to account, but he never did. We allege that the money amounted to $5,000,000 and we're entitled to 25 per cent.' It sounded so simple: 'The action against the Jeffery Estate is separate from the Yameta action which is a question of procedure. We will depose Dicker to determine who was involved. At which point we will file our Yameta lawsuit.'

If I had thought being a successful rock star had its down moments, nothing prepared me for being an ex-successful rock star. In addition to the legal funhouse, I had to deal with situations such as that thrown up by John Downing, a roadie who said he'd been promised a $1,200 bonus on the 1968 tour. He had presented the bill to Branton who wanted verification, so I wrote giving it – everyone had been promised a bonus, something which Stickells looked after. The Estate replied to the bill by saying that they had no intention of paying it and referred Downing to me. As I couldn't pay it, his lawyers threatened me with proceedings. Did I need this?

In confused frustration, I'd grab a sledgehammer or crowbar and take out my revenge on an accessible wall. Manual labour is highly recommended in these situations. At least there is something to show for the time spent. Then Ireland joined the EEC and overnight building materials more than doubled. We could still tear things down, but nothing would go up any more.

At our request, Cohen looked for and found my 1970 masters at Electric Lady Studios, where they still sit as I can't afford the storage fees payable to get them out. Jeffery had confiscated and stashed them. Mickey sent statements proving I'd personally paid for the LP, and Cohen agreed to turn them over to us, while noting that the Estate would have some contractual rights in any income derived from them.

It was now necessary to meet with my team of lawyers to have a general discussion and sign some documents. We hoped that the Estate would be grilling me soon in preparation of settlement. I flew to the States via New York to meet Lee Michaels in San Francisco – one of Mickey's supergroup ideas. I prayed something would come of my meeting with Lee. Always an admirer of his keyboard expertise, I had high expectations. We went with a drummer to his home rehearsal room which was attached to a mobile studio. He casually picked up a guitar and started to play. I picked up a bass and we plunked about for a while. Next day – same thing! I kept waiting for him to play piano, but he never touched a keyboard. It was embarrassing. The extent of his guitar knowledge seemed to be E, B, and A. Was he seriously trying to play guitar? Lee phoned to say, 'It won't work.' I agreed. Poor Lee, the play cost him a bomb. I'd had non-stop limos and a first-class flight. I was glad to be on the plane home. And it was a funny trip. Of all people, Marc Bolan and Fabian were on the flight. We had a great laugh, but I soon went back to hibernating without music.

I was being treated like a retired millionaire, and getting sick of it. Even the bootleggers were raking it in, but I was the one who got overcharged because 'he can afford it'. I was the one taking the brunt of hate-filled jealousy from strangers. I was the one with creeps showing up at my door expecting handouts and more or else.

At least I was living a country life. The crunch still comes but it comes slower, softened by the loveliness of the countryside. But how were we to pay the bills? Run the car? Or eat? The Experience and my marriage had fulfilled my dreams, but the aftermath of both had made me frightened to dream again. Slowly I adopted the aim of having a studio, so I'd still be surrounded by music even though I couldn't make it myself any longer. I counted on the Jeffery Estate to come through. How could we lose? Chas had his Barn Recording Studios in London. Jeffery had had Electric Lady. So when they settled, I should be able to afford one, too.

In the tranquillity of my new homeland, I could nearly forget the nightmare. In this world, hustlers were 'chancers' and given a wide berth, not congratulations. The most discussed topic was the weather. I rediscovered my pleasure in nature – its power and beauty put my problems in perspective. Besides flattened crops, a storm could easily mean no utilities – no water-pump for the well, no cooker, no heat except an open fire which we then cooked on, too, and no phone. But I began to find things to savour more and more each day: taking the time for a chat in each shop, the old-fashioned exchange of pleasantries, 'Anything strange? Or new? Or different?' I learned that word-of-mouth is faster than telephone. I found bits and pieces of happiness in little things that mean a lot. I passed my twenty-eighth birthday among friends.

A stranger came into my life. Dave Clarke (not *the*) pestered me until I agreed to produce a single for him. A brilliant singer-song-writer-pianist from Essex, Dave pulled me out of 'retirement' for a session for his LP, *Death of a Pale Horse* (under the name of Dave Carlsen for Spark/CBS). The session was berserk. The guitarist suffered from vertigo, went out for cigarettes and disappeared. The drummer hadn't a clue, and Dave's budget didn't stretch to redoing it with another drummer. (I love having a go on drums, but I'm no Mitch Mitchell.) We spent ages trying to mix him out and the end result, one track entitled *Snowstorm*, sounded as if a blizzard really had swept through it. Sadly, the proceeds of the track were to go the National Society for Mentally Handicapped Children, so I wish it had been a success.

The Jeffery Estate slowly gained insight into the complexities of the problems. Max Cohen maintained his pleasant facade, but the good-will my side believed he felt towards us was diminishing daily. We were reduced to scrabbling for the top of the list of creditors in case funds ran out, but we scrabbled in vain as one by one the claims put in were settled. They came as close as possible to ignoring us. A penniless, documentless plaintiff is no more than a mosquito to be splatted. Nearly a year after Jeffery's death, Uncle Max would now rather create delays than settle. I had nothing he wanted, and he had everything I wanted.

In a meeting, Dicker confirmed that Hillman had organised Yameta and owned Caicos, which itself partly owned Yameta. He also informed us that The Experience members were to have been salaried for tax reasons, not because we were 'hired'; that income received by Davidson was sent to Yameta; that Warner Brothers had met Dicker personally to say that there was a contract with Jimi but not with Mitch or me; that Jeffery had been an employee of Yameta, but had obviously been a major decision-maker – not an employee in any but a formal sense; that in July 1969 Weiss had acted for Jeffery and the group without having contracts. By this date, Hendrix and Yameta had finished. He said he hadn't a clue why the group had not received money due it. Jeffery definitely had received money. He remembered once paying $5,000 directly out of Yameta funds so that Jimi could buy a Corvette. He also made reference to a 22 September 1966, Hillman-drafted agreement between the group members and Chandler to the effect that we would receive £15 per week and the remainder of our income would go to Yameta. (We weren't a group until October of that year, so this could be a reference to the contract between Jimi and Chas.) He vaguely remembered issuing cheques to Mitch and me, but there wasn't any proof in the minutes of the arbitration. We were allowed to copy one set of notes written on stationery with a Steingarten, Wedeen and Weiss letterhead. They read:

$15,000 to Jeffery in Spain
$4,600 unexplained
$5,000 to Jeffery in Spain
$1,000 to Steingarten, Wedeen and Weiss
$2,265 to Steingarten
$33,000 to Yameta

This sort of distribution confirmed our suspicions that Jeffery had direct and easy access to Yameta funds which never found their way to the group.

Hillman had given Dicker permission to speak with us as long as Yameta was protected – especially from anything which might imply US jurisdiction for the settlement of a dispute. We needed permission from the Jeffery Estate to view any documents dealing with Jeffery, and of course such permission was not forthcoming. Hillman's position seemed to be: Good luck boys. If you find anything of interest, give us a call. Until then . . . Mickey got that sinking feeling. Anxiously he contemplated pressurising Cohen with a deposition. Push came to shove when Cohen moved to dismiss our claim entirely. Our complaint was based on a percentage agreement between Jeffery and me – both 'aliens' in US law. The Jeffery Estate was based in London. The New York Court had appointed Max, but his US citizenship didn't give citizenship to Jeffery, who only ran a business from New York. Therefore no jurisdiction was possible.

Perhaps Dicker and Hillman felt a certain sympathy for us in our totally unenviable position and so offered facts previously withheld as privileged information. Or maybe it was a spin-off from Mark Sandground's first meeting with Dicker, who was shaken and confused by the unexplained financial transactions in this case. We gratefully viewed his sparse Yameta documents: the Memo of Association; the December 1966 Hendrix/Yameta employment agreement; the 1968 arbitration agreement; the November 1968 agreement; and the 26 March 1969 agreement giving certain monies payable from SeaLark, Warners, and GAC to Yameta. Jeffery's employment agreement and Yameta's letter authorising Jeffery to act on their behalf were unavailable. There was no obvious explanation as to what Yameta did for Jimi Hendrix in exchange for their 40 per cent.

We now knew that all a suit against Yameta in the US would win us would be a stack of papers worthless in the Bahamas. Mickey suggested suing anyone on the fringe with any evidence for anything we could find. But that would mean endless years of expensive depositions when speed was the only key that could open this door. The longer we took, the more I was 'prejudiced in the eyes of the Court', because to an outsider it might have looked as if we were desperately hunting for evidence to support an outrageous claim.

We opposed Cohen's dismissal by insisting that the citizenship of the executors or administrators determines jurisdiction, and then had to wait around for the Court's decision on jurisdiction before we could get on with discovering any more details. The more time passed, the more ground we lost, and the more nervous Mickey got.

Dicker slowly got together the documents, blaming the delay on Hillman. Hillman didn't want to embarrass and alienate Dicker, and conceded some useful bits of information: that Yameta was at the time a wholly-owned subsidiary of the Caicos Trust Company Ltd; that this company never involved Jeffery, Chandler, or Jimi; that Yameta was a service company and handled the income of its employees (such as Jeffery) and employees of its employees (those signed to Jeffery) as well as non-employees (Mitch and me until mid-1968 when we became employees); that Yameta collected and distributed income according to the instructions of the people entitled to the income; that Yameta never acted on its own volition; and that, apparently, Jeffery had exceeded his authority in using Yameta as his own operation.

Dead ends. Mickey met with Weiss and was surprised to find him in good humour. Mickey showed him our Nassau files and Weiss offered to get in touch with Balin. He also offered to put me in a 'hit rock group'. He was in supergroup mode as much as Shapiro was. Spare me. As a wasted hero I was a super mark at best.

In June, the Estate offered $25,000 and my LP *Nervous Breakdown* in exchange for a complete release from all claims. Mickey suggested $50,000, hoping we'd get another $50,000 from Chas and something from Yameta. This was awful. There were four lawyers to be paid. With £200 to my name and absolutely no prospects, I agreed to consider $30,000.

Mickey visited while touring Europe. We didn't discuss the case, but his wife Bonnie worried me by saying that Mickey had been seriously threatened – she refused to say by whom. Mickey's current main aim was to get me working so the case wouldn't be so important to my existence. I'd braved a few thoughts in that direction after a songwriting session with Dave Clarke, a great lyricist even if he had to 'take a walk on the wild side' to get them out. Since I enjoy writing music, it was a good relationship. But we had no capital, so all we could plan was a long slog. I'd had enough of them.

Slightly more together, I was still not up to performing, dying of embarrassment if asked to play or sing. I avoided gatherings where I might have to do a party piece. The expectations were enormous. If I even touched a guitar, I felt I was expected to sound like the whole Experience, including drums. Very tentatively, I attempted jams with a local group, Southern Comfort, at the Monday night 'Getting To Know You' sessions at O'Donovan's Hotel, trying to conquer my fear of people, audiences, and playing. But I felt everyone was critical of my every note. I was ready to believe I could never play again.

Weiss phoned with an offer to play with his client Carmine Appice. That day, Mama Cass died in London, joining Jimi, Janis, and soon Marc Bolan. Then I dreamed of Jimi again – a similar dream to the one I had before Jeffery's death. And the next day one of the members of Slade was involved in a car crash. I had arranged to meet Carmine and Jeff Beck in London but woke up floored with a temperature of 104. I went anyway, but I should have minded the omen. I was soon fed up with all the name-dropping and references to women as this cunt and that cunt.

Mickey spread a bit of bullshit about and got enough of an advance from Anchor Records to permit a gig in London with Dave Clarke and

Pete Kircher: 'The entire band is made up of players who have been in top English groups and have taken a year or two to cool out before coming back. The seasoned attitude of these players will make the probability of success far greater than starting with a bunch of young kids.'

Mickey Gee (later Shakin' Stevens' main man) was recommended as a guitarist. Our play at Studio 51 inspired plans for a rehearsal in Ireland because I had a place where we could all rehearse and live for free. Everyone arrived but Mickey. Eventually his girlfriend rang to say he didn't like to travel unless he got £100 per week – nearly treble my current income. So we were without a guitarist. Though guitar was my first love, I had become known as a bassist and was expected to stick with it. Luckily a friend, photo-journalist Ted McCarthy, suggested Eric Bell, who had recently left Thin Lizzy – mentally and physically. Eric arrived, but Dave had split. Dave returned. Eric left. Then Pete quit. Incredibly, in between the coming and going, we'd somehow managed a full demo tape of original songs. Dave delivered it to Anchor. They lost it. And we had no copy.

A lot of my troubles were based on my growing fear that nobody gave a shit. Murray Roman, my friend, my helper, was gone in a car crash. Perhaps even I didn't care. Since I felt Mickey was dumping me, I gave him a lot of stick. He was handy. I only had to pour my ranting and fearful anxieties into a letter and post it to him. For someone who by now must have had at least a sneaking suspicion that he stood to make fuck all on this case, and that it would not make him famous, he was incredibly long-suffering. He even waived my promise to buy him a Daimler upon settlement of the case. And he waived his 5 per cent claim on my writing royalties.

Five actionless months had passed on the legal front. More complications had arisen in G&G's suit against the Hendrix Estate, the Jeffery Estate and Warner Brothers. Branton and Warner Brothers had joined forces to sue the Jeffery Estate for misrepresentation, and Branton was keen to get Cohen off his back. One of the first things the Jeffery Estate had done was to attack Branton for the 20 per cent management fee on all income. (Cohen had tried that on me, but 20 per cent of nothing wasn't really worth the trouble.)

Cohen blamed the delay on the battle between Jeffery's father and wife to be named official administrator. He said he looked favourably upon the proposal I'd made, but he was basically waiting for the court to respond to our objection to Cohen's motion to dismiss. We won that one after six and a half months and he had to change tack by presenting me with a list of fifty-two inane questions. For example: name the members of the group; tell us every sum Jeffery collected, for whom and from whom; list every performance date, place, promoter, amount, who paid, to whom were cheques made out; and on and on. I hoped someone had had a terrible Christmas getting those questions together because I had a terrible New Year trying to answer them.

It was three months before I finished, and all I accomplished was revealing to the Jeffery Estate how they could go about squashing me like a bug. They had all the documents already (they'd managed to settle with Jeffery's earlier associates); they just wanted to find out how to exploit my ignorance. Two years had passed since Jeffery's death, four and a half since Jimi's.

I was in limbo-land and not having a very good time. My lawyers were trying to do two – seemingly complementary, but that's the law for you – things at the same time: recover what I was due from having been in The Experience and recover some momentum in my musical career. I was introduced to a pair of managers – Jon Brewer and Robert Patterson – who met me in a Rolls, bought me lunch, dinner and a night in the Hilton and were keen, as Mickey put it, to make any reasonable arrangements necessary to acquire my services. After much to-ing and fro-ing, a band was put together – Les on drums, Eric on guitar, Dave on vocals, and me on bass – and we eventually made it to Steve Marriot's Essex home-studio to do our album. Marriot was in bed the first day, then stayed up all night and spent the next day watching sport on the telly. Into his hectic schedule we managed to squeeze the recording of a few tracks before one was accidentally erased. We cut our losses and headed for Island Studios where, under supervision of Muff Winwood, we did the album, *Clonakilty Cowboys*, with tracks to spare in a couple of days, after which I made a pointless one-day trip to New York to deliver the masters to RCA. I socialised, they raved, and the band was billed for the expences.

We were signed, we had an album, but we were on the wrong planet fashion-wise. Glamrock was the name of the game, and it wasn't our style at all. In mid-October 1975, we did an RCA showcase gig at Ronnie Scott's. It wasn't great, but it wasn't unbearable. Management had demanded special stage gear, for Dave a huge, ugly studded leather jacket in which he could hardly move let alone sing and play keyboards. I wore a purple satin rock'n'roll suit. Eric and Les wore sequinned jackets. Awful. Eric quit the band, then rejoined. In

December we went to the States to do PR, and returned in late January 1976 to tour, despite hourly changes of mind on the part of Dave. In Austin, Texas, on 31 January, I was doing my first American gig in six years. It was the first big gig Dave had ever done. It was the first time Eric had been in the States. Before we got on stage the tour manager informed us that our gear hadn't arrived. Nice. Jerry Garcia – whose band we were supporting – sped into the dressing room with a minuscule joint that got us all sweet and high. Fortunately the audience was smoking the same weed and we had a nice relaxed gig.

I was the uncle on this tour, passing out deeply resented wisdom to the new boys. I soon joined them in ignoring my advice to steer clear of the two main pitfalls: drugs and women. Things went smoothly, though, considering the numerous possibilities for disaster. After doing a support gig for Freddy King in Los Angeles, he sent around a bottle of his band's favourite tipple – gin – which was accepted on behalf of the band by Dave who retired to his room to drink the whole thing. As an encore, he fell over and badly gashed his head. Los Angeles was just too much of the good life and it became hard to push the band. Dave swore that he couldn't handle America, so eventually I had to confiscate his passport to keep him on board.

We managed to record the second album, but Dave was out of it. After forty-three gigs in sixty-five days we collapsed back to England in time to watch the album die. We were all short of cash and struggling hard. When we argued with our managers – which is how we generally communicated with them – Robert was fond of saying things like, 'Eric [pronounced Air-wick], I could immobilise you without moving.' He didn't realise that we were fairly immobile without his help.

We struggled on for a while, but by August I was advertising in the *Melody Maker* for new band members. Only one decent player applied. Despite the absence of a band, the office was still insisting that tours were lined up for the Noel Redding Band. The second album, *Blowin'*, was released in October to some good reviews and even some airplay, but by November my postbox was overflowing with bills dating as far back as 1975 – bills from New York guitar shops, recording studios, hotels. The office was informing all creditors that I was personally responsible and giving them my address. I started gigging with Southern Comfort and taking home seven quid a night. To cap it all, Motown released in England the record I had done for them several centuries earlier, *Road*.

I finally set eyes on our RCA contract (I still hadn't learned) and was amazed to see that our advances totalled $980,000. They were keen on a third album, but as the advance had already disappeared and there were still studios awaiting payment for the recording of album number two, there didn't seem to be much point. Endless games of darts took me through the rest of the year, and when 1977 dawned the sheriff called in to seize some of my furniture in lieu of payment for a debt. I had offered to send a local musician's demo tape to Schroeders. They had lost it when they moved office, and I was being sued by the musician. In mid-March, after struggling back onto the road several times with new musicians, the Noel Redding Band was finished.

My attempts to revive my musical career had returned me to a place I thought I had escaped. Perhaps there was no way of playing at the level on which The Experience had operated without all that apparatus of bullshit. I'd been around the track a few times, and the sights were always the same – some nice, some horrific. I didn't much fancy another circuit. I kept hearing from Warner Brothers about Experience albums that had gone gold – just to remind me of old times.

The case was grinding on, but there was no indication that a settlement was any closer than it had been years before. We applied to take a deposition from Cohen to get information on Jeffery's assets. He filed for a protective order against our request claiming it would be hardship, an unnecessary burden, blah blah blah. I took out my frustrations on poor Mickey, as usual. He explained that he had to interview the same people several times to check their stories and develop new lines of evidence. He had sent Andy Stern to take Cohen's deposition because this would permit Mickey to be a witness against Cohen should this be required. Stern had also seen Hecht and had looked at correspondence establishing my right to a 25 per cent cut and a memo of an agreement between Hendrix and Jeffery which referred to a 20 per cent share to Jeffery of all Hendrix earnings, which included Mitch and me. No copies, however, could be taken without the Hendrix Estate's permission.

The legal train was obviously running out of steam, and Mickey was getting understandably anxious about my ability to pay for his work if no settlement could be reached. He wrote to me, after I had badgered him heavily, expressing disappointment at my attitude. He must have known our relationship was nearing an end, and I think genuinely felt unhappy at the way things had turned out for both of us. Mark Sandground felt the same way, expressing the view that life would be much simpler without clients.

In retrospect, I was probably taking out my frustration and disgust with the way the law worked on a couple of guys who were trying to do an honest job for me. But I felt so let down by the whole business that as far as I was concerned anything to do with law and lawyers turned my stomach. I couldn't help feeling paranoid when I was involved in a game I didn't understand and in which I had plenty to lose.

I was sent a copy of Cohen's testimony and my temper was not improved. Having reached a state of virtually no momentum, the case now appeared to be going backwards. Cohen grudgingly admitted that Jeffery and The Experience 'knew' each other professionally. He didn't know Jeffery, but 'had heard' that he was a record producer, record company executive, publisher, personal manager, and possibly other things. He 'had heard and been told' that there was a Jeffery and Chandler Inc., but he'd never seen a partnership agreement or any other documentation. An informed music fan could have taught him a lot. Had Cohen paid anything to the Hendrix Estate? Yes, relating to Electric Lady Studios. He said that Jeffery purchased the studio from Hendrix in 1968, but wouldn't produce the documentation. Any queries regarding the 1968 purchase by Warner Brothers of a contractual relationship between Jeffery and Chandler and Yameta regarding The Experience were met with a 'don't know'. Cohen said 'don't know' so often that he sounded as if he was citing the Fifth Amendment. The deposition finished (after four hours and forty-five minutes) at a cost (to me) of $1,259.22.

My rows with Mickey had come to a head, and I was faced with changing lawyers midstream or apologising. I did the latter. The next step was to be Cohen's examination of me before trial, for which I would have to fly everyone to Ireland, plus hire an Irish lawyer. My bank account whispered a gentle 'no'. I suggested we delay until the band (Noel Redding Band) was touring in the States. I turned thirty, heading into 1976 with the pack of legal terriers snapping at my heels. A cable arrived: 'Call us urgent re: deposition. Shapiro and Stern.' It was followed by a telephone call from my manager, Jon Brewer, saying that Mickey had rung him asking how much money I had. Mickey also asked Robert Patterson if he would advance me enough money to get through the deposition for Cohen (basically paying for me to get to New York and have Stern by my side). Stern and I met on 27 January 1976 and talked for hours. Cohen had scared the shit out of me with threats of huge counter-claims. Now Stern was looking for a settlement. I stubbornly insisted that I was in the right. Cohen, recognising my fragile position, was making a derisory offer: $5,000 plus my *Nervous Breakdown* tapes. Stern counselled that he thought the offer a bit low. A bit low? When we had started on this suit we were talking $3,000,000.

The deposition took place at Hecht's office. We reviewed a few points. Jeffery and Chandler had retained Hecht during the 1968

Yameta crisis in order to keep records of all income from mid-1968. The records showed a 50/25/25 understanding and all the income which had got as far as Are You Experienced Inc. had been divided as such after a percentage had come off the top for Jeffery and Chandler. Jimi had overdrawn his account – mostly for Electric Lady Studio – and had dipped into Mitch's and mine.

Despite our long period of association, this was the first time Cohen and I had met face to face. He had a tape recorder. If we settled, he'd destroy the tape. We started at the beginning and went over well-trodden territory. He was pretty inflexible, insisting that if necessary I would have to sell my home to come up with the 20 per cent I owed the Jeffery Estate. We talked around a lot of issues and Stern finally proposed that we settle for $20,000 plus $5,000 for lawyers' fees. In exchange, I would release both the American and English branches of the Jeffery Estate. I was asked to wait outside while they negotiated. Cohen, I was told, didn't think much of my claim on money put into Electric Lady Studio. All he was thinking of as far as a settlement was a refund for my contribution to the settlement of the PPX suit.

They gave me the bad news, but I was relieved to have the whole matter put to rest. I didn't know what bad news was, though, until I actually saw it on paper: $10,000. I signed away any rights to retribution and withdrew from the suit. After settling my legal expences I took home $7,000.

I had just about run out of suits, the only remaining one being one I was reluctant to pursue, against Chas (and through him Jeffery and Chandler Inc. and Warner Brothers Records). My heart wasn't in it – I'd always liked Chas – but I had no option. The suit against Chandler had been filed in 1974 but had been put on hold pending funds. I hadn't realised that Warner Brothers had long since applied for a dismissal on the grounds that the suit was between a member of The Experience and one of his managers, nothing to do with Warner Brothers, who had been dragged in simply as a jurisdictional device. The court had agreed. Shapiro's new partner set about – with no great enthusiasm – reinstigating proceedings. Meanwhile, as though my legal life wasn't complicated and unrewarding enough, the Noel Redding Band took its management to court. It was shown that our managers had been advanced $316,000 in tour support by RCA, a mere $10,000 of which had found its way to the band. It was a good result, but we still didn't get paid. In order to have the settlement enforced I would have had to come up with thousands to pay for the legal fees. I had been down that road before.

Chapter Ten

Are You Experienced?

I hate quotations
RALPH WALDO EMERSON

IT HAD been an interesting Experience, but now what? This was the end. Finito. Nothing.

I had nothing to lose any more except our home, which was now valued at less than the purchase price and desperately in need of major roof repairs to eliminate the buckets and pans in the attic. With the loan interest gathering, the bank grew nervous. All else was gone – guitars, amps, furniture, and most devastatingly, my optimism and energies. Only bitterness and fatigue survived.

When I compared the reality with what could have been, it hurt. But I guarded that torment with perverse pride. At least it was mine. Nobody could take it away. I could wallow in it, wield it as a club. I alienated both friends and strangers. I snarled, I complained, I drank (homebrew at nine pence a pint). I resented anyone else who was making a go of it, rejected anyone who tried to cheer me up. If someone said the sun rose in the east, I'd argue it didn't. I could not see that although the world forms us, we also form our world.

Any reminders of the past or Jimi's death tore me up. I dreamt of Jimi again. A strange dream. No talking this time. He silently took a part out of his body and gave it to me. Weird.

Mitch phoned, 'Uh, Noel. Why don't we get together and sue everybody?'

As I had driven Mickey up the wall with mile-long lists of demands, I now drove my new lawyer, Paul, crazy. He reminded me that I was continuously finding myself in litigious situations when I couldn't afford the luxury of litigation. Didn't I just know it. Cancel that part of your education which says litigation is everyone's right. But I refused to quit. I still had my stubborn streak to back my bitterness.

I wrote to Alan Douglas about my tracks on the tapes which he had control of and got no reply. I wrote to Branton and my letters got returned. Thoughts of all the worldwide royalties no one would admit getting filled my mind. I hired a German lawyer to chase Polydor. No good. Hired a French lawyer to chase Barclay. No good – proof on paper or forget it. I contacted Chas and he promised to back me up with an affidavit, but he never got round to it. I still owe both lawyers their fees, which they kindly haven't chased up.

Desperate to tidy my life by tying up any loose end I could, I wrote directly to Suzanne asking for a divorce based on seven years' separation. She replied. Did I still dispute her child's parentage? I felt she'd made no attempt to make our marriage work. I could feel kindly but hardly fatherly towards a child she'd never introduced me to. Now her stand on the matter was that I'd caused all the trouble by refusing to give her a divorce so she could get social help, and that I'd left England to avoid paying her. She accused me of feeling sorry for myself. She'd been forced to finish school and work for a living because I wouldn't support her. She had another child.

I *did* feel sorry for myself, and I'd finished with being everyone's meal ticket. I had to support myself. If I didn't pull this important item together I might as well cash in my chips. This was really back to 'Go', but without the £200. In your twenties you should move from flinging, to thinking, to deciding while you have your youthful energy and enthusiasm. It may be too late by the time you reach thirty. I had so much to learn: how to concentrate and not dissipate; how to use and not abuse; how to get my intake down and my sensitivity up.

The pop music scene was somewhere else. Punk meant nothing to me. I hated the idea of doing a gig and getting spat on. Disco meant less. The new bass techniques sounded alien. There must have been some good music going on, but you didn't hear it on the radio. New LPs were way out of my budget, and old records brought back old memories. The house was crumbling, but the state of the house was lost in the state of my head. I discovered I love silence and privacy – pretty ironic for someone who earns his living breaking silence and standing in front of an audience.

I did slightly more than drop out – which in sixties talk meant slow down and take some time for yourself. I verged on withdrawal from the human race. I couldn't write any more. The music in my head was gone. I felt like I was dying. The thought didn't bother me. It seemed an easy way out.

I withdrew from music as much as possible, but I had to live and music was all I'd ever done. However, I was also well trained in the art of waiting around. Although there was nothing to wait for any more, it was a hard habit to break. Southern Comfort got very popular and Clonakilty gave birth to a great rock scene based in the Wolfe Tone Lounge. Manfred Mann brought his Earth Band (Steve Waller on guitar, Pat King on bass and Geoff Britton on drums) and the Manor Mobile over and recorded at the house for his *Angel Station* LP. We did a fantastic sneaky session there, packing the house on twenty-four hours' word-of-mouth and charging 30p entrance. We built up a no-standing-room Saturday scene at the Bandon Golf Club. I was the one who noticed the bar manager counting the takings with an ear-to-ear smile splitting his face, so I insisted we ask for a raise of £10 to £40. We got the raise.

We started working too steadily for the three members with day jobs, but not often enough for me to get by. And I wanted the additional effort of rehearsing new material. Eventually the band ran it's course. Jimmy married and moved to London, then came back to Clonakilty where he's now a great DJ. Jerry Larkin's job teaching art took him to Kerry, and then a family took his time. Jerry Lane and I tried to keep going, but drummers were hard to come by. Then Jerry (a very straight guy who resisted all efforts to get him to grow his hair longer than an inch) got married, joined a showband, started his own band, and finally was reborn as a heavy metal hairy complete with leather wristbands. It's a type of music I rarely feel inspired to play now. No one seems as heavy as The Experience anyway. Just louder – maybe.

In the spring of 1978 I tried to form another band. We bought a rattling, drafty old VW van in anticipation of carrying gear. I advertised for musicians, but they were either scattered all over the country or based in Dublin, and I hadn't anything profitable or even steady to offer. Nor were the audiences outside my local area interested in listening to me unless I had imported musicians. We did have some great nights when Les came to stay.

It was impossible for anyone to take seriously any schemes I had when I was so obviously demolished financially. I put the house on the market, but no one wanted it.

Articles and ads started to pop up regularly saying how well the Estate was doing marketing Hendrix. I was inconsolable. I didn't want to feel better. If I felt better, I couldn't hate so much.

I couldn't see any good side to this. Carol, who had doled out a lot of sympathy over the years, contended that it was very near impossible to live with me in my continually miserable frame of mind and that I had better pull myself together. My negativity was draining us both. She reminded me of Mark Sandground's suggestion to write a book and felt that it might clean me out and clear the air for a fresh start. A catharsis, an exorcism – anything was better than me wallowing in my present destructive frame of mind. After all, I still didn't really understand what had gone down, didn't know or hadn't assimilated even 10 per cent of the information presented in the earlier chapters. It had all been so overlapping, so frantic, with isolated facts scattered on an invisible framework.

We wrote to Mickey and requested my files. They were sent, with a note and a bill for the shipping. In the note Mickey reminded me how loyal he had been and told me I'd been short-sighted and abrupt, had a selective memory, and was too quick to accuse people trying to be helpful of dishonesty. He was right. I was fucking disturbed and upset. The world was no longer populated with people, it was full of bastards.

I ranted. Let's start the Musicians' Freedom Party. We'll have payments direct from companies to the artist made mandatory. And tax laws that allow for feast and famine. And car insurance which costs the same as everyone else, not double plus . . .

In August 1978, the tide stopped ebbing and started to turn. We took the box of legal files and every scrap I could find – press cuttings, documents, diary entries, letters – and put it all in chronological order. We read and sorted and wrote questioning letters and thought. The legalese bits were read out loud over and over until they made some sense, and Carol typed out a rough draft of the story that unfolded. I was amazed at what we discovered, what I began to remember when going through it all.

In September, Keith Moon died. It seemed only yesterday that we'd done a session for Dave Clarke. Clarke had hustled Moon by saying I'd agreed and gotten me by saying Moon had agreed. True to form, when the producer had decided to 'knock it on the head', Moon had a great go at knocking him on the head. And we all ended up pushing Moon's battery-dead, massively heavy, antique American car out of a no-parking zone.

I hustled Aad of Darling Agency and landed a well-planned seven-teen-town (with six doubles), fourteen-day Dutch tour, including every venue from the edge of beyond to Amsterdam. I tried to gather a group. Les was unavailable. Aad recommended Dave Donovan (ex-Roy Wood's Wizard) and he said yes. So did Dave Clarke. And Eric. It was December. We drove ourselves and self-catered and froze in a rented cottage. The music was good in concept, but Eric was so loud that when I later tried to interest the agency in organising another tour, all the venues remembered being deafened and declined. We came back with a couple of hundred each. It had been endless grumbling, and we knew we'd never tour together again.

As rhythm guitarist, I joined a Skibbereen-based semi-pro, hard rock band called White Wine. It was headed by guitarist/songwriter Pete Best (not *the*) with John Joe O'Sullivan, an excellent drummer, and Ron Bending on bass. The group was very popular, but I grew tired of mile-long versions of *Whole Lotta Love*, and of being told we were too loud. No one had ever told The Experience to turn it down. I had déjà-vu feelings, like I was reliving my earliest gigging years. I was learning guitar again too. The work with Southern Comfort and White Wine gave me back my taste for it. I love bass, but hate being limited to it. If I toured internationally, I knew I would be expected to play bass on *Hey Joe* and acid rock numbers forever. Fuck it! I wasn't earning a living playing music now, but I wasn't going into debt to play it either. Then Ron and John moved to England to work and the demands of Pete's growing family and business grabbed him.

Why did I keep expecting semi-pro players to put music first? Performing drains an incredible amount of energy, even if it's a good gig which feeds you energy at the same time. It's impossible to play and work at a full-time job for very long. Something's got to give, and eventually you will, and the music. I'd be demanding more input to the music when there were no energy reserves to draw from. After all, to them it was only a hobby, not an obsession and way of life. And dinner.

Thirty-three. How did that happen?

I juggled with a million musicians to form bands for the few gigs I was offered and started giving guitar lessons. I found the first lessons terrifying. Who was I to teach someone else the guitar? How do you go about it? But the sincere eagerness of my pupils was refreshing. I remembered how it had been for me. I grew to love teaching. A few years later I looked at the local bands and realised they'd all been my students.

Elvis Presley died and RCA, who had been up against a wall, breathed a sigh of relief. I cried. In February 1979, RCA released me. The NRB had tied me up for four years, but I was now *free* for the first time in fourteen years, no longer contracted to anyone for anything. Liberation. But then again, nobody wanted me. I was no longer considered a desirable commodity. And that was not a welcome thought.

Rolling Stone publications visited and expressed interest in the book. We sent them the first rough draft. I still meet people who read it while they had it. A letter arrived, saying no thanks – too much business.

They were only interested in doing a fan-type book.

Totally out of the blue, Roger Cook of *The Cook Report* asked to interview me for his exposé of corruption in the music business entitled 'Rock Bottom', which also featured Lyndsey DePaul, Bo Diddley, and The Small Faces. It felt good to know that somebody cared. I didn't feel so alone after listening to the bands' problems. If anyone deserves his whack, it surely is Bo Diddley. By 1986, Roger was doing his show for TV. He and his wonderful team followed the story up with an excellent documentary on rock ripoffs featuring the story of The Experience. This bucked me up a lot.

No one else wanted to know. Publisher after publisher rejected my whole story, only wanting the 'and Jimi used to wear blue underpants' type of crap. 'Forget the past, Noel,' Chas advised, 'and think about the future.' What future? My frustration was feeling, indeed knowing, that at this moment I had no future.

Our generation grew up with a no-future feeling. Ours was a Peter Pan era which equated growing up with dying, and passing thirty with brain-death. A generation of anorexics who missed sleep in preference to missing a minute of life. It is said that the louder the music the unhappier the times. Watching the changes in music is like reading the psychological history of the human race. I like to think our music was more positive than the fifties rebel sound of *Tell Laura I love Her* and *Teen Angel*. We had a great feeling of hope and wanted something to build a new world on, for the sake of our own sanity. Pictures of hippies sticking flowers in the barrels of army guns called out to protect America from its children made great front pages, but the point was ignored. Armies should be positive, peaceful forces that can give life rather than take it, to help the world, not hinder it: creative armies to turn to for help in times of need – to repair weather damage, to build emergency housing, to harvest crops before an impending storm, dig irrigation ditches, carry water and topsoil to drought-striken countries. It would certainly cost a lot less than blowing something up, then asking the government for more money to replace it.

Massive migrations of searchers and philosophers followed mystic calls to points like San Francisco, getting high on psychedelics to reassure ourselves that the place beyond words was still there, to reaffirm that there was more to life than buying and selling (even if we took a bought pill to glimpse it). We hoped to rise up gloriously from the ashes of ignorance, to make the world better for everyone. Taking drugs in the sixties was a political statement, a declaration of independence. Perhaps it still is.

There was also something very powerful in knowing that our

generation, growing up out of the tail-end of the first nuclear war, comprised more than half the total population of some countries. We felt we could change things through sheer force of numbers. We resented having to live with the everyday threat of nuclear wipeout. To our parents and grandparents who had lived through two world wars, we wanted to say, 'This is no way to live!' So paranoid, so fearful, so stunted. The Cold War bred intelligence systems so brutal and ruthless that people stopped thinking and communicating at all for fear that today's thought might get you in trouble tomorrow. We insisted there was something more than consumerism, more than a grab-quick short-sighted, shallow-minded, instant-gratification, profit-equals-happiness society. We wanted to relearn the finer wisdom of the ages. In the horrors of war, so many generations had lost so much: lost the quality of life to the quantity of life; lost the sheer wonder of existence, the sense of wonder. This was what we were trying to recapture.

If there is no tomorrow, there is nothing to lose. Life is hell unless you can feel there is something to lose, and insights to gain and therefore something good to live and care for. There is a difference in living for today and living in chaos, although a little chaos is good for the soul. Real living for today does not make tomorrow harder, if we remember that there's a difference between self-discipline and the treadmill.

I made it to thirty-four.

By 1980 there was nothing left to sell, and the survival game was a bit too real. I wanted to escape – to scream or to sleep, or to lay back and relax, or to fuck off somewhere. Anywhere. I wanted to be rich and retired like everyone assumed I was. Instead I found myself passé and penniless and wasting my time on pointless revenge.

I'd forgotten how to dream. I felt like a mother whose family has grown up, gone away and left her with empty days and too much time to think. Soon I would be thirty-five. I was forced to consider that there *might* be life after forty. Sometimes I glimpsed the possibility that there might even be life after rock-stardom. The star machinery said I'd served my time and was no longer of any use to the world except as a memory of the past, that I was redundant, like a drummer in a drum-machine world. But was I?

I hadn't become a real drug addict, but I'd had a darn good go and succeeded in becoming a very competent alcoholic. I wanted to give up but found it hard going. Carol helped me to keep trying, and did her jobs and ones that should have been mine or ours, including solo emergency roof repairs in a force ten gale, while I slept off a hard night. But even her patience and stubborn determination was faltering with her health and energy. If only I could change this festering attitude; if only I could stop striking out against people trying to help me just because they were accessible when the rats weren't; if only I could curb my tendency to begrudge anyone success, even if they'd struggled for years, because I had failed . . .

Hendrix, who hadn't died as an idol but as a guitarist, was slowly given a press build-up until you could have sworn he'd had six arms and had never ever played with another musician. He was added to the list of the Marketable Deceased – Buddy Holly, Eddie Cochran, Judy Garland, Marilyn Monroe, James Dean . . . In anticipation of the growing market, Alan Douglas (hired by Warners to revamp old tapes after the quality of material coming out of the Jeffery Estate sunk to a new low) released *Nine to the Universe*, and the creative repackaging of singles and original albums started, with expensive boxed sets beginning to appear. When it came to making a video for the re-re-re-release of *Are You Experienced*, Douglas put himself in it.

Gold and Goldstein spent endless hundreds of thousands fighting Branton's stance that they had no right to release their Albert Hall film. I prayed justice would prevail, as they were determined to share the profits with *all* the band members. Eventually they went bust, and Douglas was well able to buy it. I expect it will be released soon.

Warners charges so much for the use of an Experience track in America that it prevents European documentaries from being shown there. Polydor, which controls Europe, is much more reasonable. *She's So Fine*'s publisher is listed as Yameta. No address given.

As the years ticked by, it was to a large extent the relentless marketing of Jimi by his Estate which drove people to look me up as 'A Survivor'. The Estate now owns my face and music, but cannot buy my silence. They could have had co-operation from me by offering some concession to my part in the music, but they didn't.

The Annual Hendrix Deathday Celebrations started. Les, Eric and I played (for expenses only) at the first one – the 1980 Amsterdam Festival beautifully run by Caesar Glebbeek and Dan Foster of the Hendrix Information Centre. For the first time in ten years, I played Experience tunes. When Mitch got up to jam with me, the stage flooded with Hendrix sound-alikes who saw their chance to be Jimi fronting The Experience. Soon there was nothing but a web of guitar leads and the aural turmoil of a forest of Stratocasters. I left them to it.

Jimi had suffered a bit, but at least he had missed this ghoulish resurrection. Sadly, his legacy seemed to be lasting pain for those lives that had touched his musically. If it is possible to maintain consciousness after death, then he must be in agony.

I picked up the pieces. The Hendrix Estate picked up the cash. Periodically, newspaper articles mocked me: 'Hendrix Estate will gross $24 million this year.' Estimates of total Estate earnings have passed the $200 million mark. Ironically, all that wealth would only have been of marginal interest to Jimi. I believe he would have become a jazzer, and that is not usually a lucrative musical stance.

I still hear young bands saying, 'Well, if it goes wrong, we'll sue them.' All I can say is, 'Ha!'

Carol typed her way through 1979, 1980, and beyond. The depression caught her too as she relived it. She was forced to put it aside for a couple of years. I was amazed that it took so long to put together words, but then it took me even longer to dredge up in bits and scraps the memories I had consigned to oblivion. Some people offered help freely, some offered it under pressure, some helped by not helping or in spite of themselves. We slowly continued our research. Decisions, decisions – buy some postage stamps, or have something besides sausages for dinner? A typewriter ribbon or a gallon of petrol? We approached many, many publishers. No go. One managed to 'lose' our manuscript and the copy made the sneaky circuit of collectors who obviously felt no remorse about ripping me off either. One example was a couple of Experience demo acetates which I let one collector copy for his 'own private listening'. When I later tried to sell the acetates to raise some urgently needed cash, he'd traded copies around the world and my acetates were worthless.

The bank periodically offered to sell our home for us to cover the growing loan. Thankfully, they were more than understanding and patient when we went in to grovel and beg for time.

At this point, I became acutely aware of every cost in my life. I was *really* skint. Skint with nothing pending. Skint with thousands owing. Skint with no job. Skint with a jar of pennies for the electricity bill and a list of excuses a mile long for the creditors. So skint that when the cats killed a pigeon, we nicked it for dinner. If we saw a hare or rabbit road-accident victim, we made sure if hadn't died in vain but for a casserole. I became conscious of waste – material and mental.

If I wanted to survive, I'd have to cut down on the empty days and wean myself off the companions I called friends just because they could drink all day and I needed ears to babble to. Just because you have a multitude of forces arrayed against you, doesn't mean you must put up the white flag – though I nearly did the day we were flat broke with absolutely nothing on the horizon or in the fridge. I conquered excruciating embarrassment long enough to walk into the dole office. I nearly signed on but couldn't do it. I had never been on the dole in my life and I wasn't about to start now. I wasn't a complete imbecile. Surely I could think of something. If I could scrape by at all, I would.

Our friends and neighbours were true friends and neighbours. We traded apples for potatoes. We cleared yards of years of clutter and collected tons of burnables to feed the boiler with during the long winters. Now I can't look at a twig or bit of paper without thinking 'solid fuel'. As I collected roadside rubbish, I wondered about people. 'And what do you do for a living?' 'Oh, I collect litter.'

Diversification became the key. Carol made and sold bread, jam, jelly, and anything else anyone wanted to eat. We swept chimneys and did chainsawing jobs, cutting huge piles of tree trunks into logs. I tried agenting and promoting. Yuk! Barely broke even. I don't have the cast-iron stomach a promoter needs. We bred geese and goats but gave it up because we found it impossible to come to terms with murdering them. It was so awful chasing Christmas dinner (the slowest runner) around and shed or listening to the kids crying 'Maaaa' on the way to be slaughtered. We realised how little school had taught us about living and using what brains we have creatively, to take care of practical, everyday living problems. What an amazing variety of things there are to think about and do when you can't afford to pay someone else to do it for you. Perhaps man is a grazing kind of animal, picking at what interests him, ruminating and browsing and constantly searching. We may be fascinated by ants, but we don't make very good ones.

If what you have to do is survive, then any occupation can be fulfilling in that way. But if it comes to it that you're constantly flogging yourself to work, you should seriously consider doing something else. Immediately. You must take pleasure and satisfaction from what you spend your life doing, not just money. I hadn't any more time to waste on the Western dream, that preoccupation with acquiring things on the basis that buying will make us free. Even the biggest purchases are easier to come by than a morsel of wisdom.

The Experience became work, not music. We knew we needed to expand in our separate ways, but without cutting our ties completely. Of course, it's impossible to have a brilliant gig every night, but some later gigs were so utterly unfulfilling that the frustration followed us off stage and into the dressing room, where we'd pout, snarl and bicker like an old married couple. Some casual girlfriends couldn't understand this type of letting off steam and made matters worse by adding their own mental problems to the soup.

I got my fill of rock stardom, and I reckon Jimi had, too. It wasn't really the easy buck it's made out to be. If I could just be a simple musician again, creating music for pleasure. There is nothing like the thrill of a shooting star, but I'd certainly miss the stars that twinkle faithfully, if not spectacularly, every night. I'd started out playing music, but I'd got mixed up with success, like a kid who fell in with the wrong crowd.

I knew I'd make music for nothing again if I had to. And I did. Because of all things in my life, I needed music most – more than beer even! I needed to play, but didn't know how to go about it. There were no bands left to join. The just-ending disco era had wiped out a generation of up-and-coming musicians. With no venues, few beginner players had survived. And those who had survived, by listening to and learning from electronically regimented music, were machines themselves. What was my music? Where could it happen? I was still locked in the belief that music could only be made with electric guitars and basses and drums and volume, but it was beginning to dawn on me that small might be beautiful, since big hadn't been.

In late 1980, Jon O'Toole, acoustic guitarist and singer of Neil Young and similar songs completely alien to me, asked if I'd join him for a few sessions. It was certainly a change. I'd kept my old Gibson J-160B – the same type of guitar as the Beatles used to play. But when I played acoustic, I was certain no one could possibly hear anything I was playing, so I threw finesse to the wind and hammered away in an attempt at volume by brute force. I broke strings every night and learned how to tie them together again – if you were lucky enough to have them break at one end. Slowly my ears adjusted. I felt fortunate to be one of the few sixties musicians I know who survived with their hearing intact – not because of strong eardrums, just because I'd been lucky enough to have an earwax problem which had acted as built-in earplugs during the tour years.

Ana, Jon's wife, and Carol sometimes came along for the ride. Since RTE radio signed off at ten to two in the morning, we'd sing to while away the long and winding road home. Out of this, Tonite was born: two acoustic guitars, minimal percussion and four voices doing fifties and sixties songs we remembered and liked. We rehearsed around the kitchen table, getting dizzy from breathing all wrong and sore ribs from pushing out every last bit of breath. What got me most was the difficulty of playing one thing on guitar while searching for harmonies and vocal rhythms that were radically different.

Our first booking was the Munster Arms Hotel in Bandon. Talk about life's embarrassing moments. There were four of us trying to hide behind two mike stands. I felt uneasy with the acoustic. Powerless. Carol and Ana had never attempted anything like this before in their lives. Somehow we got through it, fluffed notes, hot flushes and all, and only a few members of the audience had fled. And we got paid – £15. I swear we each lost at least five pounds of weight in sweat that night.

In time we actually won a steady audience. We were the only group attempting any kind of complex vocal at a quiet level. Tonite lasted nearly a year, but we disagreed on what we wanted to achieve. And Ana was burning her candle at both ends, trying to work nights and raise two small children. In true country tradition we became two groups, Jon and Ana, and Noel and Carol (aka Secret Freaks). You can think up all the fancy names you want, but you only get, 'Who's that then?' 'Noel and Carol.' 'Well, why didn't ye say so?'

We kept going from sheer necessity. It was our only source of income. We were dreadful, nervous, embarrassed. Singing was the hardest. Carol and I have voices only in so far as that's what comes out of our mouths. But we worked on refining our tones and harmonic blend. I missed a second guitar, and still do. But there wasn't enough money in it to interest anyone else. For a while we tried person after person, mostly to combat our own insecurities. Some didn't mesh, some had their own dreams, and some couldn't see any future in our concept.

We held on to a couple of venues (bless Tom at O'Donovan's Hotel), but eventually found ourselves working in Shanley's pub seven nights a week with a lunchtime session on Sundays, and as long as nine hours at a stretch on holiday weekends. Even if we only earned £5 each and drinks, at least we were working and eating. And getting better. A gig is a gig.

Shanley's was a relaxed, singalong pub, where musicians were encouraged to join in regardless of their chord catalogue. Anyone could come up for a song. There were no microphones, just a smidgen of guitar amplification. The pub revolved around Moss, the owner, and the piano in the middle of the very small bar (more like a sitting room) and us sitting around him. He can play and sing along to nearly any song you can think of. In a couple of years the pub had become a huge success. Travellers from all over the world began to stop in as news spread of the great crack (from the Irish *craic*, meaning good time.) Musicians from all over the country and beyond popped in for the casual sessions that just weren't happening any more beyond the traditional Irish music crowd, who can be pretty insular. We made some wonderful friends, too numerous to mention, who made wonderful music. On a good night, the crowd would be pushed up right against us, standing anywhere they could fit. You'd be singing two inches from someone's face and they'd be swaying and singing along too. It made music real and alive for me again.

Shanley's flew it for years and one son, Bill, who at nine years old was one of my first guitar pupils, became an excellent guitarist – and he can put his hand to clarinet, piano, banjo and bass! Then they remodelled the place. We left to find our way in the world. And we found it. In vocal harmonies supported by a full guitar sound and minimal percussion.

In spite of Jimi's flash and original guitar work, I'm sure much of his lingering appeal is based on the underlying liberated and liberating feel of his music, and especially of his voice. The guitar techniques overwhelmed his whole talent only after the mechanical analysers took over, but his total sound was tied to his voice. He could shriek away on guitar all he wanted, but underneath it all his voice mellowed and relaxed you and called to you to join him.

I still feel funny about playing the few songs I've written, preferring versions of songs I love. We go for a relaxed atmosphere and hope everyone sings along. You can't do this as a completely alien sound playing completely alien songs. You have to give the audience something they can relate to until they accept your sound. At that point they will accept unfamiliar songs. I can't understand new groups getting all uppity when asked to play other people's songs. The Experience did a lot of covers – *Killing Floor, Like a Rolling Stone, Sergeant Pepper, Day Tripper*, to name a few. They were good songs for us and we liked them. In his open-minded way, Hendrix picked up on a silly English pop song called *Wild Thing* and made it his own. We didn't feel we were 'selling out'. We had our own good sound and that put our stamp on those songs.

A crunch came in 1984. The only trouble with getting drink as part of your fee is that you are inclined to fill up to boost your earnings. And drink had always been my weakness. I couldn't seem to get it into my head that less was better and more pleasurable. And even though I had completely cut out spirits and wine, I still relentlessly shoved as much down my throat as I could – and didn't appreciate a mouthful. I hadn't come to terms with starting over again. If we could only remember that we are our own worst enemies. I still harboured resentment. Resented having to hump and set up the heavy, outdated gear. Resented having an amateur as a partner. I felt the lost years and the expended energies keenly. Carol was having her own problems regarding singing and writing, fighting her own sense of 'What the fuck do I think I'm doing?' We had some very cross words. She grew tired of my constant demands for pity, and knew I was giving myself more than enough anyway. She wanted to like me, but I wanted to wallow. More and more often my dinner went back to the kitchen, only picked at. Only the dog was happy.

I found myself attending a Queen concert at Wembley, London. While meeting their very successful tour manager, Gerry Stickells, for the first time since The Experience, I had a fit, collapsed, and was hospitalised. (Thank you to the St John's Ambulance Service.) Two days of tests later, the doctor was blunt. I was there because my drink consumption had by far surpassed my food consumption. He nearly called it 'the writer's disease' – an occupational hazard in those circles.

The next day I was scheduled for another Hendrix commemorative, run by John Berry in Retford, England. The no-frills, badly attended function was utterly depressing for me in my position as the token 'musician who had played with Hendrix'. I was totally spaced from my collapse, but due to perform. With the help and support of 'Boston Bob' Dunlap, a beautifully talented guitarist from, you guessed it, Boston, who'd been visiting relatives in Ireland and doing casual gigs with Carol and I, and with Les on drums, I survived it. Al Hendrix was there, but I couldn't speak to him as I couldn't help feeling he should have helped ensure that Jimi's co-musician's were treated fairly. Tony Henderson had been good enough to drive us there from London and, bless him, he drove all night back after a quick stop for dinner which I couldn't eat. It made me sick to look at Chip Branton, son of Leo, and crowd (who could afford flights from LA) laughing and partying over their dinner. I tried to make a scene, but hadn't the energy to finish it before I passed out.

My body forced me to examine my brain. If I really wanted to live, and not just survive, I had to take a long hard look at my attitude, and my habits. There are probably some things more painful than the truth, but I can't think of any. But thinking is easier in the long run than not thinking. Everybody scrapes the bottom of the barrel in their own way. I'd been successful and I'd lost my head. I'd alienated friends and relations and attracted weirdos and bad vibes. What's worse, I was getting out of it so as not to have to think. We all love our pleasurable habits – and tea/coffee break, the cigarette/joint break, the martini, the sugary chocolate biscuit – those little rewards you promise yourself for accomplishing your work. But I'd fallen into the ritual of waking up just to get drunk enough again to go back to sleep.

Everyone alters their brain chemistry, even if you do it by jogging or chanting or jumping out of an aeroplane. But with additives the problem, *my* problem, is stopping when nicely stoned. You really only get one good buzz a day no matter what you're taking. The rest is just topping up or going over the top. Your body simply gets used to your treat, and wants more. I was never a coffee (or even tea) drinker until Carol, typically American in her love for coffee, turned me on to it. The first time I got the jitters and sweated and really sped. Not anymore. Doubling your intake and mixing drugs ruins the effect. (And that goes for medicinal drugs, too.) Cutting your intake and savouring each additive for the reason that you're taking it works. What's the point in mixing tranquillisers and caffeine when taking less of one or the other would do the same? Grass with tobacco and booze? Not unless you like the view of the interior of a toilet bowl. In the sixties drinking was considered totally unhip because it is a mind deadener. Like heroin or downers, it's a very tempting escape. I took downers simply to feel relaxed when I could no longer relax naturally. Booze is a quality-controlled downer, and legal, so you can change your brain without the debilitating paranoia of an imminent bust (when every roofrack and taxi looks like a police car and every person on the street is a plainclothes detective) or finding out your supply has been cut with poison. However, downers change your vibes. Negativity can't pull you through.

Whereas I was drinking so as not to think, I started smoking grass just to relax enough so I could think. And I thought my way through it, through every nook and cranny of the whole trip. After twenty years, I can now relax from The Experience. I'm now able to look on The Experience not as the be all and end all of my life, but as a portion of it. Perhaps that's not so much an achievement as an inevitability. The years formed a bridge and allowed me to walk away. I'm forty-four. I've missed grasping consciously many thoughts that have slipped through my mind, but I'm sure they were good for me nonetheless and I don't regret what I went through or took to have them.

You never find what you're looking for if you're so restless and dissatisfied that you can't build on what you already have. I looked around me. I had survived in spite of all this, or maybe because of it. I was making music and loving it again. I'd gone looking for sex, and against all odds found love. I made friends with animals, and slowly people. I had a roof (of sorts) over my head, and nature in the shape of West Cork constantly displaying beautiful and awesome sights for my pleasure and education. Who could ask for anything more? If I wanted to feel bad, it was my doing, but I had the choice. And I only had to change myself. Wasn't it stupid not to take what I had and make happiness out of it?

What do I want? Well, the same thing as everyone else. Time and the frame of mind to enjoy it. An interesting occupation which adds something positive to the world. Companions to share life with. Someone to care about and feel at ease with. A community to care about and feel at home in. Peace, good health, an open mind, the freedom to be creatively productive and the knowledge that we can make the world a better place for the next generations.

I love privacy, but I've bared my soul – honestly and openly I hope – to keep my sanity. Just because we lose our youth doesn't mean we have to lose our dreams. This story is not meant to take the stars out of your eyes. It's to help keep them twinkling.

Chalk it up to The Experience.

> *There's a light in the window.*
> *See it through the rain, feel the wind blow.*
> *There's a light in the window.*
> *Ain't it good to be home.*

Afterword

Carol Lines

IT GOES LIKE THIS.

Jimi, Noel and Mitch, plus Gerry Stickells the tour manager and the Rock'n'Roll Adventurer, these five are on the train from London to Manchester.

The time is spring 1967 and getting on the train to London, they have to walk along the aisle to reach their reserved compartment. The train, it is overflowing with football supporters, crazed drunk aggressive rednecks.

Jimi leads the posse and the Adventurer, he tails it. As soon as they walk into each new carriage there is, to put it mildly, a very bad vibe from the football fans, a 'Fucking long haired nigger weirdo' type vibe. These are the sort of people who turn off *Top of the Pops* when The Experience are appearing, turn it off disgusted.

The normal response would be a retaliatory 'Ah, fuck off yourself' but no, Jimi says nothing, simply beams a magnetic grin. And the Adventurer, he can feel the change. These geezers, they become transformed to go home and tell their daughters, 'Oh, I met that bloke Freddie Hendrix, he's a nice guy.'

Noel and his lady Carol, they asked me to tell this story in this book. And now Carol is gone.

'Oh Carol, don't ever steal your heart away' Chuckleberry once sang and now, now there is a different meaning to the song.

Carol and Noel, they finished this book together and the last bits, Carol had them ready on the world processor when she died.

Who are we to judge the greater plan? Yet . . . It seems so *unfair* that Carol died. Remember, her man Noel had been through all the Jimi

Hendrix Experience madness – and the many joys, too – and he survived, maybe a bit battered and certainly a bit bruised . . . But Noel, he has a stout heart.

And even more important than that, Noel found Carol. Carol Appleby was one of the kindest people I've ever met and thank God, I've met many. She was – she *is* the rainbow woman, *always* believing in the promise of possibilities.

God bless you, Carol. And thank you too.

B.P. Fallon is the Rock 'n' Roll Adventurer

Photo Credits

Since all photographs come from Noel Redding's personal collection, it has not always been possible to trace the photographers involved. The Publishers apologise for any omissions from this list.

1   Noel Redding/Richard Caylor/Folkestone Herald & Gazette
2   Ulrich Handl
3   Unknown
4   Linda McCartney
5   Ulrich Handl
6   Ulrich Handl
7   Noel Redding/Unknown
8/9 Unknown
10   Unknown
11   Linda McCartney
12   Linda McCartney
13   Mike Barich
14   Noel Redding/Herbert Worthington
15   Unknown/Unknown/Donagh Glavin, John Sheehan
     Photography
16   Unknown

Index

All Night Newsboys, 91
Allison, Mose, 141
Altham, Keith, 47
Andrews, John, 3, 4, 7
Appleby, Carol, 187, 188, 191,
    206-7, 210-11, 213, 214-15, 216-17,
    218, 220-1
Arden, Don, 20, 21
Auger, Brian, 25, 31
Avery, Mick, 110

Baker, Ginger, 127, 135
Balin, Michael, 111, 186
Banks, John, 13, 27
Barrett, Eric, 88, 105, 117, 163
Barton, Cliff, 31
Beatles, 33, 34, 36, 164
Beck, Jeff, 62, 116, 118, 131, 142, 154,
    155, 197
Bee Gees, 63, 113
Bell, Eric, 198, 199-200, 207
Bell, Madeline, 75
Bending, Ron, 210
Bennett, Brian, 6
Bennett, Cliff, 14
Bentley, John, 18
Best, Pete, 210
Black, Bill, 136, 141-2, 157
Bland, Bobby, 83
Blue Cheer, 87
Bolan, Marc, 193, 198
Bond, Graham, 100
Bonham, John, 131

Booker T, 3, 12, 18, 53, 129
Boyd, Joe, 163, 166
Branton, Chip, 217
Branton, Leo, 151, 162, 163, 168, 180,
    182, 183, 185, 188, 205
Brevitt, Marshall, 122
Brewer, Jon, 199, 202
Brody, Kathy, 150
Brown, Arthur, 87
Bruce, Jack, 127, 159
Buddy Miles Express, 91, 100
Burdon, Eric, 14, 18, 22, 23, 39, 92,
    100, 108, 125, 129, 135, 141, 146,
    169, 190
Burton, Trevor, 70-1

California, Randy, 161
Capaldi, Jim, 110
Cartwright, Tony, 13
Caruso, Paul, 140
Casady, Jack, 104, 136
Casson, Ivor, 139
Cat Mother, 91
Catini, Clem, 14
Chalpin, Ed, 60, 90-1, 94, 111,
    147, 180
Chandler, Chas, 18, 19, 20, 23-4, 25,
    27-8, 31, 33, 41, 45, 48, 51, 52, 54,
    55, 58, 60, 66, 67, 70, 72, 74, 75, 84,
    86, 87, 90, 91, 93, 94, 97, 98, 108,
    116, 117, 124, 125, 126-8, 135, 136,
    139, 144, 152, 156, 158, 165, 166,
    172, 181, 190, 194, 195, 196,
    202-3, 205

Chapman, Roger, 140
Charles, Ray, 3
Checker, Chubby, 83
Chesters, Neville, 52, 88, 177
Clapton, Eric, 59, 104, 127
Clark, Molly, 7
Clarke, Dave, 194, 198, 199, 207
Cochran, Eddie, 3, 140
Cohen, Ira, 142
Cohen, Max, 186, 191, 192, 194-5, 198, 201, 202, 203
Collins, Lynn, 136-7
Cook, Roger, 209
Cooke, Sam, 18
Corvell, Larry, 87, 98
Cox, Billy, 137, 140, 144, 159, 169
Crane, Tony, 35
Crosby, David, 78

Daltrey, Roger, 83
Danneman, Monika, 144-5, 146, 147-8
Dave Clark Five, 56
Davidson, Harold, 21, 56, 75, 172
Davis, Spencer, 58
Dee, Dave, 191
Dee, Simon, 62
DePaul, Lyndsey, 209
Dickenson, Alan 'Adge', 11, 13
Dicker, Leon, 22, 92, 156, 162, 169, 185, 186, 189, 192, 195, 196
Diddley, Bo, 209
Dillon, Eric, 13, 110, 126
Dolenz, Mickey, 78
Donovan, Dave, 207
Dorfman, Stanley, 113
Douglas, Alan, 137, 148, 205
Duffy, Warren, 157
Dunbar, Ainsley, 18
Dunlop, Jim, 48

Eire Apparent, 91, 99, 110
Emery, Martin, 187
Entwistle, John, 124
Epstein, Brian, 52, 63

Etchingham, Cathy, 36, 37, 62
Experience, 163, 170, 189, 199, 205, 219
  appear in charts, 35-6
  appear on *Ready, Steady, Go*, 34, 35
  Are You Experienced?, 50, 52, 60, 85, 90
  Big Apple Club, Munich, 33
  European performances, 42-4, 50-1, 63-4, 66, 73-4, 87-9, 113-14
  first solo LP, 50
  founding of group, 25-9
  French tour, 30-1
  Monterey Pop Festival, 53-4, 55
  Scotch of St James, 32-3
  star treatment, 42
  Top of the Pops, 34, 35
  UK performances, 35-42, 44, 45-8, 51-2, 62-3, 64-6, 68-72, 89-90, 92-3, 115-16
  US performances, 52-61, 74-87, 96-101, 107-12, 119-27
  waiting for a break, 31-4

Fallon, B.P., 220-1
Fallon, Jack, 16
Ferris, Karl, 52
Flint, Hughie, 31
Fontana, Wayne, 36
Foster, Dan, 211
Freeman, Alan, 45

Gaff, Billy, 164
Garla, Tony, 39, 75
Gaye, Marvin, 166
Gee, Mickey, 198
Gibb, Maurice, 113
Glebbeek, Caesar, 163, 211
Gold, Steve, 104, 128, 156, 211
Golding, Ron, 6
Goldstein, Gerry, 104, 128
Goldstein, Mike, 61, 75, 119, 156, 211
Goody, Mick, 3
Gordon, Jim, 187

Graham, Bill, 54, 55, 76, 104, 122
Green, Mick, 5, 6, 8, 12, 26, 32
Green, Richard, 115
Grossman, Al, 75
Gunnel, John, 33
Gunnel, Rick, 33, 70, 119
Guy, Victor, 158

Hagood, Kenny, 151, 152, 158, 162,
    163, 166, 169, 172, 173, 175, 176,
    177, 182
Halliday, Johnny, 10-11, 18, 25, 30
Hammond, Celia, 155
Hardin, Tim, 103
Harrison, George, 104
Hartford, John, 141
Harvey, Alex, 31
Hecht, Michael, 108, 135, 153, 156,
    157, 162, 166, 168, 172, 180, 201
Heider, Wally, 151
Henderson, Sir Guy, 22, 172,
    174-5, 185
Hendrix, Al, 150-1, 158
Hendrix, Jimi, 73, 105, 107, 110, 111,
    113, 220
    and audiences, 78, 89
    Band of Gypsies, 138, 142, 169, 180
    blackness, 83-4
    changes name from Jimmy James, 23
    contracts, 34, 39, 44-5, 51, 52-3, 60,
        80, 85, 90-2, 107-8, 139
    death, 145-8, 204
    drugs, 80, 113-14, 123-4, 133, 142,
        145-7
    early career, 24-5
    Electric Lady Studios, 138, 140, 143,
        154, 170
    entourage, 128-9
    equipment, 44, 89
    estate, 149-52, 157, 162, 180, 192,
        202, 206, 212
    Experience reunion tour, 137-41,
        144-5

    experiments with guitar sounds, 66-7,
        85-6
    family, 78, 148, 150
    fans, 42, 47, 71-2
    films, 115-16, 137, 162-3, 189, 211
    funeral, 149
    guitar set on fire, 47, 53
    lawsuits, 108, 116-17
    letter of apology, 120-2
    as marketable deceased, 211-12
    money problems, 38-9
    moodies, 43-4, 57
    and Mrs Redding, 36-7, 116, 144
    plays guitar with teeth, 89
    refusal to play, 109
    singing, 26-7
    songwriting, 49
    Wildman image, 45, 48
    see also Experience
Hendrix, Leon, 78
Herman and the Hermits, 56
Hill, Vince, 6
Hillman, John, 22, 91, 107, 156, 158,
    169, 171-2, 185-6, 189, 195, 196
Hiscox, Bob, 4
Hobbs, John, 173
Hopkins, Jerry, 150, 186
Hopkins, Nick, 131
Howard, Ed, 151, 152, 168, 169, 172,
    176, 177, 182 Hughes, Ken, 127
Humperdinck, Engelbert, 13, 14,
    16, 46

Isley Brothers, 24

James, Jimmy, 23
Jansch, Bert, 64
Jansen, John, 174
Jeffery, Gillian, 186
Jeffery, Michael, 16 6, 20, 22, 23, 27-8,
    33, 44, 50, 51, 52, 54, 56, 57, 70, 72,
    75, 80, 85, 86, 90, 91, 92, 93-4,
    101-2, 103-4, 106, 107, 108, 111, 115,
    116, 117, 124, 126-8, 129, 137-8,

139, 141, 150-1, 152, 154, 156, 157, 158, 159, 160, 162, 163, 165, 167, 169-70, 172-3, 174, 175, 179, 180, 182, 185, 189, 192, 194, 195, 196, 198, 201, 202-3
Jimi Hendrix Experience, 27, 107-8
Jimi Hendrix Foundation, 150
Jones, Brian, 53
Jones, Deacon, 125
Jones, Nick, 46
Jones, Tom, 14, 15
Jorgensen, Sebastian, 64
Juried, Michael, 140

Katz, Dick, 18, 94
Kay, Des, 7
Keane, Micky, 46
Keeley, Andy, 154
Keith, Linda, 23
Kellgren, Gary, 55, 87
Kenzie, Phil, 12
Kessell, Danny, 126
Kidd, Johnny, 6, 7, 13, 18
King, Freddy, 200
King, Martin Luther, 83-4
Kingsley, Billy, 15, 35
Kircher, Jan, 61
Kircher, Pete, 2, 3, 5, 8, 10, 11, 12, 13, 32, 62, 198
Klein, Alan, 163
Klein, Warren, 170
Knight, Curtis, 24, 60
Knight, Derek, 7, 13, 32, 49
Knights, Dave, 26
Korner, Alexis, 31, 213
Kramer, Eddie, 55, 154, 174
Kruger, Jeff, 167

Laine, Denny, 12, 52, 62, 118
Lambert, Kit, 33-4, 50
Landon, Neil, 4, 6, 7, 8, 10, 11, 12, 15, 16, 32, 38, 93, 100, 135, 140, 141
Lane, Jerry, 206
Lang, Kevin, 8, 10, 11, 12-13

Larkin, Jerry, 206
Lawrence, Sharon, 162, 165, 170, 171, 189
Lawton, April, 159
Led Zeppelin, 5
Lennon, Freddy, 14
Lester, Howard, 162
Leverton, Jim, 6, 13, 16, 32, 45, 110, 125, 135
Levine, Bob, 75, 139, 150, 156, 181
Lexon, Lotta, 58
Little Richard, 24
Locking, Licorice, 6
London, Laurie, 3
Lulu, 113

McCarthy, Ted, 198
McCartney, Linda, 76
McCartney, Paul, 52, 53
McQueen, Steve, 61
McVey, Terry, 39
Mann, Manfred, 116, 141, 206
Marriot, Steve, 199
Marshall, Jim, 8
Mason, Dave, 67, 105
Merseybeats, 13
Meyer, Roger, 44
Michaels, Lee, 105, 193
Miles, Buddy, 105, 130, 137, 149
Miller, Pamela, 61
Miller, Russ, 173
Milligan, Spike, 52, 110
Mills, Gordon, 13-14, 15, 16-17, 25, 46, 94
Mitchell, Mick, 45
Mitchell, Mitch, 13, 26, 28, 29, 31, 32, 38, 41, 51, 58, 59, 65, 66, 71, 73, 74, 75, 77-8, 80, 88, 91, 93, 97, 100-1, 104, 105, 111, 117, 129, 136, 139, 140, 142, 149, 150, 154, 155, 158, 159, 161, 162, 166, 167, 174, 175, 195, 204, 211, 220
Monay, Zoot, 14
Monkees, 54, 56, 57-8
Moon, Keith, 58, 77, 124-5, 207

Morgan, Nigel, 156
Moriarty, Michael, 150
Most, Mickey, 20, 22
Mothers of Invention, 56, 87
Motown, 157, 160, 162, 171, 173

Natural Resources, 157, 173
Nelson, Ricky, 3
Nero, 18
Nimoy, Leonard, 82
Norman, Kevin, 10
NuNu, 8, 32

O'Donnel, Hugh, 6
Oldham, Andrew, 21, 53
O'Neill, Bob, 140
O'Neill, Mike, 18
Oskar, Lee, 125
Osmonds, Colin 'Buster', 4, 5
Ostin, Mo, 116, 127, 154, 157, 175
O'Toole, Ana, 214-15
O'Toole, Jon, 214-15

Page, Jimmy, 131
Patterson, Robert, 199, 200, 202
Paul, Steve, 56, 87
Perkins, Wayne, 187
Phillips, John, 55
Pile, Susan, 170
Pinera, Mike, 161
PPX, 80, 90-1, 93, 109, 116-17, 147,
    165, 203
Presley, Elvis, 3, 103, 208
The Pretty Things, 135
Price, Alan, 75
Prichard, Barry, 8

Raven, Genya, 21
Redding, Anthony, 1
Redding, Margaret, 1, 5, 7, 12, 14, 19,
    36-7, 110, 111, 116, 142, 144,
    171, 186
Redding, Noel, 220-1
    The Animals, 20-4

bass guitar, 41
book, 207, 208-9
breaks arm, 158-9
The Burnettes, 6-17
contracts, 39, 51, 85, 91-2, 93-4,
    107-8, 126-8, 160, 165-6
divorce, 143, 153, 187-8, 205
drinking, 6, 33, 43, 77, 133, 171,
    187, 210, 216, 218
drugs, 11, 31, 53, 54, 57, 113-14,
    120, 141-2, 153, 155, 171
English accent, 78-9
equipment, 48, 55, 67, 89, 98
fans, 42, 47, 71-2
Fat Mattress, 95, 101, 110, 115, 119,
    120, 125-8, 134-6, 139, 152, 153,
    176, 179
Gold Disc, 96
Hendrix' funeral, 149
house, 186-7
lawsuits, Chapter 8, Chapter 9, 125,
    153, 156-8, 163-4
learns of Hendrix' death, 145
The Lonely Ones, 3-6
The Loving Kind, 32
marriage, 134-5
meets Jimi Hendrix, 18-19
money problems, 38-9, 140-1, 142
Noel Redding Band, 199-201,
    202, 203
Road, 157, 158, 162, 166
Rolls Royce, 117-18
schooldays, 1-5
Shanley's pub, 215-16
songwriting, 49-50, 84-5, 86-7,
    102-3, 108-9
The Strangers, 3, 4
tax, 139, 141, 142, 143
see also Experience
Redding, Vicki, 1, 136
Reid, Terry, 159
Reiss, Barry, 156-8, 162, 180
Relf, Keith, 35
Richard, Cliff, 3

Richards, Keith, 66
Roben, Joyce, 156
Roberts, Al, 177
Robertson, Phil, 71
Robinson, Dave, 70
Roemer, Richard, 108, 124, 139,
    153, 156
Rolling Stones, 34, 164
Roman, Michelle, 157
Roman, Murray, 61, 1, 134 141, 156,
    166, 198
Rose, Tim, 23, 93, 162
Rosen, Peter, 125
Rosenblatt, 172
Row, Fritz, 75, 114
Rubini, Michele, 187
Russell, Tony, 188

Salyers, 161, 171
Sampson, Les, 154-5, 157, 158, 160,
    161, 162, 166, 170-1, 173, 177, 188,
    199, 207
Sandground, Mark, 166-7, 168, 169,
    171, 173, 175, 179, 181, 185,
    196, 207
Schroeder, Aaron, 22
Shapiro, Bonnie, 170, 197
Shapiro, Michael, 165-8, 170, 171,
    172, 173, 174-6, 179-80, 181-4, 185,
    187, 188, 192, 193, 199, 201, 202,
    203, 204, 207
Sheridan, Bernard, 188
Simon and Garfunkel, 53
Sinatra, Frank, 44
Small Faces, 63, 66
Smith, Russ, 161
Solomon, Bernie, 128
Sperber, Betty, 94
Stamp, Chris, 33-4, 39, 101, 106
Standford, Chris, 13
Starr, Freddie, 13
Steingarten, Henry, 91, 150, 151-2,
    156, 162, 169, 174, 189
Steptoe, Bob, 154, 155

Stern, Andy, 186, 201, 203
Stevens, Cat, 46
Stewart, Al, 12
Stewart, Rod, 12, 93
Stickells, Gerry, 33, 36, 38, 41, 55, 71,
    77, 79, 88, 89, 101, 107, 111, 112,
    132, 144, 148, 156, 163, 174, 220
Stigwood, Robert, 70, 126, 127
Stokes, Dennis, 4
Sullivan, Jim, 6
Sullivan, John Joe, 208
Sullivan, Tommy, 161
Sullivan, Trixie, 109
Sutch, David 'Lord', 131
Sutton, Trevor, 7-8
Suzanne, 110, 114, 133, 134-5, 136-7,
    139, 143, 153, 187-8, 205

Tarrant, Robert, 160
Tearell, Dave, 2
Thorpe, Jeremy, 64
Thunderbolts, 6
Tiny Tim, 56
Tremeloes, 98-9
Trevor, Alex, 174
Troggs, 35

Valenti, Fernando, 108
Vanilla Fudge, 99
Viatkin, Serge, 5
Vincent, Gene, 3, 7
Vinnedge, Char, 160

Wadmore, Teddy, 6
Walden, Snuffy, 177
Walker, Tim, 64
Waller, Mickey, 110
Warner Brothers, 91, 115, 126, 133,
    138, 139, 148, 151, 152, 154, 157,
    160, 162, 163, 167, 175, 182, 183,
    192, 195, 198, 202, 203, 211
Weiss, Steve, 54, 74-5, 115, 148, 167,
    168, 169, 172, 174, 175, 176, 181,
    188, 190, 195, 197, 199

Whiting, Lawrence, 8, 32
The Who, 33-4, 54
Wibley, Mick, 4
Wildcats, 44
Wilde, Marty, 6
Wilke, Derry, 21, 112
Williams, Trevor, 41
Wilson, Devon, 139, 146
Wilson, Tom, 157, 173
Winters, Bernard, 139
Winters, Johnny, 141, 149
Winwood, Muff, 199
Winwood, Steve, 86
Wonder, Stevie, 65

Wood, Chris, 86
Wood, Ron, 93, 110
Wright, Tappy, 156
Wyatt, Robert, 98

Yameta, 22, 34, 44, 75, 91-2, 93, 103,
    107-8, 140, 168, 169, 171-2, 174-5,
    180, 185, 189, 192, 195, 197,
    202, 211
Yardbirds, 56
Young, Neil, 214
Youngblood, Lonnie, 24

Zappa, Frank, 158, 159

All Pan books are available at your local bookshop or newsagent, or can be ordered direct from the publisher. Indicate the number of copies required and fill in the form below.

Send to: **CS Department, Pan Books Ltd., P.O. Box 40, Basingstoke, Hants. RG21 2YT.**

or phone: 0256 469551 (Ansaphone), quoting title, author and Credit Card number.

Please enclose a remittance* to the value of the cover price plus: 60p for the first book plus 30p per copy for each additional book ordered to a maximum charge of £2.40 to cover postage and packing.

*Payment may be made in sterling by UK personal cheque, postal order, sterling draft or international money order, made payable to Pan Books Ltd.

Alternatively by Barclaycard/Access:

Card No.

Signature:

Applicable only in the UK and Republic of Ireland.

While every effort is made to keep prices low, it is sometimes necessary to increase prices at short notice. Pan Books reserve the right to show on covers and charge new retail prices which may differ from those advertised in the text or elsewhere.

NAME AND ADDRESS IN BLOCK LETTERS PLEASE:

....

Name————————————————————————————

Address————————————————————————————

————————————————————————————————

————————————————————————————————

————————————————————————————————

3/87